Children
and
Television

Random House / New York

Children
and
Television

Lessons from Sesame Street

by Gerald S. Lesser

FOREWORD BY JOAN GANZ COONEY
INTRODUCTION BY LLOYD MORRISETT

Library of Congress Cataloging in Publication Data
Lesser, Gerald S
Children and television. Includes bibliographical references.
1. Sesame Street.   I.   Title.
PN1992.77.S43L4   791.45'7   73–20554
ISBN 0-394-48100-3

Manufactured in the United States of America
9 8 7 6 5 4 3 2
First Edition

Grateful acknowledgment is made to the following for permission to reprint previously published material:

M. J. Arlen and McCall's: For an excerpt from "A Few Sensible Words About Children's TV," by M. J. Arlen which appeared in the February 1971 issue of McCall's. Copyright © 1971 by McCall's.

Children's Television Workshop: For various reference materials, charts, and drawings published by the Children's Television Workshop.

Educational Testing Service: For an excerpt from "The Discovery and Development of Educational Goals" by H. S. Dyer. Published in Proceedings of the 1966 Invitational Conference on Testing Problems. Copyright © 1967 by Educational Testing Service. All rights reserved.

John Holt and his agent, Robert Lescher Literary Agency: For excerpts from "Big Bird, Meet Dick and Jane" by John Holt. Copyright © 1971 by John Holt. (This piece first appeared in The Atlantic Monthly.)

The New York Times: For a chart, "The Impact of Sesame Street," from the January 28, 1970, New York Times. Copyright © 1970 by The New York Times Company.

*To my son Ted—for
sharing with me his
enjoyment of* Sesame Street

And shall we just carelessly allow children to hear any casual tales which may be devised by casual persons, and to receive in their minds for the most part the very opposite of those which we should wish them to have when they are grown up?

Plato,
The Republic

It's becoming obvious that no one knows what the world is going to be like when the time comes for the younger to live in it, so perhaps the kindest thing we can do is to try not to burden them with the quaint details of today's beliefs and customs, but just attempt to get across a few principles of how things interact, what is basic in human life, and to acquaint them with as thorough a cross section as possible of persons, places, and things as they now stand. After this we can only give them a pat on the shoulder and wish them well.

Clark Gesner,
Prospectus for the Children's Television Workshop,
1968

Preface

Television for children has no recorded history. Although twenty-five years have passed since television arrived, and few other experiences pervade and invade our children's lives as deeply, we have little understanding of its effects. Programs vanish almost as soon as they appear. Nothing is so ephemeral and perishable, nothing is used up so fast.

Not only do the programs themselves vanish, but even more important, the processes by which they were created are unrecorded. Some thought—logical or illogical, creative or prosaic, educational or economic, constructive or exploitative—must have guided what television has presented to children over the past decades, but whatever the rationales have been, they now are lost to us.

This book records the history of thought behind one television series for children, a series called *Sesame Street*. As such, it is the property of my colleagues at the Children's Television Workshop who created *Sesame Street*. I have collected and recorded their acts of creation and their store of insights about children and television: Edward L. Palmer, Samuel Y. Gibbon, Barbara Reeves, David Connell, Joan Ganz Cooney, Jon Stone, Evelyn Davis, Jim Henson, Jane Henson, Jeff Moss, Vivian Horner, Joe Raposo, Norton Wright, Joan Lufrano, Sharon Lerner, Barbara Fowles, Joyce Weil, Naomi Foner, Lutrelle Horne, Lloyd Morrisett, Edith Zornow, Robert Davidson, Frank Oz, Christopher Cerf, Robert Oksner, Bob Hatch, Jane O'Connor, Bobbie Miller, Stuart Aubrey, Charlie Smith, and others.

Children's television never has been regarded by people in universities as a topic for serious study, yet my jobs over the last twenty years have been in universities. To my colleagues at

Harvard, I am grateful for their (sometimes bemused) tolerance of my interest in children's television. Some even went so far as to help in *Sesame Street*'s planning: Sheldon White, Courtney Cazden, Jeanne Chall, Carol Chomsky, Leon Eisenberg, Chester Pierce, Jerome Kagan, Burton White, Roger Brown, Lawrence Kohlberg, Keith Connors, Marion Walter, Knowles Dougherty, Daniel Ogilvie, Marshall Haith, Thomas Pettigrew. One colleague in particular at Harvard was convinced of television's potential as a way to learn about children and as an important force in American education. Luckily, this colleague, Theodore Sizer, was dean of my faculty and gave me the academic and personal support I needed.

Before the Children's Television Workshop was formed, Craig Fisher in 1961 invited me to help in the production of his children's program *Exploring* at the National Broadcasting Company. Through him, I was alerted to the great benefits of reducing to a minimum the paraphernalia of research on children and simply talking with them and watching them as they watch television. Herbert Schueler, who invited me to join the faculty of the City University of New York (where he is now president of Richmond College), gave me the chance to see television from another point of view, as a tool for training children's teachers.

Without Joan Ganz Cooney, president of the Children's Television Workshop, *Sesame Street* never would have happened and I would not have had anything to write about. Without Lloyd N. Morrisett, chairman of the Workshop's Board of Trustees and president of the John and Mary R. Markle Foundation, *Sesame Street* never would have happened and I would have had neither the moral nor financial support to write about it. The Markle Foundation and Guggenheim Foundation gave me the time for reflection and writing. Funds provided by the National Center for Educational Research and Development of the U.S. Office of Education (OEG-0-72-1264) allowed us to train young researchers by involving them in our work.

My gratitude to Jason Epstein, vice-president of Random House, for insisting that I try to write this book for a general audience instead of only a professional one. He not only insisted, but as editor he tried to show me how. I hope that, between us, we have had some measure of success.

Each of my colleagues at the Workshop probably would write the story of *Sesame Street* differently. By presuming to write it for them, I may distort their stories. Writing things down tends to tidy them up, to impose an immaculate appearance on what was and is a rumpled reality.

Contents

Foreword

BY JOAN GANZ COONEY

When we first made plans for the Children's Television Work-shop back in 1967, we could easily have got long odds that one of the central premises of the enterprise simply would not work. Namely, the forced marriage of educational advisors and professional researchers with experienced television producers.

Few people who had known and thought about creating a highly entertaining, well-financed educational TV series for pre-school children had any serious reservations about its chances for at least moderate success. We knew that young children watched a great deal of television in the years before they went to school (and only slightly less during their elementary school years). We knew also that they liked cartoons, game shows, situation comedies; they responded to slapstick humor and music with a beat—and above all, they were attracted by fast-paced, highly visual, oft-repeated commercials.

The wasteland of children's programing was too vast for a major effort not to attract at least some attention and audience. We had an idea and we felt confident that it would work. Even though it had not been tried before, there was nothing very radical, after all, about using various popular television techniques to try to teach preschoolers some basic cognitive skills like recognition of letters and simple counting.

However, from the beginning we, the planners of the project, insisted that the show be designed not merely as a broadcast series (stamped with the inevitable imprimatur of some "name" individual or institution in early childhood education) but as an experimental research project that would bring together educational advisors, researchers and television producers as equal partners. To an unprecedented degree, the creative, educational and research components were to function as inseparable parts of the whole.

"Researchers helping producers design a show? You must be kidding!" came the reaction of practically everyone in TV willing to give a real opinion. As Gerry Lesser points out in this book, producers believe, or always had until CTW came along, in intuition, taste and experience as the means to successful shows. And luck, always luck, as the *sine qua non* of any big hit.

What *we* were proposing was that material, as it was produced, be tested on the target audience for both appeal and educational value; that researchers report back to producers; and that producers modify or discard material based on these almost continuous reports from the field. In other words, we were suggesting that luck not be allowed to rule with quite such an arbitrary hand—that its role be cut down, however slightly (though we hoped it would be more than slightly), by something very much akin to science.

Looking back, I guess it was not the concept which raised so many doubts. Rather, it was the thought of the *reality* of the situation—temperamental, creative people working with outside advisors and inside researchers on the educational goals of the series. It meant that long before the series went on the air—where a mass audience of children, newspaper critics, parents and teachers would judge it—social scientists would in fact tell the producers whether the material was "good" or "bad" in terms of the goals of the show and the reactions of a sample of young children.

To the amazement and near disbelief of outside (and some inside) observers, the courtship went smoothly, if not always lovingly, and the marriage has been a howling success.

When I have been asked why I think this marriage of research and production has worked so well, I always answer without hesitation: "Personalities."

There can be no question that the personalities, patience

and know-how of Gerry Lesser as Chairman of the Board of Advisors and Ed Palmer as Director of Research were critical to winning the "hand" of the production department. Let me hasten to add that the receptivity of our producers to research input, their very gameness in agreeing to try a new model for producing shows, remains one of the cornerstones of the house that CTW built.

But in the creation of the model we had to start somewhere, and that somewhere was with Gerry Lesser. By the time Lloyd Morrisett and I were ready to select a Chairman of the Board of Advisors, I had interviewed scores of academics all over the country in connection with the 1966 Carnegie Corporation study I had conducted. Lloyd through his position at Carnegie, knew personally most of the leading people in the field of educational psychology. When we drew up our list of "possibles" for the chairman role, we hardly discussed our first choice. It was understood that Gerry was it.

It is interesting to note that if enthusiasm for the project had been a criterion for selection of the Chairman of the Advisors, Gerry would have come in at some midpoint on the list. Known as a bit of a Cassandra, Gerry brought the same skepticism to my emotional conviction that television could educate that any good scientist brings to an amateur's passion. But because he was one of the very few educational psychologists around (Ed Palmer was another) who had had the good sense (or brilliance) to take a professional look at television and its effects on children, Gerry said yes, he would become a partner in our effort to try to educate children via mass communications.

I remember at the first of our five curriculum seminars thinking what a good choice we had made. In a perfectly comfortable air-conditioned room, Gerry took off his jacket, rolled up his sleeves and proceeded to tell the participants representing both creative and academic life in America that researchers, educators and producers were going to set the curriculum goals together and that the goals were going to be tailored to television and not the classroom. While the latter point seems obvious, one of the most difficult problems in consulting nontelevision people is getting them to think television rather than face-to-face teaching. Gerry, himself an academic, anticipated this. He forced the attention of his colleagues on this point. But what was most impressive about Gerry's performance in those early days was that he never looked back. He never betrayed to anyone, including me, the slightest doubt that research could and would play a critical role in the creation of a highly successful television production, and despite the reservations that I knew existed in his own mind, there was never any question that he wanted to be any other place.

And he was all over the place. He did not confine his interest in CTW to the educational and research issues. There was no administrative, personnel, community or public information problem that came my way that I could not share to advantage with Gerry. If he couldn't help in some concrete way, he would cluck sympathetically, and this was no small thing. For in effect he was commuting between two demanding jobs—one at Harvard and the other at CTW. Countless times he flew down from Cambridge on almost no notice because I would call and say, "We've got a problem and need your help." I am, of course, speaking of *my* phone calls to Gerry. There were also those from Dave Connell, Sam Gibbon and Jon Stone who had the primary job of creating the show. And, of course, there was endless communication with Ed Palmer, whose responsibility was to design and execute the formative research for the series and work with Educational Testing Service on the design and execution of the summative research.

I do not know where Gerry found the time or good will to involve himself so completely in the Workshop, but I do know that if you're ever starting an enterprising educational television series, find yourself a Gerry Lesser. If you can!

Look for reputation and expertise in the field of interest, of course; add the willingness to give more time than anyone has. Find someone who rolls up his sleeves with the toilers in the vineyard, and above all, insist on someone that you can laugh with a lot, because I think without Gerry's sense of humor, the project could not have worked—or at least we couldn't all have meshed so well together, and the meshing somehow made it work.

After five, going on six, years I couldn't begin to measure how proud I am to be Gerry Lesser's colleague and how happy I am to know the pleasure of his company.

Introduction

We first began to plan *Sesame Street* at a time in the 1960's when there was great concern about preschool education for young children. Nursery schools and kindergartens provided some systematic educational experience for children, but many schools did not offer kindergarten education, and nursery schools were available to only a small fraction of three- and four-year-olds. Moreover, while traditional preschool experience emphasized play and emotional and social development, there was new evidence that a child's intellectual development is extremely rapid in the preschool years and of vital importance to his later learning.

There were at the time experimental attempts to add cognitive content to early educational experience, but most such efforts depended upon structured preschool education in the form of kindergarten training or intensive summer programs before the beginning of first grade. Given the relatively slow spread of nursery school and kindergarten training throughout the United States, it was apparent in the 1960's that these experimental efforts would slowly, if at all, reach many of the children who needed them, particularly underprivileged children for whom preschool facilities might not be available. Television, on the other hand, provided a way to reach many, if not most, of the children who were in need of such help. The question was whether or not television could be used to benefit children before they went to school—and particularly whether poor, nonwhite city children could be aided in this way.

The idea that television might benefit children is a tribute to the fantastic development and spread of the medium. Television developed in the United States so suddenly and became pervasive so rapidly that we sometimes forget that before 1947 it was practically nonexistent. In 1947 it was a rarity. Only about 14,000 families had sets. By 1950 almost four million American families, or 9 percent of the total number of United States homes, owned television sets. From that point on television quickly became omnipresent in American society. Today over 95 percent of American households in all sectors of the country and of all income levels own at least one television set. Now more families own two television sets (approximately 38 percent of all households) than owned one in 1950.

This is the age of television not only in the sense of wide ownership of television sets, but much more in the sense that children are growing up in a time when television is available to them and widely used. Henceforth, practically speaking, no child in the United States will reach maturity without ready access to television and all it can bring to him. This is becoming more true each day all over the world. South Africa is the only industrialized nation where television has not been introduced, and it will be introduced there in the next five years.

1950 was a watershed year. Children in the United States who were born, went to school and became adults before 1950 did so without television as part of their lives. After 1950 we came to take television for granted and began organizing our lives in both obvious and subtle ways around the reality of one, or perhaps two or three, television sets in our homes. Mealtimes were changed. Families planned their recreation in order to allow the viewing of favorite programs. The time-honored newspaper at breakfast was often replaced by the early morning news and weather. Late-night movies brought entertainment to the insomniac. A good television personality became an important political asset. For children, television often became the central element in their cognitive lives.

Almost 30 percent of the people in the United States are under thirteen years of age, including almost 12 percent under six years of age, and children spend more of their time watching television than any other age group. Preschool children up to the age of six are the single heaviest television viewing audience in the United States. And while viewing falls off slightly after children enter school, those between six and thirteen are still very heavy television viewers. For the preschool child estimates ranging as high as an average of fifty hours per week of watching television have been given. Even if one discounts these estimates, it becomes clear that for young children the one activity that engages most of their time, aside from sleeping, is watching television.

The idea that children have special needs as television viewers and deserve special treatment is not new. But although this responsibility has for many years been specifically stated by the broadcasters and the Federal Communications Commission, it has yet to be reflected in the overall quality of children's programing. Part of this failure is due to lack of concerted and continued action by broadcasters and advertisers. Part is due to lack of leadership by the Federal Communications Commission. Part is due to lack of sufficient public protest. Many more people need to ask and demand answers to questions about the nature of television's responsibility to children and how this responsibility can be fulfilled.

There are signs that the public is beginning to be made aware of the need for improved television programing for children and demand better fare. Public organizations such as Action for Children's Television (ACT) have emerged as significant voices for improved children's programing. The reports of the National Commission on Causes and Prevention of Violence and the Surgeon General's Scientific Advisory Committee on Television and Social Behavior both highlight some of the relations of television to the emotional and social development of children. Finally, the success of *Sesame Street* convinced many people that it was possible both to produce entertaining programing for children and at the same time to make that programing beneficial to them.

Despite these encouraging signs, most people would still agree that quality television programing for children, both in terms of entertainment and education, is sadly lacking in the television schedule. Why isn't there more children's programing? Why isn't there better children's programing? Why has not the example of *Sesame Street* stimulated the development of other programs designed to entertain and educate young children? The answers to these questions are, I think, largely economic.

The cost of research, development, production and broadcast for the first year of *Sesame Street* was approximately seven million dollars. A curriculum had to be carefully constructed, translated into production ideas, and tested to make sure that the resulting show both entertained and educated. Talented performers and advanced production techniques were necessary to appeal to the child viewer already sophisticated by our television culture and ready to switch channels when confronted with an unappealing program. Since programs were designed particularly to help children in poor areas and the inner cities, special efforts were made by teams of staff members to develop viewing audiences in fourteen major cities. All this was costly.

The original funds for *Sesame Street* were provided by the federal government through the Office of Education, private foundations—mainly Carnegie and Ford—and the Corporation for Public Broadcasting. The sharing of cost was 50 percent from the government and 50 percent from the other sources. When we began to try to finance the project we had found it impossible to do so in commercial television. Current support for *Sesame Street* and *The Electric Company* comes from the Corporation for Public Broadcasting, the Office of Education, self-generated income, and a small amount from private foundations.

Public television has made a notable attempt to provide a children's service and indeed does provide at least ten hours per week of quality children's programing. But public television is still troubled by insufficient financing, lack of attention to its potentialities, and an overabundance of UHF television stations that are poorly received and infrequently watched. Today, as before, public television is in a continuing financial squeeze. Under these circumstances, it is difficult to see how a very much greater proportion of public television's limited funds and limited air time can be devoted to children's service.

Commercial television is caught in a different kind of squeeze. The commercial networks which overwhelmingly dominate television are dependent upon a system of financing that comes almost exclusively from advertising revenue. Broadcasters are required to provide some children's programing by the station licenses granted by the Federal Communications Commission. But children as an audience are not the primary target of many advertisers. Advertising revenue comes predominantly from adult programing and not from children's programing. Under these conditions it is quite natural that adult programing receives by far the greater part of the commercial broadcaster's attention. Unless change is required, the economic advantages of attending to commercial broadcasting's adult audience will undoubtedly keep more funds from flowing into children's programing. This in turn will prevent talented people from working in this area. There are steps which the networks could take to improve their children's programing and to share the competitive disadvantages of providing improved children's service. For example, each of the three networks might agree to take primary responsibility for one hour of children's programing on Saturday morning at a different time than the other networks. In this way resources could be concentrated to produce better programing while freeing some time for other purposes. Given the past history of commercial broadcasting, it seems unlikely, however, that this will ever take place unless a much greater public outcry occurs or the Federal Communications Commission requires these actions.

Even what must seem like radical proposals may be very conservative when measured against the real needs of children. If broadcasting is to meet its obligations to children, what is needed is quality children's programing available at all hours when children are likely to be watching. Children have the right to be served by television when they can view it. This means that a child should have available to him at whatever hour he normally watches television a quality program designed for his benefit: for his education, for his entertainment, for his enjoyment. This will not happen until a wealth of television channels are nationally available combined with diverse sources of financing. Only then are television's priorities likely to be reordered.

Our experience with *Sesame Street* and later with *The Electric Company* has confirmed our initial hope that it is possible consciously to use children's television to their benefit. To the degree that these programs have been successful, it has been because they have combined the technology of television with the art of entertainment and specific pedagogical aims. *Sesame Street* is not "the answer" to early education problems or to deficiencies in children's television programing. It is one effort and a more successful one than we originally dreamed, to use television to benefit children's development.

The real answer to problems of early education is for the total culture of childhood, including television as an important element, to work in harmony with the family and later the school. The environment in which children live needs to foster constructive cognitive and emotional growth from birth onwards.

Looking ahead, it may be that further developments in communications technology will bring the benefits of television more fully into the service of children. Cable television—transmission of television signals through a wire to the receiving set rather than over the air to a home antenna—is rapidly becoming one of the primary means of delivering television signals to the home. Already about six million American families have cable television, but the growth of cable television is about 15 percent per year, so that in five or ten years, if this rate of growth continues, many more millions of American families will have this form of signal delivery. While at first glance cable television seems to be merely another form of delivering television signals to the home, it is to be expected that in the future it may bring about other changes in our television technology.

In the short run, cable television will bring many more program possibilities to the set owner. Where television reception is now limited to a maximum of seven VHF channels in either New York or Los Angeles and many less in most other parts of the country, cable television will make possible the delivery of ten, twenty or more clear television signals to each set. This means that the family may have a wider range of choices for viewing than it now has at present, and it is to be expected that the amount of television viewing by children will not diminish under these conditions. Rather, it is to be hoped that along with more choice, new special programing will be developed for children, so that more will also mean better. It is possible that a wealth of television channels may lead to a children's television service—at least one channel that carries only material produced or chosen to meet children's needs and interests. Cable television may fractionate the audience so that television becomes an industry like magazine publishing. In that case it could become economically viable for there to be a commercial television service for children or economically possible for there to be a noncommercial service.

At the time *Sesame Street* was being developed, we did not know if entertainment and instruction could be combined in a program format that would appeal to an audience of children and hold their attention. We did not know if such a program could indeed produce beneficial learning in the audience. The challenges at times seemed so great that one or another of us had to buoy the confidence of our colleagues. Now we know these things can be done; the original challenges are behind us, but *Sesame Street* should be only a beginning.

The lessons from *Sesame Street* that are here chronicled so well by Gerald Lesser provide a partial basis for further improving television programing for children. They should be combined with the experience gained from other projects and from the other efforts of public television and commercial television so that in ten years *Sesame Street* of the early 1970's can be viewed as a horse-and-buggy version of television programing for children. With sufficient funds and the dedication of talented people, children in the United States in 1980 should be vastly better served by television than they were in 1970. Television is pervasive, fascinating to children, and viewed very heavily. The lessons from *Sesame Street* show that it is possible consciously to use television to benefit children directly rather than to harm them with it, let it be a neutral instrument in their lives, or leave the results to chance. The failure to further capitalize on the potential of television would be a tragic waste.

Section One: A Proposal

Let me draw your attention to the fact that everyone talks about bad television programs and the effects which they have; but actually it would be much more constructive and enlightening to experiment with good programs. Why shouldn't it be possible to get reformers and writers together, and have them devise programs which everyone thinks would be desirable, and beneficial? Would children listen to them? Would they have good effects? And even prior to that, do we really know what we mean by a good program? Are there people around who could write them? It is such a simple idea, but consider what has to be done to carry it out. You have to get psychologists and writers to meet and work together. You have to have funds to provide programs for experimental purposes, regardless of whether a television station or network is willing to put them on the air. But the aridity and the negativism of much of the discussion which takes place today can be overcome only if it is shown that there is something like a good program, that there are people who can be trained to write and produce them, and that children are willing to listen to them.

Paul F. Lazarsfeld,
Testimony to Kefauver Committee,
1955

In 1966 a television producer and a foundation executive decided that the time had come to test television's usefulness in teaching young children. Joan Cooney was the producer. Her early training had been in education and her subsequent work in journalism and noncommercial television production. Lloyd Morrisett, the foundation executive who since has become president of the Markle Foundation, is a psychologist who had taught at the University of California at Berkeley and, in 1966, was an executive at the Carnegie Corporation. With television so pervasive in our society, and with children so addicted to it, they wondered why so little had been done to test its potential for educating young children.

Joan Cooney took on the task of preparing a report in 1966 for the Carnegie Corporation and other possible sources of financial support. She held discussions with everyone she believed could illuminate the prospects of teaching young children through television, talking with preschool teachers, television and film producers, pediatricians, and psychologists and educators who had studied the development of children. The following year several potential funding agencies expressed interest in the report, and Carnegie asked her to prepare a detailed proposal for action. She and Lloyd asked me to help on research aspects of the proposal.

My own professional background is in the study of how children develop. In addition, as a psychologist at Harvard's Graduate School of Education, I had been trying to teach university students not only basic facts and theories of developmental psychology but also how these ideas might be applied to the education of children. Joan Cooney's proposal clearly was calling my bluff. Could what we know about children actually be of any use in creating a television series for young children that would both catch their interest and teach them something?

I had had extensive opportunities starting in 1961 to observe young children watching television, and had found these experiences to be an illuminating source of ideas about how children learn. It was the time when Newton Minow, then head of the Federal Communications Commission, uttered his now legendary accusation that the television industry had created "a vast wasteland," an episode recorded in detail in Erik Barnouw's *The Image Empire* (1970). Each network responded by quickly developing plans for a high-quality children's series that would proclaim the network's commitment to public service. The National Broadcasting Company assigned an outstanding news producer, Craig Fisher, to produce *Exploring*, a weekly one-hour series for children. He asked if I would watch with groups of children as the show was being produced to see what I could learn that would improve the series from week to week. The arrangement provided him with immediate access to children's reactions and provided me with an opportunity to observe children closely and to see how television programs were created. It lasted for the four years that *Exploring* was on the air.

When Joan Cooney and I met, we discussed not only the prospects for her proposal but also the next steps that might be needed once the proposal was funded. She outlined her reasons for thinking that the project should be tried and that it might succeed. She argued that the shortage of organized educational programs for preschoolers was not going to be remedied overnight and was having especially damaging effects on children from low-income families, despite the heroic efforts of programs such as Head Start. Yet, in contrast, there was no shortage of television sets in American homes or of young children watching them. If the obvious need and opportunity attracted funding for the project, she felt that she would immediately face certain crucial decisions—hiring the right creative staff, locating researchers who could work with producers, finding ways to attract a large national audience to an educational program, deciding upon procedures for evaluating educational effects, and so forth. High on her list of critical next steps was finding a process for deciding what the educational objectives should be. She asked if I would help her to design this process.

Like most psychologists and educators, I had received similar invitations before. Professionals often are asked to perform a ceremonial laying on of hands by a program developer who assumes that criticism can be diverted by showing that members of the professions participated in planning the program. Having performed this service, the professionals appear only on the letterhead of the project's stationery. Professionals actually have been known to make real contributions, and program developers have even been known to listen to them, but such outcomes are not the primary purpose of these relationships.

It took a short time for me to recognize it, but Joan's request was different. She was serious. She knew that some rational system for generating goals had to be found, and that she wanted to include people who knew children from diverse points of view. As we began puzzling over how a system could be created, it was clear that professionals would be asked to provide more than window dressing. We also talked about the role of research in the project, including how observations of children should not only be made to evaluate the impact of the series after it had been broadcast but also to feed the producers and writers with ideas about how to improve the show from day to day. The project was beginning to make excellent sense.

If anyone could give a project of this magnitude an honest try, Joan Cooney and Lloyd Morrisett were as good a pair as could be found. Instead of following the public-television tradition of timidly pleading for funds for educational projects, they decided that they would either obtain enough funding to go all out or would drop the project completely. Commercial television spends enormous sums to produce its slick, fast-paced programs, and a series with educational goals would need the same well-produced, expensive appearance to compete for the children's attention.

Joan and Lloyd seemed convinced that sufficient money

could be found, or at least they were acting with the kind of confidence that reflects conviction. They also seemed to know how to spend the money if they raised it, planning to create an organization that would combine production and research with activities in inner-city communities to encourage the use of the shows among low-income families. Beyond all these attributes, I was convinced of their staying power. There are so few precedents in using entertainment in the service of education that we could not expect to immediately find the right routes. If we did not quickly discover this magic formula, we would not be likely to collapse.

But faced with the pending reality of the project, and being by nature somewhat less optimistic than Joan Cooney, I had misgivings. Our society seems more and more uncertain about why we are educating our children, and I had begun to share that uncertainty. If I were to help to formulate the goals for this specific educational project, I would be forced to resolve my doubts and clarify my thinking about the aims of education in our society. I was not sure that I could do this soon enough or well enough to help launch the project. What is education for, anyway?

Although my thinking about the larger goals of education was unsettled, it was drifting in the direction of Joan's thinking about the specific goals of the program. It seemed to me that education had been asked to take on too much, to assume responsibility for personal and social problems that were beyond its ability to solve. Educators cannot solve all the emotional problems of students. They cannot remedy the injustices to minorities in our society or create new life styles or new communities to replace deteriorating ones. Yet they sometimes act as if they think they can. Educators have been far too willing, not only to acknowledge the importance of these problems, but to make rash promises beyond their means. They have not delivered and are suffering the inevitable loss of credibility.

Education could, however, be asked to teach children to understand symbols—to read, to calculate, to write, to communicate—and to use these symbols to reason logically and to solve problems. It might also be asked to convey some useful knowledge about what the world is like and how things operate within it. These were the same functions that Joan Cooney was considering. Without excluding the prospect that television might eventually be used more broadly, she chose to focus her proposal on the teaching of well-defined language skills, mathematical concepts, reasoning and problem solving.

There were other reasons to question the prospects for the project, but they seemed to me more abstract and less threatening than the requirement that we be clear about our educational goals. The project was unprecedented in its effort to combine education and entertainment in a national television series for very young children. There have been decades of talk about how limited television is as a teaching tool—its passivity, its vicariousness, its one-way transmission that does not permit the child to respond. There have been decades of talk about how harmful television is to our society, inciting us to violence and interfering with human interaction. Against all this, however, was the potential that the apparent natural addiction of children to television could be turned to constructive educational use, especially for very young children of the inner cities. And so it seemed worth a try.

Chapter One

Why It Should Be Tried

Some Men by the unalterable Frame of their Constitutions are Stout, *others* Timorous, *some* Confident, *others* Modest, Tractable, *or* Obstinate, Curious, *or* Careless, Quick, *or* Slow . . . *Begin therefore betimes nicely to observe your Son's Temper . . . See what are his* Predominant Passions, *and* Prevailing Inclinations; *whether he be Fierce or Mild, Bold, or Bashful, Compassionate or Cruel, Open or Reserv'd, &c. For as these are different in him, so are your Methods to be different.*

John Locke,
Some Thoughts Concerning Education, 1693

Behind all the recommendations of Joan Cooney's plan, "Television for Young Children: A Proposal," was a plea for help for all children, but especially those in inner cities who are locked into lives of poverty. She saw little advantage in limiting the effort only to children of the poor; the series was intended for national distribution to any child across the country who cared to watch. But despite the desire to reach as large a national audience as possible and to teach something to any child who watched, her central purpose was clear: If the series did not work for poor children, the entire project would fail.

We spend over fifty billions of dollars a year to maintain a massive educational superstructure which holds captive over fifty million children, yet we still have remarkably little understanding of what this system is doing and why it is doing it. It is difficult to estimate just how poor a job the system is doing. Estimates of damage range from assertions that it is systematically murdering our children to only slightly less severe indictments. Since we are unclear about what we would like education to accomplish, we can make no realistic estimates of our failure—except to acknowledge that we are making a great many children unhappy. That we are failing to educate our children, either disastrously or to a degree no worse than the failures of other social and political institutions, is almost beyond dispute.

Why have we not done better? What prevents us from learning—even little by little—how to educate our children, and how to make them suffer less (or even enjoy themselves) in the process? The usual reasons given are the staggering size of the educational enterprise, our unwillingness to invest enough money, our inability to attract creative people into education, and the environmental disadvantages of the children. Each surely is true, yet even if these problems did not exist, we still have not decided how we would want our system to change and what we would want it to achieve.

The Lack of Defined Goals

Since schools and schooling have existed for centuries, we might suppose that the question of what purposes they serve would be at least partially resolved. It is startling to admit that, despite the history and magnitude of educational activities, basic questions about why schools exist still are unsettled. Perhaps these decisions never should be settled finally, giving each new generation its chance to reassess the aims of education. Even so, our ideas about the goals of education remain vague, unanalyzed and whimsical.

There even are arguments that the explicit specification of these goals is neither possible nor desirable. In his book on *The Schools* Martin Mayer asserts that "in the context of the classroom nobody except an incompetent, doctrinaire teacher is ever going to worry about the 'aims of education.' " He quotes a leading educator who says that the effort to define educational objectives is on a par with the attempt to explain the universe. But granting the difficulties involved in being clear about the goals of education, consider the consequences of avoiding the question. Henry Dyer, a veteran evaluator of educational programs, describes them:

> As you watch the educational enterprise going through its interminable routines, it is hard to avoid the impression that the whole affair is mostly a complicated ritual in which the vast majority of participants—pupils, teachers, administrators, policymakers—have never given a thought to the question *why*, in any fundamental sense, they are going through the motions they think of as education. In spite of the tardy recognition in a few quarters that there are some ugly situations in the schools of the urban ghettos and rural slums, the general attitude still seems to be that if we are spending 50 billion dollars a year on the education of 50 million children, and if over 40% of them are now getting to go to college, as compared with less than 20% a few years back, then "we must be doing something right," even though we haven't the remotest idea of what it is. [1966, p. 13]

What do we have instead of objective, explicit statements about why our educational system exists? Dyer suggests that we have resorted to "word magic." For example:

> The first goal in education for democracy is the full, rounded, and continuing development of the person. The discovery, training, and utilization of individual talents is of fundamental importance in a free society. To liberate and perfect the intrinsic powers of each citizen is the central purpose of democracy, and its furtherance of individual self-realization is its greatest glory. [President's Commission on Higher Education, 1947, p. 9]

A more modern form of escape from the problems of setting educational goals is to delegate these decisions to the children themselves, especially in some forms of "open education" that are being tried here and abroad. This is not all bad; certainly pupils should not be excluded from deciding why they should attend school at all. However, young children surely cannot contemplate the full range of educational options available to them, and to place the responsibility for defining their educational aims either entirely or primarily in their hands is a clear sign of defeat and abdication by adults. Increasing the child's ability to make intelligent decisions is a desirable goal, but this is not equivalent to imposing upon the child the full burden of deciding the purposes of his own education.

The Need for Additional Options

Massive size, inadequate financing, scarce creative manpower, and the absence of clear purposes—all contribute to our problems in education. But our worst failure is to persist in the simplistic idea that a single, best educational approach exists for all children, and if we can find it, all educational problems will be solved. We remain stuck in a mindless pursuit of the one best system instead of searching for a diversity of educational approaches to fit the diversity of our children's needs, abilities and interests.

Having focused all our resources on the schools, we have failed to search for the other formal and informal opportunities for children to learn. Schools and classrooms surely provide only one site where children can learn. We recognize how much children learn informally from each other when we permit and encourage it, and this is slowly being incorporated into programs where older children teach younger ones, apparently to their mutual benefit. Clearly some of the child's most important learning takes place when adults find time to bring him into their activities as a contributing, if junior, partner. Against these influences of peers and adults, television may not appear to be a powerful added option. But given its prominence in children's lives today, it seems worth experimenting to see how useful we can make it and how the peers and adults surrounding the child can reinforce its influence.

The need to provide new options, including television, is especially critical for our youngest children. There are about twelve million American children between three and five years old; less than 20 percent of all three- and four-year-olds attend any form of preschool and less than 75 percent of five-year-olds go to kindergarten. For those families who want it, some form of early education should be available. Head Start facilities can be expanded and used as a step toward creating even more powerful forms of assistance to the children of poor families. If, in addition, effective means are found to use television to educate, another option would be available. Given what little we have, even one limited form of educational experience during a child's early years surely seems better than none at all.

Inner-City Children

All children deserve a greater range of educational options than we have given them. But the children who not only deserve more, but also need these opportunities desperately if they (and we) are to survive, are those we have been calling, over the past decade, "disadvantaged"—children who live in inner cities, usually poor, usually black or Spanish-speaking. Can television be used to help these children enter school more comfortably and to move along more rapidly once they get there?

Once in a while, the school problems of inner-city children are interpreted to mean that they are less able intellectually than others. This interpretation is rightly challenged by those who claim that poor children are not less bright but perhaps may be even more capable than others in nonschool ways, that anyone who can survive in a chaotic and hostile environment must have a natural acumen that is not demanded in more protected surroundings. But in ways that count in school—that is, in the rapid learning of symbolic skills used in reading, writing, mathematics, and other school activities—there seems little question that many poor children experience problems when they enter school and that these problems are likely to persist throughout their school careers.[1] Even before they enter school, young children may have been stymied by the poverty of their surroundings.

Unlike Head Start, which could be offered to the poor and yet legitimately withheld from middle-class families by requiring the demonstration of financial need in order to qualify, our television series was planned to reach as large a national audience as possible, including middle-class children as well as the poor. Since we hoped that all children would watch and learn, we did not aspire to reduce the differences between poor and middle-class children. But we did hope that our series would help to prepare poor children to do well in the schools as they are now organized and operated.

Some critics totally reject these schools—as they are now organized and operated—and in turn reject the value of better preparation for participation in them. They claim that existing schools are so narrow and mindless in their purposes, so inferior and irrelevant to the poor, that even vastly improved preparation will be worthless to poor children. They insist that we not tinker with the preparation of children for schools as they are, but instead develop new approaches to teach what schools do not teach and probably never will. In the *Atlantic Monthly* John Holt put this argument clearly and concluded that television will lose its opportunity unless it strikes out in entirely new directions:

> The operating assumption . . . is probably something like this: poor kids do badly in school because they have a "learning deficit." Schools, and school people, all assume that when kids come to the first grade they will know certain things, be used to thinking and talking in a certain way, and be able to respond

[1] This phenomenon is one of the few well-documented facts in educational research (e.g., Bloom, 1964; Coleman, 1966; Deutsch, 1965; Stodolsky and Lesser, 1967) and was correctly accepted as a rationale for the establishment of the Head Start Program (Cicarelli, 1969).

to certain kinds of questions and demands. Rich kids on the whole know all this; poor kids on the whole do not. Therefore, if we can just make sure that the poor kids know what the rich kids know by the time they get to school, they will do just as well there as the rich kids. So goes the argument. I don't believe it. Poor kids and rich kids are more alike when they come to school than is commonly believed, and the difference is not the main reason poor kids do badly when they get there. In most ways, schools are rigged against the poor; curing "learning deficits," by Head Start; *Sesame Street*, or any other means, is not going to change that.

The program asks, "How can we get children ready to learn what the schools are going to teach them?", instead of "How can we help them learn what the schools may *never* teach them?" This is the first of its lost, or not yet seen, opportunities —to be very different from school. [1971, p. 72]

Schools do need changing. But in one form or another they probably are here to stay. While we seek ways to make them more useful and humane for all children, television perhaps can help to prepare poor children to take advantage of the education that exists.

The Need to Experiment

Despite years of effort by educators and researchers, little is known about how children learn. We know even less about the educational possibilities of television. Attempting to use television to teach young children is based on so little real evidence that it is almost purely an act of faith.

With this scarcity of reliable information about children's learning and the effects of television, all we could have done when we began planning our television series (and all we can do even now) is to keep trying, in any intelligent way we can think of, to look for what will help children to learn. We are not ready to conduct this search entirely in the systematic manner preferred by science, but we can "experiment" by trying a variety of approaches to teaching young children and seeing what works and what fails.

Several meanings (nondictionary) exist for the verb "to experiment." Scientists generally mean that the behavior of a group that receives some special attention or treatment will be compared with that of a similar group receiving no such treatment in order to see if the treatment really matters. Despite some useful efforts in early education to experiment in this sense, we have not progressed very far by using this approach. When nonscientists say they are going to experiment, they often mean simply that they are going to try something that they had not tried before; even scientists sometimes use the term in this way. Since we really know so little about how to teach children effectively, the need is inescapable to experiment in the sense of trying something new and seeing how it goes.

Sadly, we have not been able to show in any conclusive way that any program of early education has definite or lasting effects on children. Encouraging data are reported from time to time,[2] but on balance no one can claim to know how and why we educate young children. Maybe we simply need more time. Maybe we need more sensitive instruments to detect the changes that are taking place. Maybe early education never will matter very much in the child's life, even if we have more time and money to explore its possibilities. But probably—and this simply is an article of faith—our failures in early education exist because we don't know enough about children and how they learn, and in the case of television, we don't know enough about the medium and its capabilities. Here then is the need to experiment: if we can begin to understand why certain children become competent and happy while others do not, if we can try a variety of ways of reaching them and see how these ways work, perhaps some of the mysteries of early education will begin to dissolve.

For those of us who do experiment in the uses of television

---

[2] For example, Bereiter and Engelmann, 1966; Ball and Bogatz, 1970; Karnes, Teska, and Hodgins, 1970; Weikart, 1967.

with children, a hidden impulse operates. Suppose we fail completely to discover anything more about how children learn; suppose television's capabilities and limitations remain a mystery despite our best efforts. Even so, once in a while (with a little luck) we connect and a child laughs. That sound is worth most of life's satisfactions rolled into one.

Chapter Two

Why It Might,
or Might Not, Work

*May Allah believe me, I don't think children's pro-
grams should always be true, beautiful, inspirational,
or spiritually enlarging . . . But this empty, empty,
prissy, bumbling, sing-songy stuff is something else,
and I can't see that it adds up to much of anything.
Grown men ought to speak in their own voices when
they speak to children, and they ought to pretend to
be awake. That doesn't seem to ask a lot.*

Michael J. Arlen,
Living-Room War, 1969

Not only were Joan Cooney and Lloyd Morrisett seeking
enough money to do an educational series that could compete
with expensive commercial programs, but their sources would
be noncommercial, a combination of government agencies and
private foundations. Since the government and foundations
usually see their roles as providing start-up money for promising projects and not prolonged support, this decision would
later create problems of locating continued funds for the organization. At the outset, however, we would be protected from
the pressures that affect the erratic course of the commercial
networks as they waver capriciously between economic forces
and the sporadic demands upon them for public service.

Beyond money, Joan and Lloyd also were seeking enough
planning time to develop and test a detailed blueprint before

proceeding. By ordinary television standards, an eighteen-month planning period is luxuriously long, but this was precisely what they were requesting. With confidence in their own abilities, they were reserving their right to create their own organization, independent of any pressures that the money sources might choose to exert. Most important, they were reserving the right to create their own programs, rejecting the lowest-common-denominator approach so pervasive in television of giving the public what it thinks the public wants. They insisted on pursuing the idea that when it comes to providing high-quality children's programs, the public will not know what it really wants until someone comes along to show it to them. On the surface, this assumption does not seem especially radical, but the most ancient of television's traditions is its defense of mediocre programs on the theory that this is what the public wants. In creating our series, we would rely heavily upon the reactions of children and their parents, but we were not going to rely upon them to tell us what kind of series to initiate.

Ubiquitous Sets, Endless Hours

Current statistics on the amount of television viewing by young children are familiar and somewhat chilling. Although all these figures are only estimates, the conclusion is inescapable: Young children watch an awful lot of television (and consequently a lot of awful television).

Over one hundred and eighty million Americans (about 96 percent of the total U.S. population) have television sets in their homes. More families have television sets than have bathtubs, telephones, toasters, vacuum cleaners or a regular daily newspaper. Even in households with less than five-thousand-dollar incomes well over 90 percent own at least one television set. For example, in the "hollers" of Appalachia, where the median income is well below five thousand dollars, over 95 percent of the families have sets. Few of these children have ever visited a zoo or a library or a fire station, but they do watch television up to eight hours a day.

Nationally these television sets are on in the homes of pre-school-aged children from approximately fifty-four hours per week in the fall of the year to forty-six hours a week in the spring (Neilsen Television Index, 1967). By the time these children graduate from high school, they will have spent on the average about 12,000 hours in school and about 15,000 hours watching television, having devoted more of their young lives to watching television than to any other single activity except sleep. They will have given roughly two full years, twenty-four hours a day, to sitting in front of the television screen.

The figures raise one of the oldest of human dilemmas. What do we do about unseemly habits among the young, such as television addiction? Exposing American parents to these figures usually induces a state of numbed shock, followed quickly by a guilty, determined resolve to break the habit (in parent as well as child), by means of physical force if necessary. In a more delayed response, parents are apt to recognize that society probably is not about to abolish television, and that despite heroic efforts to wean or force the child from the set, some residue of the habit will remain and is almost certain to reappear from time to time. Then can viewing be put to any constructive use? If it can, television might teach the child something useful, or might at least expose him to parts of the world he has never seen before. It might also expose him to some good programs so that he can learn to discriminate between good and poor programs and become more selective in how he spends his time. This seems to be asking a lot, but possibly the child can learn both substance and taste from television.

The Logic behind the Experiment

There is no real evidence that all the television sets and viewing hours make a difference in how much children learn, but certainly much informal learning does take place. No child can be bombarded by images of energizing cereals, bumbling fathers in family comedies, exciting toys, and excited mothers winning prizes in game shows without acquiring some stereotypes about people and products.

We have never lacked for reports, and verified reports at that, of children who learn to read from commercials, quiz shows or weather reports or children who suddenly display some other advanced intellectual skill that they could have learned only from television.[1] Any adult can supply anecdotes about children whose first spoken words were "Budweiser," "Namath," "Clairol" or "Axion" or who learned to spell "Mickey Mouse" or "Batman" before they could spell their own names.

Most of what is learned—mindless advertising slogans—is not worth knowing, so even if all the anecdotes are true, they do not provide any real testimony for television's educational values. But they do suggest the extent to which children can learn from television even when it is not deliberately designed to teach. These remarkable feats of learning may occur precisely because the televised message was not deliberately designed to teach and precisely because no adult was presiding over the learning. Even so, the stories should entice us to imagine the potential of learning from television shows when they are carefully designed to teach children.

Television as Recreation

The child associates television with pleasure and recreation. No coercion is necessary to get him to watch; he initiates and seeks out opportunities. Why this is true is not clear. Surely the child has watched many dull programs that lack wit and imagination. Despite this, television seems to retain its seductive appeal.

Many decades ago, psychologists used to say that teaching should provide "mental discipline." We were supposed to study Latin and Greek and mathematics not because the subjects

[1] For example, Culkin, 1970; Durkin, 1966; Torrey, 1969.

were interesting or useful, but rather because they were so dull and obscure that they would teach us to persist in tasks that had no inherent interest. This persistence (if we ever did learn it) was to serve us later in life. The less we liked something, the better it was supposed to be for us. This theory fit well with our American ethic that anything worthwhile should not come easily, that we should have to work hard to get what we want or it cannot be much good. The main trouble with this view of "mental discipline" is that it does not work. We do not learn well what we are forced to learn unless the force is so overwhelming and persistent that our lives are made to depend on it. Indeed, as most adolescents will eagerly testify, we are more likely to acquire a strong aversion from forced learning. Instead, we learn well what we search out on our own initiative. For whatever reasons, children seek opportunities to watch television, providing us, in turn, with opportunities—as yet unused—to put their spontaneous pleasure to use.

School attendance is compulsory; watching television is not. It is a good bet that this difference between compulsion and free choice matters. It may come down to this: Most education —going to school, for instance—is doing what someone else wants you to do; watching television is doing what you have decided you want to do.

Television as Nonpunitive

Television's impersonality is one of its obvious weaknesses. It stares unblinking at everyone alike, making no accommodations to differences among members of its audience. Yet its impersonality, and especially its nonpunitiveness, is also one of its special strengths. We look ahead to the advantages of two-way television communication which will allow the viewer to engage in some sort of dialogue with what he sees on the set. These advantages are likely to be substantial, but there still may be a great deal to be said for just looking at people on the television set and knowing that they cannot look back at you, cannot criticize you or make you face up to your responsibility to make proper, expected responses. In a culture where children spend much of their time trying to do (or trying to avoid doing) what others expect of them, it is possible that children give the most when nothing is demanded of them, when they are left to respond as they will. Periodic liberation from duty to the expectations of others may be just what attracts children to television and frees them to learn from it.

Learning has become for many young children simply a vehicle for pleasing others, for gaining the attention and affection of parents and teachers. We hope that eventually this early motivation to learn in order to please others will disappear and that the child's pleasure in learning for its own sake will take over. Sometimes this happens but often it does not. Whether or not this shift occurs, learning in order to please others carries a heavy overload of emotion: Succeed and you are valued and esteemed, fail and you are unworthy. Since the only way to win is to do better than anyone else, winners are few and losers are many.

This emotional game is played out in the open, with grades and records exposed as matters of public record. The prizes are controlled by others, and while a child may be able to influence a teacher's judgment through the quality of his performance (especially if he is good at giving the teacher what she wants to hear), these decisions are essentially beyond the child's control. The central ingredients of the system are public exposure, control by others, and the continuous threat of failure and humiliation if you falter.

Television contains none of these emotional overtones. A child may watch and learn by correcting his mistakes without fear of the public exposure that occurs in classrooms. He can control his involvement simply by flipping a switch, turning the set on or off at his own discretion. Television's impersonality removes the constant threat of humiliation.

Most educators believe that emotional relationships can facilitate learning, and surely they sometimes do. A parent's personal influence or a teacher's individual attention probably have no match. But too much or too steady a diet of personalness and emotion can block learning, especially when the child is losing more often than he wins. Then private, noncompetitive, unthreatening experiences, operated under the child's own control, can provide a retreat, a temporary sanctuary. We may regret the conditions in our society that make sanctuaries necessary and must guard against a child's permanent retreat into them, but sanctuaries are needed, and television is one of the few shelters children have.

Television and Modeling

Imitates

What psychologists call "modeling" occurs simply by watching others, without any direct reinforcement for learning and without any overt practice. The child imitates the model without being induced or compelled to do so. That learning can occur in the absence of direct reinforcement is a radical departure from earlier theories that regarded reward or punishment as indispensable to learning. There now is considerable evidence that children do learn by watching and listening to others even in the absence of reinforcement and overt practice. Opportunities for modeling have been vastly increased by television.

Albert Bandura, a leading researcher on this topic, illustrates modeling with this story:

> A lonesome farmer decided to get a parrot for company. After acquiring the bird the farmer spent many long evenings teaching the parrot the phrase, "Say Uncle." Despite the devoted tutorial attention, the parrot proved totally unresponsive and finally, the frustrated farmer got a stick and struck the parrot on the head after each refusal to produce the desired phrase.

> But the visceral method proved no more effective than the cerebral one, so the farmer grabbed his feathered friend and tossed him in the chicken house. A short time later the farmer heard a loud commotion in the chicken house and upon investigation found that the parrot was pummeling the startled chickens on the head with a stick and shouting, "Say Uncle! Say Uncle!" [1967, p. 42]

Parrots teaching chickens probably has little direct bearing on how children learn from television, and cats learning by watching other cats may be no more relevant, but an experiment by John, Chessler, Bartlett and Victor (1968) provides an excellent example of modeling. One group of cats watched as another group of cats was taught to press a lever each time a light went on in order to obtain milk. When these "watcher" cats were placed in the box with a lever, they learned the behavior more quickly and easily than cats who were trained without first observing veteran lever-pressing cats in action.

By watching televised models, children learn both socially desirable and undesirable behaviors. By observing altruistic models on film and television, children learn to model altruistic behavior and kindness toward others. Watching models who display courage, self-sacrifice or affection induces these behaviors in the viewers. Modeling also affects self-criticism, self-control, the tendency to be reflective rather than impulsive during problem solving, the moral judgments of children, the tendency to initiate social contacts with peers, and the inhibition of deviant behavior.[2]

Aggressive behavior also is affected by viewing televised models, but—despite the periodic public furor over the effects of televised violence—just what these effects are is disputed. Most educators claim that when a child views aggressive behavior, he is more likely to become aggressive himself. Others contend the opposite, that the child will become less aggres-

[2] On altruism: Bryan and London, 1970; Bryan and Schwartz, 1971, Krebs, 1970. On kindness toward others: Rosenhan, 1969; Rosenhan and White, 1967. On courage: Bandura, Grusec, and Menlove, 1967; Bandura and Menlove, 1968. On self-sacrifice: Bryan and Walbek, 1970; Walbek, 1969. On affection: Frybear and Thelen, 1969. On self-criticism: Thelen, 1969. On self-control: Bandura and Mischel, 1965; Stein and Bryan, 1972; Stein and Friedrich, 1972. On the tendency to be reflective rather than impulsive during problem solving: Debus, 1970; Ridberg, Parke, and Hetherington, 1971. On the moral judgments of children: Bandura and McDonald, 1963; Cowan et al., 1969. On the tendency to initiate social contacts with peers: O'Connor, 1969, 1972. On the inhibition of deviant behavior: Slaby and Parke, 1971; Walters, Leat, and Mezei, 1963; Walters and Parke, 1964; Walters, Parke, and Cane, 1965; Wolf, 1972.

sive.[3] Almost all agree that while aggressive models will induce aggression in many viewers, each child will respond according to his personality and the particular conditions of his viewing.[4]

Thus, a model's behavior can either "incite" or "defuse" the viewer, can either increase or decrease the likelihood that the viewer will behave like the characters he sees on television. Psychologists suggest three modes to explain how incitement occurs. Models can show viewers what behaviors are possible, appropriate or permissible, and reinforced in the situation: for example, that one may injure another, that it may be appropriate or permissible for one man to injure another in self-defense, and that in some conditions it may even be praiseworthy for one man to injure another, as when an antagonist threatens harm to a third person. The opposite defusing effects are explained in a somewhat parallel way; models also show viewers what responses are inappropriate or prohibited, and display the likelihood of negative consequences of such acts. Inherently, television neither incites nor defuses. It can do both or either.

A specific case illustrates the alternatives. Television should be able to alert young children to physical dangers in their environments. They must learn not to cross streets at the wrong time or place, to avoid harmful foods and medicines, and to recognize the many dangers beyond their understanding and control. Parents ordinarily have great difficulty teaching these lessons, often with tragic consequences. But no one has discovered how to teach these lessons on television either. To expose the potential danger, television must simultaneously expose the act itself. For example, how can television show the dangers of taking drugs, in the hope of discouraging this behavior, without

[3] Those who claim that viewing aggression incites violence include Bandura, 1969; Berkowitz, 1962; Bryan and Schwartz, 1971; Dubanoski and Parton, 1971; Liebert, Neale, and Davidson, 1973; Surgeon General's Report, 1972. Those who claim that viewing aggression defuses violence include Feshbach and Singer, 1971. Those who report no discernible effect of televised violence upon antisocial behavior include Milgram and Shotland, 1973.

[4] For example, the similarity of the televised characters and the viewers (e.g., Feshbach, 1961; Rosekrans, 1967), the degree of the viewer's frustration (e.g., Berkowitz and Geen, 1966), and the viewer's sex, with boys showing more film-induced aggression than girls (e.g., Bandura, Ross, and Ross, 1963; Hicks, 1965; Maccoby and Wilson, 1957)—all affect the degree of aggressive modeling.

displaying these acts, and thereby risking incitement to them? Nobody has found a way. What remains clear is the powerful effect of models in influencing learning, whether those influences provoke or inhibit the behavior of the viewer.

Television as Transportation

In addition to showing a variety of people and behaviors, television has another inherent property that deserves experimentation: its remarkable ability to transport, to take children to events, places and experiences that they have never seen before and are unlikely ever to have the opportunity to see in person. Young children, especially those confined to inner cities, necessarily move within a very narrow neighborhood. Television can and should take them beyond these boundaries.

Television and Shared Experience

With this ability to show people and events to large numbers of children simultaneously, television can become an unprecedented source of shared experience. Even now television provides the single greatest common experience of American children. The classic instances of television's impact (for example, in showing assassinations, riots and war, the excitement of space exploration) almost force us to share events as they occur.

There are no historical precedents to this universal sharing. Newspaper accounts of critical events inevitably are delayed and reach only a selected audience. Radio provides immediacy, but lacks the graphic quality of television, which is totally new in reaching almost everyone with visual portrayals of events as they occur. We now take this capability for granted, ignoring its historical uniqueness.

This has special implications for the American family. Among our scarcest commodities are opportunities for parents and children to share experiences that they both can enjoy and discuss. Indeed, we even seem to have lost the impulse to seek these opportunities. On those rare occasions when parents are forced by circumstances to share experiences with their children (or even worse, when children are forced to include their parents), both parents and children either are bewildered about how to behave or, once in a while, find extraordinary, unexpected pleasure in the confrontation. Television viewing remains an unpressured and natural occasion for sharing within families.

Television's Economy

The tragedy of inadequate education is so intolerable that one hesitates to defend an educational service because of its low cost. But since financial support for education is not unlimited, every approach must consider its costs against its benefits, and if we are going to discuss balance sheets, television looks good. When a series attracts a large national audience, its cost per child per viewing hour is reduced to a very low figure. Even with the Children's Television Workshop's comparatively luxurious allowance of eight million dollars for its first two years of planning, programing and broadcasting, the cost of reaching each child in its audience of preschoolers was less than one cent per child per viewing hour.

Why Our Series Might Not Work

There were as many reasons to expect our series to fail as there were favoring it. Almost everything that needed to be done would be new and untried. No one had combined entertainment and education in a national series for children. No one knew how large an audience could be attracted to such a series. No organization had ever been created to achieve this purpose. Although the form that the organization would take was without precedent, Joan Cooney knew the kind of people she would need and knew that they would be scarce. This perhaps was the greatest obstacle of all.

For creative producers and writers, working in children's television always has been near the bottom of the prestige ladder. It is regarded as a place to apprentice in learning the trade or as a stepping stone to more elevated status. Producing educational programs is regarded as even worse, a refuge for untalented technicians. Finding talented producers and writers who wanted to make a long-term commitment to an educational series for children would require miracles.

Researchers with experience observing children also would be needed, and here the prospects were even worse. Not only would the researchers need to invent ways to observe children's reactions to television, but they then would need to convey their insights to the production staff in a form that would guide efforts to build better shows. Since researchers with these experiences and skills were nonexistent, we would be forced to guess who might be able to grow into the job.

Joan Cooney's plan also included people to work with parents and organizations in inner cities. Public television's record of attracting large inner-city audiences is notoriously bad, and before anything else could be achieved, we had to get the children and their families to watch. Existing inner-city agencies are so overburdened with their own projects that we could not expect them to do our work for us. New approaches had to be found, and we would need our own staff of community workers to find them.

Every other necessary step was just as untried. We needed a process for deciding on the educational goals of the series. Since no organized network of public-broadcasting stations existed at the time,[5] we needed to convince each of the then approximately 180 public-broadcasting stations individually to broadcast the series and to carry it during times when preschoolers would watch. We had no idea where long-term financial support could be found; the first-year budget carried no

---

[5] Since then, the "Public Broadcasting Service" has slowly gained "network" status, providing a major distribution service.

obligation by the foundations and government agencies to continue funding even if the series were successful. There was almost nothing that could be based upon established practice.

All these obstacles were specific to our series. Critics of television in general have provided a full catalogue of grievances, all of which deserve to be considered when programs for children are planned. Profoundly destructive effects of television are hypothesized and deplored, especially the teaching of violence and physical passivity. Claims for almost every possible effect of televised violence—incitement to aggression, its defusing through television viewing, or the lack of any discernible effect whatever—have been made, and each has some support. Critics complain that even if televised violence does not always lead to aggression, whenever this does occur, it is to be deplored, and many parents agree.

Another parental objection to television is its seductive appeal to children. One parent observes: "The main disadvantage of television for children is not so much what it inspires them to do, but what they miss by sitting down and watching television. It takes time away from reading and outdoor activities, which is why we limit it. It is a form of entertainment in which they do not participate [quoted by Steiner, 1963, p. 94]." According to this argument, the better the programs, the more insidious the effects upon children. Good programs will seduce children into distraction and passivity even more than bad programs. This in turn relates to a larger complaint: that television creates an attitude of spectatorship, a withdrawal from active participation in events and experiences.

Hard evidence on these effects is unavailable, and the objections often seem overstated. For example, in 1969 an article in the Boston *Globe* quoted Dr. S. Hayakawa (semanticist and past president of San Francisco State College) as saying: "The kinship of the LSD and other drug experiences with television is glaringly obvious: both depend upon turning on and passively waiting for something beautiful to happen." The kinship that Hayakawa sees between television and drugs may be "glaringly obvious" or only semantically obvious.

Other objections stress television's limitations as a teaching tool. Psychologists and educators have worked hard to try to identify the conditions that promote efficient learning.[6] These researchers have had their problems even in the laboratories, and when they move into classrooms and the child's natural environment, they have even more trouble. Even so, they have still come up with some favorite themes: two-way exchange between student and teacher, sequencing of the material to be learned into small steps of increasing difficulty, evoking active participation from the learner, and providing clear reinforcement of the right responses and quick correction of the wrong ones.

If indeed these are necessary conditions for learning, television in its present form cannot be expected to accomplish much. It is mostly one-way communication, at least until two-way television technologies are refined. Rarely is televised material carefully sequenced in small ordered steps, active physical responses are not demanded, and the child can be reinforced by television only in the most impersonal way. But if television does not supply these necessary conditions, most of the young child's natural environment does not supply them any better. His world is simply not organized neatly into sequences, into ordered opportunities for active responses, or into reinforcements that are finely adjusted to his behavior. Yet the young child does seem to learn, often at a remarkably rapid rate.

Even under controlled laboratory conditions, sequence and other presumed conditions of learning have been brought into question. The random scrambling of sequenced instruction often produces results that are indistinguishable from carefully ordered instruction. Several studies[7] conclude that there are few differences in performance between groups who have been exposed to logical, systematic instructional sequences and groups who have taken illogical, random or scrambled sequences.

[6] Some leading contributors include Gage, 1963; Gagné, 1965; Miller, 1957; Skinner, 1958, 1971.
[7] For example, Cartwright, 1971; Hamilton, 1964; Levin and Baker, 1963; Payne, et al., 1967; Roe, et al., 1962; Wodtke, et al., 1967.

There are other reasons for suspecting that television is not an ideal teaching tool. Psychologists stress the value of involving all of the child's senses (seeing, hearing, touch, smell) in learning.[8] While television can capitalize on sight, sound, and their combination, it excludes the use of other modalities. In addition, the combination of sight and sound—television's primary strength—is difficult to achieve in practice. It takes planning and careful execution to combine sight and sound so that they reinforce each other instead of conflicting, with each distracting the child's attention from the other.

Some objections to television go far beyond attacking the bad habits it may induce and its limitations for teaching—for example, the argument that television is a major contributor to the dehumanizing technological orientation of our society. According to this argument, television has made us lose contact with each other, and to seek and accept solitary vicarious spectatorship as the normal course of human activity. Not only does it destroy relationships between people, but its bombardment of commercialization—its use in selling products both to adults and to children—forces us to regard each other as markets instead of people, diminishing us both as individuals and as a society.

Our series would confront all these risks. Through careful planning, it might avoid some of them. For example, even if televised aggression were found to be effective in holding children's attention, we would simply refuse to use it. By being aware of the common use of television as baby-sitter, we would seek ways to get parents and older children to share in the young child's viewing. Risks would remain, but the need to create additional educational alternatives is imperative, and there were enough good reasons to justify the experiment.

[8] For example, Bissell, White, and Zivin, 1971.

Section Two: Planning

~~~~~~

Grownups never seem to understand anything by themselves, and it is tiresome for children to be always and forever explaining things to them.

Antoine de Saint-Exupéry,
The Little Prince

On March 15, 1968, several government agencies and private foundations announced their joint support for Joan Cooney's proposal "Television for Preschool Children." Among them, they had put together a grant of 8 million dollars to cover an eighteen-month planning period and a year's series of 130 one-hour programs. In a joint statement, Alan Pifer, president of Carnegie Corporation, McGeorge Bundy, president of the Ford Foundation, and Harold Howe, then U.S. Commissioner of Education, said:

> This is an enterprise that needs and deserves public and private support. Our three organizations are glad to join forces in experimenting with the use of television for early childhood stimulation . . . The question is . . . whether the kind of entertainment that children like on television can be put to educational purposes.

In a statement of his own, Harold Howe restated two basic questions that the project was setting out to answer, and then added the sobering thought that predictions of success perhaps were premature since the project had not yet begun.

> Can a daily television program filled with elements of learning attract and hold the attention of four- and five-year-olds—particularly those from deprived homes—in free competition with animated cartoons and "shoot-'em-ups?" If the series can win and hold this attention, will the children learn basic skills?

> There's a lot of open water between today's launching and a successful landing. No one can predict success—partial or unqualified. But it is a test we must make unless we want to admit, in advance, that television with all the attention it commands from small children cannot serve more than a babysitter's role.

Although the commercial networks were hesitant to endorse a television effort supported by noncommercial funds, even they added their verbal if not their financial blessings. For example, Michael Dann (then vice-president of the Columbia Broadcasting System, later to join the Children's Television Workshop) hailed the Workshop as one of the most important breakthroughs in the history of the mass media.

This was not the first time in television's history that brave promises had been made for the just-around-the-corner benefits that the medium was soon to bestow upon children. The present sources of the announcements—government and foundation agencies—were new, but similar words had been heard before. Soon-to-appear new-and-improved children's programs had been proclaimed periodically by the commercial networks throughout their twenty-five-year history. Each time the call to action was sounded, the words were just as well-intentioned, but they never resulted in any sustained accomplishment, any persisting elevation of quality. As soon as public pressures receded, children's programing fell back into its gentle stupor.

If things were to be different this time, the right creative producers, writers and researchers would have to be found. This clearly was the most difficult problem the project would ever face. We got lucky. If we hadn't, *Sesame Street* never would have happened.

Ultimately, the task simply was to find the right people and then to make certain that they would be protected from outside pressures while creating the series. We had a few criteria in mind in conducting the search. Producing five shows, each one hour long, for twenty-six consecutive weeks is a vast undertaking. It takes years of experience to solve the continual crises that arise in daily production and to recover in time for the next day's production. People with this experience are scarce and usually have moved out of children's programing into activities that bring more prestige and more money. David Connell was the best choice for executive producer because of his ingenuity, practical good sense and eleven years of experience as producer of *Captain Kangaroo*, a daily CBS morning program for preschool children. But at this time he was comfortably and profitably settled in the film business and seemed genuinely alarmed at the prospect of returning to the grind of a daily series for children. What convinced him to return is unclear. He claims it was Joan Cooney's charm and persuasiveness, and this surely was the case. But this was abetted by Dave's own lurking hope that we actually might achieve something useful to young children. With his acceptance of the job, the pieces of the puzzle began to fall into place as he and Joan Cooney started to assemble the group of producers and writers who were to create the programs.

Samuel Gibbon, who had worked with Connell on *Captain Kangaroo* and had left that show earlier, was hired as producer because he had the excellent technical skills needed to sustain the pace of a five-show-a-week schedule and because he could work under pressure. There was nothing in his previous experience, however, to predict his extraordinary grasp of the ways academics think about the development of children and the ways in which their ideas might connect with television production. Most of us expected that before the season ended, the brutal schedule would burn out several producers. Sam survived, a perfectionist who wore a perpetually worried look that we took to mean that he felt that everything was always going wrong. He often did feel this way, but the worry also contained a force that sustained him, a compulsive urge to probe television's effects upon young children and the sense that this mystery always was just beyond reach.

The head writer, Jon Stone, also was hired at this time. Jon had worked with Connell and Gibbon, and he brought his own worried frown to the Workshop's atmosphere. His worry, however, was a sense of personal pain and outrage at the world's injustices—poverty, wars, the way we treat old people, the way we treat our environment. He had retreated with his family to a house in Vermont, but once again the temptation that television might help young children was too great.

In turn, Matt Robinson, a black producer and writer of black-oriented public-affairs shows in Philadelphia, was added to the creative staff. When the producers later found it difficult to locate a black actor to play Gordon—the strong male character on the program—Matt was asked to audition, and immediately conveyed the combination of casualness and authority that the producers were looking for. A later key appointment was Jeff Moss, who had written book, music and lyrics for two Princeton Triangle reviews and had acted in them as well, had written for *Captain Kangaroo,* and then had withdrawn in frustration to do some "serious writing" when Connell and Stone enlisted him for the writing staff.

Two other major decisions were made. Joan Cooney had suggested in her proposal that puppets be included in the series. Some members of the creative staff were generally skeptical about the use of puppets. However, they had long admired the work of Jim Henson, creator of the Muppet puppets, and he was asked to join in our early planning. Henson and his associates had created an array of puppets that came in all shapes, sizes and guises. Connell, Gibbon and Stone all guessed that the variety, charm and vitality of these Muppets would provide the writers with a wide field for their imaginations. In addition, some of the production techniques and Muppet characters that Henson had earlier created for special children's programs, commercials and adult variety shows seemed to have great potential for presenting educational content in an entertaining manner. For example, in a piece that had appeared on the *Ed Sullivan Show,* Henson created a "thought balloon" technique in which one Muppet character tries to convey an idea to another. As the first Muppet talks, his version of the thought appears visually in a balloon above his head while the other Muppet's balloon displays his own interpretation of what he is hearing. The producers guessed that such techniques (later used in some of our animation sequences), along with the Muppets themselves, would fit our purposes well, a guess that was correct almost beyond belief, as Bert and Ernie, Kermit the Frog, Big Bird, Oscar the Grouch, Cookie Monster and others, some of whom were newly created for *Sesame Street,* were to become the heart of the series.

Less visible than the Muppets, but as crucial to *Sesame Street,* is its music. Joe Raposo was known by the producers to possess an amazing instinct for creating music that was at once sophisticated and uncluttered. His musical training had started with his bandleader father and continued with Walter Piston at Harvard and Nadia Boulanger in Paris. He wrote music for summer theater, taught at the Boston Conservatory, and then wrote music for off Broadway, Broadway and television, including a show for ABC called *Hey, Cinderella* with Stone and Henson. His music reflects his character, full of infectious enthusiasm and affection for children along with a true instinct for musical composition and performance. The variety in Joe's music is enormous, yet its distinctive flavor gives *Sesame Street* a cohesiveness that binds its elements together.

Later in the planning period, Connell, Gibbon and Stone also assembled the cast of *Sesame Street*'s adult inhabitants. Since we stressed the importance of providing characters with whom inner-city children would identify, we decided that two cast members would be a black husband and wife. Loretta Long, a singer who had earlier taught school, was cast as Susan, and after prolonged efforts to locate a black actor to play Susan's husband, Matt Robinson switched from his production job to play Gordon. Bob McGrath, an experienced singer, joined Susan and Gordon on the street as their white neighbor. Will Lee, a character actor with forty years of experience, completed the adult cast as Mr. Hooper, the candy-store owner.

It was no easier to locate researchers for the Workshop, but there was one trained psychologist, Dr. Edward L. Palmer, who at this time was actually studying children's reactions to television. With a doctorate from Michigan State University, Ed was working at the Oregon State Division of Higher Education, where he was developing measures of children's attention to television. Not only did he have the right training and interests, but he was gifted in communicating his observations to producers and writers. In the summer of 1968 Ed joined the Workshop and engaged in planning the educational goals, defining the Workshop's research activities, and assembling his research team.

We also knew that our work with parents and organizations in inner cities would have to be carefully planned. This would demand at least as much ingenuity as production and research, and we would need someone with a special knowledge of the inner-city communities themselves. Some of us had experience working with community people in inner cities, but at this time our staff was mostly white and mostly middle class, and we needed all the help we could find from people more experienced in community activities. Alerting these communities to the existence of *Sesame Street* would be only part of the job. What we especially wanted was to discover the types of educational services that could and would reinforce the program's effects, in store fronts, living rooms, community centers and wherever children could watch in the presence of sympathetic adults and older children. Later during this planning period, an experienced community worker, Evelyn Davis, joined the Workshop from the New York Urban League, and she formed a staff to work with local community people in inner cities throughout the United States.

Reaching families in inner cities would be difficult. A national effort would also be needed to distribute advance information elsewhere around the country. The Workshop retained the services of the Carl Byoir agency and asked them to assign to us the man we knew would bring imagination and energy to the job, Bob Hatch. With a background in journalism and in public relations, Bob had just returned to Byoir from a four-year tour with the Peace Corps. Without overselling a series that was not to appear for another eighteen months, Bob and his small staff began letting people around the country know that the series was coming.

Every organization needs someone who knows everything that goes on within it and can do almost any of its jobs. During these early days, the Workshop was small enough for Joan Cooney to play this role herself, but she knew that the growing demands on her time would soon prevent her from staying in close personal touch with all Workshop activities. She had worked at Channel 13 in New York with Bob Davidson, whose quiet competence seemed perfect for the job. Clearheaded and very bright, he seemed willing to unobtrusively track all activities and to help solve the daily operational crises that surely would erupt. Joan appointed him assistant project director (he later became corporate secretary), and Bob immediately became the glue that held the organization together. His first major responsibility was to obtain the consent of the then roughly 180 public-broadcasting station managers around the country to carry the series at a morning time when preschoolers were likely to watch. He and I also began working closely together to plan the meetings to decide upon our educational objectives.

The timing of these appointments was critical. Producers, researchers and community personnel all had to participate in the planning of educational goals if that planning were to be of any value when the programs actually were produced and distributed. Educational programs often fail because they are planned by one group and implemented by another. We decided that both the design and implementation of *Sesame Street* had to be carried out by a single group working in unison, and that the creative staff would work closely with educators and other advisors from the outset.

By the summer of 1968 we had hired most of this creative staff and we were ready to think hard about what the specific goals of the series should be. Joan Cooney had outlined some general areas in her proposal, including language skills, number concepts, reasoning and problem solving, and social development. These would need more detailed specification before they could be useful for television production; this was one of the responsibilities for which I had joined the Workshop—to help to define our objectives precisely and to set priorities among them.

Chapter Three

Goals

*Our inventions are wont to be pretty toys, which dis-
tract our attention from serious things. They are but
improved means to an unimproved end, an end which
it was already but too easy to arrive at; as railroads
lead to Boston or New York. We are in great haste to
construct a magnetic telegraph from Maine to Texas;
but Maine and Texas, it may be, have nothing important to communicate.*

Henry David Thoreau,
Walden

As we began to think about what we should try to teach on
television, we found ourselves working in almost a complete
vacuum. We had no plans for how our ideas could be translated into production, what the series would look like, or even
what the name of the show would be. Later, as the format and
style of the shows became clearer, our ideas about what to
teach became clearer too. But in the beginning we were forced
to work abstractly, and although we found a great many intelligent advisors who were willing to help us, we struggled to find
some firm ground on which to stand.

Joan Cooney's proposal to the funding agencies suggested the
formation of a National Board of Advisors, and I was to chair
this board's activities. Establishing such a group is customary
procedure, but her suggestion was unusual. The board would
not act to kosher a product created by others but would actually contribute substantially to the design and implementation

of the project. With only a few tremors of shocked surprise by board members asked to provide more than window dressing, the Board was formed,[1] went to work, and began to construct a base of ideas about educational goals and methods from which a creative television staff could begin to operate. Here is how this happened.

The Board of Advisors has been helpful in many ways, including giving advice on educational questions, reviewing plans under consideration, and offering suggestions for staffing, organization and other operating procedures. Their first project was to identify what we should teach the children who watched the shows; it was my responsibility to organize and conduct a series of seminars at which these goals would be decided. In the spring and summer of 1968 we held five three-day seminars. Many additional seminars and informal meetings would follow before *Sesame Street* began broadcasting in November 1969, but as an initial step toward establishing its educational goals, each seminar considered one of these topics:

1. Social, Moral, and Affective Development
2. Language and Reading
3. Mathematical and Numerical Skills
4. Reasoning and Problem Solving
5. Perception

Two of the seminars were held in a large meeting room at Harvard University, an atmosphere that was somewhat staid but presented few distractions. The others were held in large hotels in New York City, which was both more interesting and more distracting to the participants. New York City's activities

[1] The original Board of Advisors, with their affiliations in 1968, included: Leon Eisenberg, Massachusetts General Hospital; Stephen O. Frankfurt, Young and Rubicam; Allonia Gadsen, The Emerson School; Dorothy Hollingsworth, Seattle Model Cities Program; J. McVicker Hunt, University of Illinois; Francis Mechner, Institute of Behavior Technology; Glen P. Nimnicht, Far West Laboratory for Educational Research and Development; Keith Osborn, University of Georgia; Chester Pierce, Harvard University; Elmo Roper, Roper Research Associates; Maurice Sendak, author and illustrator of children's books; Paul K. Taff, National Educational Television.

exerted a faint but continuous pull on the advisors, who came from various parts of the country. For those advisors and workshop staff who lived in New York City, being within easy telephone distance of their offices posed some diversion. However, the meetings did not seem to suffer much from these distractions, as most participants showed great stamina and commitment to the job we were trying to do.

Before most seminars a small planning group met to decide on examples of the skills to be discussed, some ground rules for conducting the seminar, and the roster of people to be invited. We decided that at each seminar we would have as many different points of view as possible, including those of preschool teachers, psychologists, film makers, psychiatrists, artists, musicians, children's book writers, performers, sociologists, puppeteers, television producers and creative advertising personnel. This might create some difficulties in communication, but we also expected that we would get more varied contributions.

The Process

Professional educators and psychologists have fallen into bad habits at conventions and conferences, where meetings often are given over to the clever swapping of words. Elegant practiced speeches are given to display expertness before the group, zigzagging conversations are typical when consecutive comments by participants are unconnected, and Talmudic haggling is common over old professional controversies. We had a specific job to do in our seminars, however, and could not afford to have it sink beneath the weight of these customs. To keep the discussions from wandering in all directions, we not only organized our procedures carefully, but at the beginning of each seminar we offered some guidelines about television and about children.

Although several participants attended more than one seminar, different people were invited to discuss the different topics. To give each group some orientation, I began each meeting with a statement of our general purposes and our immediate need to develop a specific curriculum to guide television production. Joan would then describe some boundaries that the use of television would impose upon us, stressing that television had unique features of its own. If we tried to force it into another framework, such as the classroom, it would lose its integrity as a medium and become an imitation of something it is not. Television, she would say, is but one among several forms of experience and cannot replace or compete with other educational opportunities. It can only complement whatever else the child has available, and therefore our curriculum would need to be selective, acknowledging that television can never give the young child everything he or she needs educationally. Joan emphasized that the series had to be entertaining in order to compete with existing programs and to attract a large audience of preschoolers. To attract these preschoolers, it also would have to appeal to their older brothers and sisters, who are more likely to control the set. Although we would try to get parents to watch with their children, Joan made it clear that the series could not depend upon adult participation. These remarks would set some clear boundaries for the discussions that followed.

At most of the seminars Dr. Sheldon White, a Harvard psychologist who provided valuable direction to the seminars and later collaborated closely with the producers in designing *Sesame Street*, would then describe some upper and lower boundaries in the learning of three-, four-, and five-year-old children. In other contexts both Shep and I had participated in many fruitless professional discussions that tried to describe the characteristics of the "average disadvantaged four-year-old," passing over the fact of wide variation among children. As an alternative, Shep discussed the range of skills in these ages, what sorts of things we might aim to accomplish given this range, and what must surely be beyond our expectations. During the seminar on numerical skills, for example, he indicated that the concepts of multiplication and division were beyond their grasp, that simple enumeration, addition and subtraction might be within the reach of many, while a few children would already have some rudimentary ability to count in sequence. These observations provided a valuable orientation for the participants who lacked direct experience with young children and also set additional boundaries upon subsequent discussions.

Within these boundaries the members of each seminar began suggesting specific goals for the series. Each seminar of approximately twenty participants proceeded in a similar fashion. First, the entire group formulated as comprehensive a list as possible of what might be taught on their particular topic, without regard to the organization, order or priority of importance of these ideas. During the first day of the seminar on language skills, for example, over one hundred ideas were suggested, ranging from reciting the alphabet to recognizing the sounds of individual letters and several letter combinations to learning to listen and to ask questions. These suggestions were assembled into three or four loose clusters of related skills, and on the second day small groups were formed to consider each cluster, to identify the important suggestions and to begin considering production possibilities. Each small group was composed of a cross section of the people at the seminar. On the third day the full group reconvened to discuss the ideas developed in detail by the small groups.

The reality of the meetings was far less orderly than this account suggests. None of us had a firm idea of where we were going or of what the profitable directions would be. Inevitably, the sessions often rambled or swirled wildly. All of us were confused much of the time, and bored or tired some of the time. But eventually we did define a curriculum to guide *Sesame Street*'s production. Not only did we identify specific goals, but as the seminars wore on, our premises became clearer.

The Premises

We strongly endorsed the fundamental purpose of preparing children for school. While this may seem to be an obvious goal, there is considerable opposition to it. Some people see the schools as so useless and inhumane that preparation for them shares their uselessness. None of us believed that the schools were everything they should be, especially for children living in city ghettos, but we could not expect that they were going to change overnight. For better or worse, they were a fact of life. When the positive reasons for stressing school preparation seemed insufficient, some seminar members described the other side of the argument, the individual suffering and frustration of the child who is unprepared to face the school's demands. None of us thought we really knew how to prepare children for school, but we assumed that one likely route would be to build an appetite for learning based on real accomplishment and its recognition. One premise, then, was to suggest skills that might help prepare a child to enter school quickly and comfortably, skills that would be recognized by people important to the child as something worth knowing.

What we meant by school preparation is illustrated in the choice of one of our simplest but most controversial curriculum objectives, teaching the alphabet. Eventually, we decided to teach the child to "recite the alphabet," though howls of repugnance arose over our use of the new technology to teach what appears to be an arbitrary and useless skill. Why should we bother? Our answer was to refer to the relationship between alphabet learning and success in early reading in school.[2] Surely many other skills more important than alphabet recitation are required before children are ready to read, but if they can learn the sights and sounds of letters in part by learning to recite the alphabet, if we can make it fun for them to learn, and if there is reason to believe that it will facilitate later learning, then we figured that we would try it.

Another criterion for selecting goals became clear during the seminars: what inner-city parents say they want for their children. Although inner-city parents may suspect that schools do not function to their children's benefit, they want what most other parents want—reading, writing, arithmetic and any other

2 For example, Bond and Dykstra, 1967; Chall, 1967.

skills that will equip their children for later life. We know that inner-city families feel strongly about educational achievement, even if they aren't sure how to motivate their children, help them to set realistic goals or show them how to succeed. After many years of seeing inner-city parents work to gain greater educational opportunities for their children, we should not need research studies to document this commitment, but they exist anyway.[3]

To meet these aspirations, inner-city parents take a utilitarian view of education and seek for their children the basic intellectual skills that have broad currency in our society. In an article entitled "It's into Cognition, Baby," Clayton Riley writes:

> And if you talk to Black parents in a city like New York, any program intended to give their kids a leg up in the reading, writing, and arithmetic sweepstakes, any program that will help their kids compete on sensible, perhaps *even* terms has got to make sense, has got to be a project that's on the case. Radicals can scream brainwash, but what is the mother whose experience with the school system tells her that changes, innovations, and any other things offering educational assistance are needed —just what is she talking about? Moreover, there isn't a militant on the scene who doesn't know the value of having read his own classics: Malcolm X, Chairman Mao, Cleaver, Huey Newton, Guevara . . . the revolution is learned, is read, has been written. Take the positives, the help, wherever you can find it. "By any means necessary" wasn't written to be stared at dumbly by people who needed to know what it meant but couldn't figure out what it said. Check it out. [New York *Times*, February 8, 1971]

There were objections in the seminars that these basic skills teach the children *what* to think instead of *how* to think. Some psychologists distinguish the thought "product" and the

---

[3] For example, Baughman and Dahlstrom, 1968; Cloward and Jones, 1963; Deutsch, 1965; Gurin and Katz, 1966; Herriott and St. John, 1966; Reiss and Rhodes, 1959.

thought "process," concluding that the quality of the process is crucial to a child's development while the correctness of the product is inconsequential. For example, Lawrence Kohlberg, a psychologist from Harvard University, argued that when a child is able to think causally instead of magically—when he develops a sense of why one event (teasing an animal) leads to another (getting scratched)—a definite developmental advance is made, in contrast to the trivial accomplishment of learning the meaning of vocabulary words like "envelope" or "amanuensis," the kind of miscellaneous information tested in standard measures of intelligence. At our seminars, we decided to try both the what to think and the how to think. We did not see any incompatibility between the two, so we took as another premise that information probably is worth having if only to provide thought processes with material to manipulate.

Three related aims thus began to emerge: school preparation, the inner-city families' stress on basic skills, and the effort to teach both what and how to think. We also had decided to ignore the "average" child and what he is like at a particular age, and consider the range of skills in the three-to-five-year-old audience. We eliminated certain skills from consideration because most three-year-olds already possess them (for example, the words that label certain parts of the body), and there seemed no need to teach them. (Some advisors argued cogently that some very simple skills should be included anyway, to give even the youngest child the confidence that comes from seeing something that he already knows. We decided that with so much to teach that at least some children do not know, we should not concentrate on skills that all children already possess.) In contrast, if we knew that no five-year-olds yet possessed a certain skill, we concluded that it may well be beyond the reach of our audience and we should not include it.

During the seminars, we argued about whether we should depict the child's world as it is or as we might want it to be. Since we had already decided to reach inner-city children, this came down to the question of whether we should present the realities of the ghettos as they are or as they might be if we really cared to have something better. Some participants said that we must show people acting with kindness and decency toward each other, that even young children already know about life's harsh realities, and if they don't now, they will learn soon enough. Others disagreed, claiming that we would mislead gullible young children into expecting that everyone will be decent to them when instead we should be preparing them to cope with indecency and harshness. We decided to try it both ways, to show the world as it is and some aspects of the world as it could be.

We decided not to be constrained during the early planning by what we felt the producers and writers might not be able to do. Instead, we asked advisors to offer whatever educational ideas came into their minds, leaving it ultimately to the creative staff to invent ways to translate the goals into television programing. Furthermore, we asked the advisors to suggest whatever production possibilities occurred to them as they listed potential objectives. This was not done to impose the burdens of production upon them (their contribution, after all, was to create a curriculum), and we did not anticipate that their production ideas would be of direct value.[4] But looking for these ideas forced the educators to make the meaning of their educational suggestions clearer to the creative staff.

We did not order the curriculum from simpler to more complex skills. No matter how entertaining the show might prove to be, many children would view irregularly, and they would differ widely in age, background and prior experience. The kind of sequencing that is possible with captive audiences is impossible with television, and we concluded that no single

---

[4] It turned out that some production suggestions were of direct value, for example, building characters around the ideas that making mistakes is no catastrophe (later to become Big Bird) and that different people perceive the same situation differently or feel differently about it (later to become Oscar the Grouch). There were also, of course, good production reasons behind the decision to develop these characters; when production began, it became apparent that the live characters on the street of *Sesame Street* would need to be bolstered by other interesting characters, such as Big Bird and Oscar the Grouch. Most other production ideas from the educators were not used—for example, having viewing children copy letters and numbers shown on television by drawing on the screen with crayons or magic markers.

program could require that its audience had seen any preceding program.

A final premise that we rejected has broad implications. One common basis for deciding what should be taught in preschool is the presumed differences between advantaged and disadvantaged children. With middle-class characteristics as a standard, some preschools are designed to bring disadvantaged children up to that standard. Aimed at giving the have-nots what the haves already possess—it must be good or why would the haves have bothered to get it?—these conpensatory education programs are based on what has been called the "deficit model." We rejected this model.

Everyone in the seminars agreed that what the middle class has is not uniformly good. No one believed that our only social problem is the insufficient distribution of middle-class paraphernalia throughout our society. But no one thought that we should romanticize the presumably great benefits that poverty confers, the spontaneity, generosity and brotherhood that oppression supposedly creates. Surely it is hard to believe that people are poor because they want to be.

A more covert flaw in the deficit model is the assumption that class differences identify the cause of the problems of the disadvantaged. If the inner-city children are more present-oriented, or live in more crowded conditions, or speak an inferior nonstandard English,[5] it does not mean that correcting any or all of these conditions would make them middle class or even that they have any desire to undergo this particular transformation.

If the logic of the deficit model were better, the absence of empirical evidence still would prevent its use. Since discussions of the disadvantaged have become fashionable, an incredible array of proclamations has appeared on the differences between the advantaged and the disadvantaged. Most writers pick their favorite candidate for the principal deficiency of disadvantaged children. Others decide that it is neither really so great to be

---

[5] On present-orientation, see Banfield (1970); on crowdedness, Hunt (1968); on non-standard English, Deutsch (1963), Green (1964), Hurst (1965).

middle class nor really so bad to be poor, and then develop long romantic descriptions (e.g., Cheyney, 1967) of all of the special strengths of the poor as compared to the presumably flabby, coddled middle class. But in our opinion neither favorite deficits nor presumed superiorities had any empirical justification.

The unfortunate chronicle of preschool efforts guided by this deficit model began over a decade ago and still is going strong. Guessing that the poor child's primary problem is his inability to use language effectively, compensatory preschools set out to build language skills. Betting on the absence of tender, loving care at home, other preschools tried to compensate by the teachers' giving of this care. Also lacking facts, other preschools assumed that the environments of poor children are chaotic; these programs presented a structured, tidy atmosphere. Assuming that the poor child's inferior reasoning skills were his major disadvantage, preschool programs provide training in the understanding of cause-effect relationships. There may not be special preschools to correct each of the following deficits, but each has been proposed at one time or another as the special source of difficulty for the disadvantaged: low motivation for educational achievement, weak self-concept, inability to defer gratification, absent fathers, inadequate mothers, poor nutrition, insufficient medical care, lack of hope, insufficient language stimulation, crowding, poor teacher expectations, inability to read, inability to think abstractly, too much stimulation, too little stimulation.

All of these "compensatory" programs aim to make amends —to give the disadvantaged children whatever it is that will make them like everyone else. But neither logic nor experience endorsed this deficit model. Our contrasting premise is to give disadvantaged children what they need in order to learn to cope with their environments and improve their lives.

The Seminars: Lost in Space

By and large, the seminar discussions stayed within the guidelines we had set, although several unforeseen events occurred.

Although the members' various professional backgrounds elicited the desired diversity of suggestions for educational goals, it also brought problems of communication, some real and some imagined. No participant had previously tried to design a curriculum for a children's television series. No precedents exist on who should do it and how it should be done. Each group—academics, teachers, artists, children's book writers, and so forth—had a crucial but only partial contribution to make. Each participant was in an unfamiliar role, evoking various forms of accommodation, some beneficial and others destructive. Crosscurrents came from both professional and personal differences among seminar members:

- Academics versus nonacademics
- Practitioners with direct, daily contact with children versus those with only irregular contact
- Creators of ideas and materials versus critics, analysts, evaluators
- Research versus teaching versus social action
- Professionals with sufficient confidence in present institutions (including the schools) to advocate working within them versus those viewing present institutions as so corrupt that only their demolition will permit our survival
- Professionals accustomed to "word-swapping" versus those less practiced in verbal debate
- Professionals whose work derives mainly from intuition versus those who depend upon explicit, analytic problem solving
- Professionals whose disciplines contain a specialized vocabulary and language versus those whose professional language is common parlance

"Why Don't You Speak English?"

It is infuriating when a professional talks in his specialized jargon and seems unaware of its unfamiliarity to others. Probably all professionals are at least vaguely aware that their special vocabulary is not shared universally, but habits of thought and language may be so strong that they ignore the discrepancy. Confrontations over language occurred at each seminar, sometimes on several occasions. Their timing was unpredictable, but they often occurred when academics had lapsed into word-swapping skirmishes with each other. These exchanges never were allowed to continue for long, but they exceeded the patience of some nonacademics who asked, in one form or another, "Why don't you speak English?" The academics typically would reply that they were speaking English, that the artists and practitioners could easily follow the meaning and relevance of the discussion if they would only try. Although the nonacademics' protests often seemed justified, they sometimes assumed a stylized form that suggested that debating points were being won by those who attacked the academics' language. Sometimes these confrontations cleared the air a bit, if the exchange contained some humor and good faith. Sometimes the accusations remained unresolved until quieter discussions could be arranged between the people most involved.

To Think or Not to Think

A recurrent conflict arose over the use of creative intuition or deliberate analysis in designing material for children. The artists, children's book writers, film makers, performers—those professionals who must rely upon and trust intuition—vehemently protested imposing objective analysis upon their creativity. They contended that any creative product must be conceived intuitively and lovingly, with the creator drawing freely upon his own fantasies and feelings. These protests often occurred when the academics and educators appeared to be dissecting not only the creative product but the child himself, dividing and classifying his mind and heart into "symbolic representations," "cognitive processes," and "self-concept."

Since the seminars' purpose was the rational selection of educational goals, no progress could be made without settling this objection. In a series of temporary armistices, academics and educators (presumably the thinkers and analyzers) acknowledged the necessity of intuition but argued that analysis need not smother intuition. The protesters were skeptical of this compromise but were also eager to avoid a stalemate. They agreed to proceed in the unlikely hope that thought and intuition are not inevitably incompatible.

Having agreed to plan and analyze, the artists and children's book writers made heroic efforts to do so and did indeed contribute greatly. A few felt that their participation in these analytic procedures would compromise both personal integrity and professional trust in intuition; they retreated either physically or mentally from the meetings. Others reluctantly agreed to offer what they could. Taking collective deep breaths, and holding their noses, they did surprisingly well. They contributed substantively and also added a sense of whimsy and humor to the discussions that prevented them from becoming ponderous. Their presence also was a constant reminder that our ultimate purpose was to design creative television programs for real children.

Periodically the analytic discussion failed to hold the full attention of artists and writers. Maurice Sendak, an original member of the National Board of Advisors, attended most of the seminars and captured his reveries in doodles based on the elements of discussion that drifted through his unconscious. These doodles also capture many themes (sex roles, penis envy, sibling rivalry) that entered the discussions but were not included in our goals or program content.

Like the artists and writers, the academics found that their participation in the seminars placed unfamiliar, even uncomfortable demands upon them. Outstanding academics make their reputations by producing original ideas and new findings. Once their work becomes known, they often are asked to serve as critics or evaluators of the work of others, and to act as general-service gurus. Their role then is to criticize, to expound on the contributions of others. In being asked to construct a preschool curriculum for television, academics were being asked to initiate instead of react, to work against a dead-

Sex Roles

Sibling Rivalry

Sex Roles

line, to be constructive instead of critical, to be tolerant instead of judgmental, to work in a group instead of individually, and to be agile in thinking toward a purpose for which their professional knowledge did not prepare them directly because no existing knowledge was directly relevant. Some academics rose to these unusual demands magnificently; others folded.

Before extending invitations to the seminars, we asked ourselves what kind of participants we wanted. We didn't know who the effective members would turn out to be, but we used criteria such as prior productivity on a related topic; eagerness (or at least willingness) to think hard about television for chil-

Interactional problem Solving

Parent Participation

dren, a topic that many academics might dismiss as trivial; sense of humor and agility of mind; ability to think cooperatively with nonscholars outside their academic field; the inclination to avoid converting meetings into debates where points are won and lost but the job does not get done. By themselves, these are stringent criteria, but still others appeared during the course of the seminars.

Academics who contributed constructively used their professional knowledge as background music; the information was in the backs of their minds and they used it when it was relevant, but they drew on anything that might help. They refrained from giving the eloquent, practiced speeches that display expertness but do not push the group's planning ahead. In a large group, people inevitably cannot talk when they want to and it is difficult to carry on a consecutive conversation where comments build upon each other. Constructive participants avoided fragmented discussion and rarely offered ill-timed speeches.

Some of the academics tried to explain to the full group what psychology and child development really are all about, concluding that educating children in any basic ways through television is impossible. To others in the group, this conclusion seemed premature. As example, these issues were debated in one seminar:

- The impossibility of defining the term "perception." (Other participants asked: "So what? Who cares?")

- The absence of studies on differences in perceptual skills between advantaged and disadvantaged children. (Other participants commented: "These differences are not a useful guide to choosing goals, even if we had the evidence.")

- The absence of studies showing that perceptual skills can be trained. (Other participants commented: "No one said it would be easy.")

This arguing over issues that academics perennially debate among themselves both delayed and undermined useful conversation. One practical guide did emerge, however. Among the few invitees who were reluctant to attend, some doubted their professional or personal qualifications to contribute. When this seemed to stem from false modesty, we encouraged attendance and sometimes were successful. Out of these experiences, we formulated a guiding principle: When a person says that he cannot be helpful, believe him.

Despite major differences between television and classroom instruction, we knew that preschool teachers were essential to our curriculum planning. No other professional group has the same sustained daily contact with young children, the same intensity of prolonged interaction. However, status differences arose between academics and teachers. Many of the academics were widely known for their scientific contributions, and their accustomed relationship with teachers has become standard: The academic speaks and the teacher listens. Without good reason, this relationship has evolved and congealed through the years. As the meetings proceeded, occasions for informal conversations melted some of the customary status barriers and the teachers began to draw upon their knowledge of children to contribute valuable ideas to our planning.

The participation of the workshop's creative staff reminded advisors of their practical task of constructing goals that could be understood clearly and converted to television programing. Whenever esoteric jargon was used, the producers and writers, sounding like a Greek chorus, would intone repeatedly "What do you mean by that? What do you mean by that?" until a simple explanation was given or they concluded that none would be forthcoming. Since the staff's questions were made in a sincere attempt to understand (with only a slight tinge of testiness), the advisors always tried to clarify their meanings and often succeeded. Thus by participating in the seminars, the staff had the opportunity to understand both the intent and the meaning of the goals. Instead of being handed a curriculum and being told to teach "visual discrimination" or "differences in perspectives," they knew that they would be trying to teach children how to sort objects by size, form or function, or to understand that different people may have different reactions to the same situation.

Priorities among Goals

The seminars generated many more educational goals than could be incorporated into a single television series. When they ended, the workshop's creative staff met with Sheldon White and me to decide which goals were most important. The staff's stake in making selections it could live with was obviously great, and they needed full freedom to decide what goals might be workable for program production. By this time in the fall of 1968, almost the full production and research staffs had been assembled, and priorities were set through a process of individual advocacy by each staff member.

From a list of all the suggested educational goals, each staff member independently placed his bets on roughly the six or eight specific goals that he judged most important and that seemed most promising for television. In pooling our judgments, we easily found consensus on several language and numerical skills (those marked by asterisk in the curriculum[6]). We were more uncertain about what reasoning skills and social concepts to emphasize. We had little idea about how these could be taught on television, and we could no longer suspend judgment about what was feasible. By this time the first inklings of the format of *Sesame Street* were beginning to emerge, and the staff's intuitions about what could be taught through that format began to come into play.

Since one major premise was the preparation of disadvantaged children for school, I argued that the most useful ammunition we could give the child was the ability to "read" the teacher, to pick up the small, covert clues in the teacher's behavior that would allow him to guess what the teacher wants to hear. Simply alerting the child to this implicit rule of the game played in school, without necessarily teaching the techniques for playing it successfully, could equip him in a fundamental way for doing well in school. But even if we share the

---

[6] Dave Connell dubbed our priority-setting sessions "You Bet Your Asterisk."

conviction of others[7] that this is exactly at the core of what goes on in school, the argument implies considerable cynicism: that teachers have fixed ideas about proper school performance, that they credit only those responses that correspond to their fixed ideas, that a child will succeed in school by manipulating these preferences of the teacher and thereby create a false but pleasing impression of being docile, well prepared, and willing to play the school game according to its traditional rules. The argument implies the still more cynical conclusion that all this can happen without the teacher's awareness, that the child succeeds without the teacher ever knowing what hit her. The creative staff did not disagree that this happens in classrooms, but I was overruled as they rejected it as a legitimate premise for deciding what to teach young children through television. We did eventually decide to give priority to teaching children to take another person's point of view, but not as a means of manipulating the teacher.

Now that we had defined the goals, we had to begin worrying about how to measure the outcomes. Earlier we had suspended this restriction, assuming that if a goal was educationally important, some measurement of whether it was achieved could be devised. If not, the goal should not be discarded for this reason alone. Some goals customarily elude objective measurement (self-concept, ability to take another person's point of view, cooperation, etc.) but seem important nevertheless. Others are less significant educationally (recognition of letters, counting to ten, etc.) but are more susceptible to reliable measurement. We decided to include both, accepting the risks that we might teach certain significant skills and attitudes effectively without being able to precisely estimate our success, and that we would include some less significant goals because they could be measured directly.

Finally, we decided that at least during the early period of the experiment we would emphasize cognitive skills rather than the social and emotional aspects of development. We would not ignore social and affective growth, but both the de-

---

[7] For example, Henry, 1955, 1963; Postman and Weingartner, 1969.

mands of the schools and the desires of parents, especially in inner cities, pointed toward basic intellectual competence. In addition, we wanted to teach skills that the child could display to others and feel good about knowing, perhaps creating in the child a sense of competence, and in his teachers, parents and older siblings a change in expectations about what the child could learn under the proper conditions. We also decided to emphasize cognition because we were uneasy about dealing with social, emotional and moral issues on a mass medium. We worried that our efforts to defuse emotional problems (fears, anxieties, hostilities, and so forth) might act only to incite further difficulties. Television indiscriminately reaches anyone who cares to watch, without guarantee that each child will have a competent adult or older child with whom he can discuss unresolved feelings that the show may have stimulated.

With these decisions made in the fall of 1968, our priorities were determined. They were to be modified continuously throughout the project, but we now had prepared the ground for proceeding; we had stated what we would try to teach and our reasons for making these selections. We still had a year of planning time before broadcasting would begin, but we needed to know much more about the young children we were going to try to teach with television.

The Instructional Goals of Children's Television Workshop

I. Symbolic Representation

The child can recognize such basic symbols as letters, numbers, and geometric forms, and can perform rudimentary operations with these symbols.

A. Letters

(Note: For most of the following goals, the training will focus only upon a limited number of letters. The entire alphabet will be involved only in connection with recitation.)

*1. Given a set of symbols, either all letters or all numbers, the child knows whether those symbols are used in reading or in counting.

mauric Sendak

*2. Given a printed letter the child can select the identical letter from a set of printed letters.

*3. Given a printed letter the child can select its other case version from a set of printed letters.

*4. Given a verbal label for certain letters the child can select the appropriate letter from a set of printed letters.

*5. Given a printed letter the child can provide the verbal label.

6. Given a series of words presented orally, all beginning with the same letter, the child can make up another word or pick another word starting with the same letter.

7. Given a spoken letter the child can select a set of pictures or objects beginning with that letter.

8. The child can recite the alphabet.

B. Numbers

*1. Given a printed numeral the child can select the identical printed numeral from a set.

*2. Given a spoken numeral between 1 and 10 the child

can select the appropriate numeral from a set of printed numerals.

*3. Given a printed numeral between 1 and 10 the child can provide the verbal label.

*4. Given two unequal sets of objects each containing up to five members the child can select a set that contains the number requested by the examiner.
Ex. Where are there *two* pennies?

*5. Given a set of objects the child can define a subset containing up to 10.
Ex. Here are some pennies. Give me *two*.

*6. Given an ordered set of up to four objects, the child can select one by its ordinal position.
Ex. Where is the third book?

*7. The child can count to 10.

8. The child can count to 20.

9. The child understands that the number system extends beyond those he has learned, and that larger numbers are used to count larger numbers of objects.

C. Geometric Forms

1. Given a drawing or a cut-out of a circle, square or triangle, the child can select a matching drawing, cut-out or object from a set.

2. Given the verbal label, "circle," "square" or "triangle," the child can select the appropriate drawing, cut-out or object from a set.

II. Cognitive Processes

The child can deal with objects and events in terms of certain concepts of order, classification and relationship; he can apply certain basic reasoning skills; and he possesses certain attitudes conducive to effective inquiry and problem solving.

A. Perceptual Discrimination

*1. Body percepts
The child can identify and label such body parts as elbow, knee, lips and tongue.

2. Visual discrimination

a. The child can match a given object or picture to one of a varied set of objects or pictures which is similar in form, size or position.

b. Given a form the child can find its counterpart embedded in a picture or drawing.
Ex. Given a circle the child can find the same shape in the wheels of a car. (This could be done with letters and numbers as well.)

c. The child can structure parts into a meaningful whole.

Ex. 1. Using modeling clay and beans the child can fashion a head.

Ex. 2. Given two triangles and a model the child can construct a square.

Ex. 3. Looking at a picture of children with presents and a cake with candles the child can describe the picture as a birthday party.

* 3. Auditory discrimination

    a. Initial sounds

      The child can match words on the basis of common initial sounds. (see I.A., nos. 6 and 7, above)

    b. Rhymes

      The child can match words on the basis of rhyming.

    Ex. Given two or more words that rhyme, the child can pick or supply a third.

    c. Sound identification

      The child can associate given sounds with familiar objects or animals.

    Ex. Car horn, wood saw, moo of a cow.

    d. Copying rhythms

      The child can copy a rhythmic pattern.

B. Relational Concepts

  * 1. Size relationships

    Ex. Big, bigger, biggest; short, tall; skinny, little.

  * 2. Positional relationships

    Ex. Under, over, on top of, below, above, beneath.

  * 3. Distance relationships

    Ex. Near, far away, close to, next to.

  * 4. Amount or number relationships

    Ex. All, none, some; same, more, less.

  5. Temporal relationships

    Ex. Yesterday, today, and tomorrow; early, late; fast, slow; first, last.

6. Auditory relationships

Ex. Loud, louder, loudest; soft, softer, softest; noisy, quiet, high, low.

C. Classification

*1. Given at least two objects that define the basis of grouping, the child can select an additional object that "goes with them" on the basis of:

               —Size: Height, length.
               —Form: Circular, square, triangular.
               —Function: To ride in, to eat, etc.
               —Class: Animals, vehicles, etc.

2. Given 4 objects, 3 of which have an attribute in common, the child can sort out the inappropriate object on the basis of:

               —Size: Height, length.
               —Form: Circular, square, triangular.
               —Function: To ride in, to eat, etc.
               —Class: Vehicles, animals.

3. The child can verbalize the basis for grouping and sorting.

D. Ordering

1. Given the largest and smallest of five objects which are graduated in size, the child can insert the three intermediate objects in their proper order.

2. Given pictures of the earliest and latest of five events in a logically ordered temporal sequence, the child can insert pictures of the intermediate events in their proper order.

E. Reasoning and Problem Solving

1. Inferences and causality

*a. Given a situation the child can infer probable antecedent events.

Ex. Given an apple with a bite missing the child can indicate that someone was eating it.

*b. Given a situation the child can infer probable consequent events.

Ex. Given a man stepping off a ladder, and a bucket of paint beneath his foot, the child recognizes that the man is going to step into the paint.

c. Ordering on the basis of causality

Given two or more events which are causally related, the child can place them in their appropriate causal order.

2. Generating and evaluating explanations and solutions

*a. The child can suggest multiple solutions to simple problems.

*b. Given a set of suggested solutions to a simple problem, the child can select the most relevant, complete or efficient.

3. Attitudes toward inquiry and problem solving

a. Persistence

The child persists in his efforts to solve problems and understand events despite early failures.

b. Reactions to lack of knowledge

The child exhibits no undue frustration or embarrassment when he must admit to a reasonable lack of knowledge or when he must ask questions.

c. Impulse control

The child understands that reflection and planning may pay off where premature problem attack will not.

III. The Physical Environment

The child's conception of the physical world should include general information about natural phenomena, both near and distant; about certain processes which occur in nature; about certain interdependencies which relate various natural phenomena; and about the ways in which man explores and exploits the natural world.

A. The Child and the Physical World Around Him

1. The natural environment

a. Land, sky, and water
The child should realize that the earth is made of land and water, and that the earth's surface differs in various places.
Ex. The child can identify puddles, rivers, lakes and oceans when shown pictures of them, can tell that all of them are water, and can tell how they are similar and different in terms of size and depth.
The child can identify mountains and rocks although they differ in size and shape.
The child can identify and give salient facts about objects seen in the sky.
Ex. The sun provides heat and light during the day; the moon and stars provide light at night; airplanes carry people; rockets explore space.

b. City and country
The child can distinguish the environment and natural life of the city from those of the country.

c. Plants and animals
The child can classify a group of objects as plants although they differ in size, shape and appearance.
The child can tell that plants are living things, and that they require sun and water to grow and live.
The child can name some plants that are grown and eaten by man.
The child can classify a group of objects as animals although they vary in size, shape and appearance.
The child can tell that animals are living things, and that they need food and water to grow and live.

The child can associate certain animals with their homes.

Ex. The child can associate birds with nests; fish with water; bears with forests.

d. Natural processes and cycles

(1) Reproduction, growth and development
Given pictures of various kinds of young, the child can tell what they will be when they grow up.
Ex. Calves and colts become cows or horses; tadpoles, frogs; caterpillars, butterflies; boys, men; girls, women.

The child can identify such seeds as corn, acorn, bean, and knows that after one of these has been planted a new plant will grow.

The child can identify birth, growth, aging and death as stages in the life process of individual plants and animals.

(2) Weather and seasons
The child can describe the weather and activities which are associated with summer and winter.
Ex. In summer the weather is hot and sunny, the trees all have their leaves, people wear lightweight clothing and may go swimming; in winter the weather is cold and snowy, many trees have lost their leaves; people wear heavyweight clothing, and may go sledding or ice-skating.

2. The man-made environment

a. Machines
The child can identify automobiles, trucks, buses, airplanes and boats, and can tell where and how each is used.

The child can identify such common tools as a hammer and saw, and can tell how each is used.

The child can identify basic appliances such as refrigerator and stove, and can tell how each is used.

b. Buildings and other structures

The child can identify some of the different types of buildings which serve as family homes, schools and stores.

The child can identify some of the materials used in building, such as bricks, wood and concrete.

The child can identify as man-made such structures as bridges, dams, streets, and roads.

IV. The Social Environment

The child can identify himself and other familiar individuals in terms of role-defining characteristics. He is familiar with forms and functions of institutions which he may encounter. He comes to see situations from more than one point of view and begins to see the necessity for certain social rules, particularly those insuring justice and fair play.

A. Social Units

1. Self

a. The child knows his own name.

b. The child can specify whether he or she will grow up to be a mother or a father.

2. Roles

Given the name of certain roles from the family, neighborhood, city or town, the child can enumerate appropriate responsibilities.

Ex. The child can name one or more principal functions of the father and mother, mayor, policeman, baker, mailman, farmer, fireman, soldier, doctor, dentist, baker, schoolboy or schoolgirl.

3. Social groups and institutions of concern to children

a. The family and the home

The child views such activities as reading, playing of games, and excursions as normal family activities.

The child recognizes that various types of structures all serve as homes.

b. The neighborhood

The child distinguishes between neighborhood areas that are safe and unsafe for play.

c. The city or town

The child recognizes various structures, spaces and points of interest which make up the city or town.

Ex. The child is familiar with the concepts of a zoo, park or playground, airport and parade, and with stores where various types of common items may be purchased.

The child understands that there are many different cities, that they have finite boundaries, that various goods or products must be transported in and out, and that various modes of transportation are employed.

The child identifies the respective functions of such institutions as the school, post office and hospital.

Ex. The child knows that people go to school to

learn how to read and write; to the hospital if ill or having a baby.

B. Social Interactions

*1. Differences in perspectives

The child recognizes that a single event may be seen and interpreted differently by different individuals.
Ex. Given a picture showing one boy in a bathing suit and another boy in a snowsuit, the child can express the feelings of both boys in the event of snow.

*2. Cooperation

The child recognizes that in certain situations it is beneficial for two or more individuals to work together toward a common goal.
Ex. Two girls want to bring chairs to the table, but can only lift and carry them by working together.

3. Rules which insure justice and fair play

a. Behaving by rules

The child is able to behave according to the constraints of simple rules presented either verbally or by models.

b. Recognizing fairness or unfairness

The child can distinguish simple situations representing fairness from those representing unfairness.
Ex. The child can say whether a particular form of praise or punishment is or is not appropriate in a particular situation.

c. Evaluating rules

Given a rule, the child can tell whether it is good or bad, and why.

d. Generating rules

Given a situation involving interpersonal conflict, the child can furnish an appropriate rule for resolving it.
Ex. Told that two boys both wish to play with the

same toy, the child must formulate a rule that is equitable (neither may have it; they can take turns; etc.).

Chapter Four

Children and Learning

"I taught them that, but they didn't learn it."

A teacher quoted by
Postman and Weingartner,
*Teaching as a Subversive
Activity*

No sooner had we made our decisions about what to teach than Arthur Jensen,[1] a respected psychologist from the University of California, announced that compensatory education programs had failed and that this failure was related to genetic differences in learning ability between white and black children. Almost all Jensen's assertions were contested by other researchers, with no party in the controversy being able to marshal any real evidence to support his positions. All the pronouncements, for and against, tried to sound as if they were based on fact, but they served only to emphasize once again how little we really do know about children's learning and the conditions that bring it about.

While many educators began struggling to decide what they knew about children that would help them to settle the Jensen controversy, we had the special problem of deciding what we thought we knew about children that would help us to use television to teach them. A few ideas had taken form during the seminars—for example, the limited attention spans of preschool

---

[1] Arthur Jensen, 1969.

children. Almost all research confirmed this, suggesting that we use many short segments (mixed with only a few longer ones for variety) and varied styles and techniques (mixing animation, puppets, live-action films, pixilation, and any other visual devices the producers could invent). Though by and large, how children learn remains a mystery, we still needed some operating assumptions and felt enough confidence in a few ideas to put them to work.

Our Assumptions about Children

Jerome Bruner (1971) observes correctly that any decision to concentrate on the very young is made in the form of a wager that early education will be of some real benefit. The odds on this wager are not obvious. They depend upon a series of overlapping arguments, each giving us only a rough estimate of what we can hope to accomplish with any program of early education, including television.

• A child's learning capacity is only partly predetermined by biology or genetics, and is to some degree plastic and responsive to the opportunities provided by his environment.

• This plasticity is greatest during the earliest years, the period of most rapid learning.

• Therefore, the earlier we reach the young child, the better, with one objective being to accelerate his development.

Even while raising the specter of genetic inferiority of blacks, Jensen admitted that a deprived environment can stunt intellectual development and that a good early environment can largely overcome the effects of deprivation, thus "permitting the individual's genetic potential to be reflected in his performance." He insisted, however, that no child's learning capacity could ever be pushed beyond his biological and genetic limitations. Jensen was reacting against what he believed to be the prevailing view in recent years, the belief in the almost infinite plasticity of development and the denial of biological and genetic boundaries.[2] Just how plastic is a child's development, anyway? No one knows, but amidst the overheated rhetoric, both sides overlook their fundamental agreement on what to do: try alternative educational programs, fitting them as best we can to the child's individual characteristics, and see how well we make out.

The Earlier, the Better?

Whatever the absolute degree of human plasticity, learning is so rapid during the early years that, according to Benjamin Bloom of the University of Chicago,[3] before a child reaches age five, roughly as much intellectual growth has taken place as will occur in the next thirteen years. Early learning is not only remarkably rapid, but it is also remarkably predictive of later competence. Knowing how far a child has progressed intellectually by age five allows a fairly accurate prediction of how far he will progress as an adolescent or adult, suggesting that the earlier we reach young children with programs designed to accelerate their development, the better.

This logic is all right, but not perfect. Perhaps it is in these years of most rapid learning that children most need protection from the forced learning of what adults decide children ought to know—decisions that are at best somewhat arbitrary. To exploit this rapid learning fully, perhaps young children must be free from adult demands and most open to initiate their own encounters with the world, to follow their curiosities on their own. Maybe the best thing we can do is to stop pestering them to learn whatever we happen to consider important at the moment.

Anyway, why should we bother to accelerate the acquisition of knowledge that a child will sooner or later learn in school?

[2] Zigler (1968), Eysenck (1971) and others share this indictment of "unbridled environmentalists."

[3] Bloom, 1964.

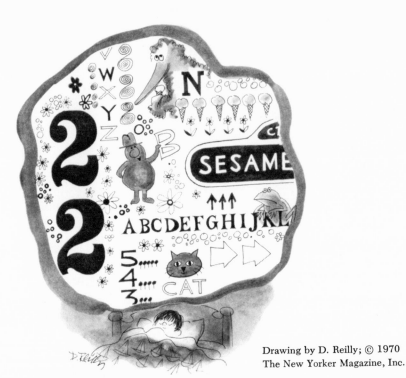

Drawing by D. Reilly; © 1970
The New Yorker Magazine, Inc.

The only apparent outcome is that children will perform certain skills earlier than they would otherwise. And if these skills
—usually those involved in manipulating the symbols of words,
numbers, shapes and forms—are of dubious value even when
taught later in school, why bother teaching them even earlier?

Assume that schools as we know them (despite their many
faults) are here to stay, more or less in their present form
(despite our efforts to change or even abolish them), and that
preparing inner-city children for school is a plausible undertaking. Then the reasons become clearer for the early teaching
of symbolic skills and the early effort to help the child build
positive feelings about himself. Development to one level
facilitates development to the next. For example, the earlier a
child learns an elementary set of symbolic skills (e.g., recognizing numerals and learning to count), the earlier he can use
them to build more advanced symbolic skills (e.g., learning to
add, subtract, use numbers to order and classify objects, and so

forth). The earlier he learns these symbolic skills, the more likely he is (with a little luck) to convince a teacher, when he gets to school, that he can do the things the teacher values.

Are there other reasons to bother with early learning? Merely alerting the child to the fact that symbols exist in his world and that they are invariant (the letter W always remains the letter W) will alert him to the appearance of these symbols in his environment and may in turn create a curiosity about the world, an appetite for further learning that can become a child's pivotal asset. No one knows how to create this appetite, but it is likely that when a child learns something new, and knows that what he has learned is valued by the people who are important to him, he will be motivated to learn still more. Learning is acknowledged currency in our society, and the more a child learns, the better he begins to feel about himself, the more he regards himself as capable of further learning. When based on real accomplishment, this sense of personal competence becomes a source of self-esteem. When real learning does not occur, the outcome differs:

> In this, children cannot be fooled by empty praise and conde-scending encouragement. They may have to accept artificial bolstering of their self-esteem in lieu of something better, but their ego identity gains real strength only from wholehearted and consistent recognition of real accomplishment—i.e., of achievement that has meaning in the culture. [Erikson, 1950, p. 208]

Parents and Older Siblings

When the aim is to reach young children, there are good reasons to reach their parents and older siblings at the same time. First, these older folks—adults or children—generally control the television set. The common viewing pattern seems to be that the older children select the family situation comedy or the adventure series, and the younger children string along with this choice, understanding as much as they can of programs that are at least somewhat over their heads. This actually may turn out to be a pretty good system in forcing the young child to stretch to understand programs designed for older audiences.

No single set of television programs, or any other single educational approach, can be expected to produce a substantial effect by itself, unless the experiences are tied to other aspects of the child's life. Whenever a parent or an older sibling talks with the young child about what they have seen or done together and encourages him to elaborate upon the experience, a multiplier effect is set into motion. Even just keeping a young child company while he watches a television program probably has its own reinforcing properties, since it represents a rather uncommon sign of crediting his activities by the parent or older sibling. Also, having the opportunity to actually see a child respond and learn may lead the older family members to expect more of him, and the beneficial effects of these expectations are well-known.[4]

Inner-City Children and Others

To succeed, a national television series must attract as large a national audience as possible, including children from all social classes and cultural groups and from all geographic regions. This restricts television's potential to "narrow the gap" between children from inner-city and well-to-do families. What national television can aim to achieve is to provide some useful educational experiences for all children who watch.

To reduce the educational gap between children from poor and well-to-do families, national television would need to meet either or both of two implausible conditions: Either poor children would have to watch more than middle-class children; or if poor children did not watch more, they would have to learn more from the same amount of watching as middle-class chil-

[4] Robert Rosenthal, 1971.

dren. Our intention of reaching as large a national audience as possible automatically violated the first condition. Although we were going to take measures to encourage maximum viewing in inner-city areas, we certainly were not going to discourage or prevent viewing by middle-class children in order to assure greater viewing by inner-city than middle-class children, and thereby narrow the gap.

We also did not expect to produce more learning among poor children than middle-class children in response to the same or lesser amounts of viewing. We hoped that poor children would learn as much and that the gap would not be widened, despite the fact that almost all comparisons of educational progress show middle-class children proceeding more rapidly. We would try to make our series so appealing to inner-city children that they would learn at least as much as children with a wider range of early educational opportunities.

Some Assumptions about Learning

During this planning period, the producers' efforts to develop program materials, and the researchers' observations of children's reactions to them, brought our ideas about children's learning into sharper focus. As the producers began producing program segments, the researchers began observing children reacting to them, trying to discover what these children saw, heard and understood as they watched. In doing these child observations, researchers were looking for the signs of the appeal of the segments and their value in teaching the specific skills they were designed to teach. Children were observed individually in their homes or in small groups in nursery schools, day-care programs, and other viewing centers.

For example, we observed wide variations among children in their viewing styles. However, the different styles did not seem to relate closely to how much a child learns. Each style seems to depend upon how the child uses it. The research staff described some variations:

Some children can view television for hours with their eyes rarely leaving the set. We were so struck by this viewing style when we first began doing research on appeal that we coined the term "zombie viewer" to refer to the child who sat seemingly hypnotized, in front of the set. Other children constantly keep a check on all outside activities in the room while they view. We found these styles to be no guarantee of how much the child was absorbing from the program. [Reeves, 1970, p. 11]

In one viewing pattern, children seem able to watch television while simultaneously keeping track of other interesting events around them.[5] What may appear as distractibility may in fact be the ability to monitor many events simultaneously. Of course, in other children what appears to be distractibility is just that. Similarly, "zombie viewing" may reflect either intense concentration or stupor.

Another common viewing style displays overt active physical and verbal participation in the televised action. Certain children sing or talk along with (or even talk at) the televised characters, reply to questions directed toward the children on the program or toward the viewing audience, yelp or tremble

[5] Researchers such as Maccoby (1967, 1969) and White, Watts, et al. (1972) describe this pattern as "dual attention." It seems to characterize highly competent young children.

in mock fright at monsters or cliff-hanging sequences, offer delighted or disdainful comments on what they see, and generally respond with a high level of both physical and verbal activity. Although we try to encourage active participation through numerous programing devices, we do not yet know how this facilitates or inhibits learning. It does insure the child's orientation to the set, interrupts periods of physical passivity, and reflects active rehearsal by the child. On the other hand, participation can become so engrossing in itself that some children seem carried away by their own activity, losing contact with the material that initiated their participation in the first place.

Learning from Format as Well as Content

Each communication medium has its conventions. Starting with the simple convention that books written in English are read from left to right, with lines read in descending order, many more subtle conventions affect the ways in which books are written and read. Television's conventions seem to have evolved without deliberate design, but operate strongly to expedite a viewer's understanding. Certain conventions have become so commonplace that their triteness now intrudes upon the viewer's attention; swelling music, dramatic pauses, fade-outs and zoom-ins and freeze-frames elicit groans from adolescents who have grown up on television and regard these conventions as unimaginative and archaic.

But format cues can provide important prompting devices for learning. For example, the producers of *Sesame Street* designed speech balloons that appeared in ten-second segments to teach letter names; soon viewers learned that the appearance of the balloon itself was a signal to the learning of letters. To teach children that their minds can perform several essential functions (including pretesting alternative solutions to problems imaginally before acting, planning a sequence of steps to solve a problem, and guessing intelligently from progressively revealed clues), the producers developed another convention to signify the mind at work. The televised thoughts appeared above the character's head, signaling the viewer that the character was thinking and working through a problem in his mind before acting.

The educational uses of other common television conventions remain to be exploited. Can zoom-in techniques teach a child who has difficulty in discriminating salient cues to attend more selectively? Can the format in which a speech balloon appears above a character's head to display his thoughts be used to teach children the value of thinking in solving problems? Can slow-motion techniques help an impulsive child to develop a more reflective mental pace? Split screens can visually juxtapose two or more events that actually are distant from each other; can the technique teach the child to juxtapose events in his own mind? We are familiar with the use of television-format conventions to supply a setting for learning (e.g., the consistent use of a song or a particular visual display), but we have not experimented yet with their possible effects on a child's mental operations. Will the visual representations of television foster corresponding mental representations in the child? It seems overly simplified to expect such direct effects upon a child's thinking, but given the importance assigned to the development of mental representations (or Piaget's "schemata"), it probably is worth finding out how the visual and mental representations connect.

In contrast to these positive cases, format clues, including music, can be distracting and interfere with learning. For example, a child may concentrate on the music or on the quality of a voice and miss what the speaker is saying. When Lauren Bacall read a story, her voice "sounded funny" to many children, and they concentrated on this voice quality instead of the story itself. These children may have been engaging in significant incidental learning about variations in vocal patterns, but their attention had been diverted from the intended focus.

Modeling

Our early observations of children watching television contained innumerable instances of specific modeling or learning simply by watching others. Children frequently imitate the physical movements of televised characters. When *Sesame Street* cast members count on their fingers or use their fingers or other parts of the body to shape letters or forms, many children copy them. In particular, one device used on *Sesame Street* has evoked a remarkable amount of physical imitation: All the viewer sees on the screen is a hand trying in various ways to make a noise. As the hand tries snapping its fingers and making other movements, children often imitate these actions. When the hand delightedly discovers that with the cooperation of the other hand, it can make a clapping sound, the hands of young viewers tend to share in this gratifying experience. Giggling, washing, scratching, hopping, rubbing and various comical actions also evoke considerable imitation. If a character on television does something absurd, such as stepping in a bucket, children may get up and pretend to walk around with buckets on their feet, too.

Modeling, of course, extends far beyond simple physical imitation. Modeling of effective verbal communications has guided many of our writing and production methods. For example, on *Sesame Street* we show children asking questions as a way of acquiring information, talking together until they solve a problem, or simply enjoying the feel and the sound of words. Since modeling is strengthened through children's identification with the character they are watching, we decided to introduce varieties of speech forms on the program, including some dialect and a considerable amount of informal street language. For similar reasons, we also showed several forms of Spanish speech and culture.

Observational learning does not require direct teaching in order to be effective. Simply displaying activities that convey an implicit attitude also can produce effective modeling. In this way, altruism, kindness, courage and tolerance can be communicated indirectly through the actions of the televised characters, without explicit labeling. The discovery of writing and production methods that will convey these attitudes effectively to young children had only just begun during the planning period, but the importance of modeling was conveyed succinctly by the young black child who exclaimed while watching *Sesame Street*, "Look! He looks like me and he knows the answers!"

Narrow Focusing

In communicating a message to a young child, the less "noise" masking the message, the better. In many learning situations, preschool children have difficulty discriminating what is essential or relevant from what is incidental or irrelevant to the specified goal, and this certainly is true when they respond to film or television. Young children are readily distracted from the central content of a program and often respond to peripheral details. As children get older, they become more capable of attending selectively to those features that have the greatest potential utility and can more easily pick out what matters in a confused situation and ignore what does not.[6] Since we know that young children have difficulty making such discrimi-

[6] For example, Collins, 1970; Gibson, 1969; Pick, Christy, and Frankel, 1972; Pick and Pick, 1970; Stevenson, 1972.

nations and attending selectively, special care must be given to make salient what the child is expected to learn.

Television can be designed to screen out irrelevancies, reducing the extraneous material, either visual or auditory, that confuses the child and causes him to lose interest. An example on *Sesame Street* of the exclusion of irrelevancies is the "dot bridge," designed to teach rhythm and the anticipation of elements in a sequence. A series of these consists of dots marching onto the screen, one at a time, to a musical background. The dots form a pattern, but a single dot goes awry to spoil the pattern. The children in our research samples readily understood the problem, found it amusing, and expressed relief when the pattern was finally formed correctly in the last episode of the series. Another example, "The Triangle and the Square," involves these two animated geometric forms moving against a solid background. To a musical accompaniment, they each demonstrate what they can do and how they differ from each other in an episode that is deliberately bare of irrelevant or peripheral detail.

Total stripping of irrelevance from the material to be learned must be handled judiciously. What is irrelevant to one child may be another child's primary source of learning, and this especially may be true when an adult decides what is irrelevant to a child. Total stripping also may render the material so bare and unembellished as to be simply uninteresting. When a televised episode is repeated and children see it a second or third time, they seek new meanings, and sufficient embellishment is necessary to supply them. If an entertaining way cannot be invented to teach the central content, and a nonessential but amusing feature can be added to hold the child's attention, the risk of adding this peripheral element may be worth taking. Then the production problem is to tie this nonessential feature to the central content, or at worst, to keep the peripheral content from totally distracting the child from the content to be learned. Whatever the risks, however, television can provide the young child with a precise focus on central content, carefully eliminating irrelevancies and distractions.

Cross-Modal Reinforcement

Another of the perennial either-or arguments in which researchers have entangled themselves is "Which works better,
words or pictures?" This one has not been resolved either.[7]

The search continues, however, based on theories[8] that human information processing is characterized by low capacity
and a single-channel transmission system, suggesting that there
is no advantage to supplying redundant information through
more than one sensory modality and thus flooding the learner
with more information than he can handle. According to these
views of information processing, messages fed simultaneously
through two modalities will tend to interfere with each other.
Although there are rare occasions when television will present
either pictures or sounds, one without the other, its special capacity is in their coordinated combination. For instance, in a
segment designed to teach letter discrimination, Big Bird, an
eight-foot-tall feathered puppet who tends to get confused
easily, is shown painstakingly drawing an E and an F side by
side on a blackboard. Viewing children attend to Big Bird's efforts until the letters are completed (they are alert to Big Bird's
tendency to make mistakes, which they enjoy correcting); then
their interest fades. Soon, however, while Big Bird watches in
befuddlement, the bottom line of the E migrates mysteriously
to the neighboring F, making an E of the F and an F of the
original E. As the bottom line of the E begins its magical move,
a slide-whistle sound effect accompanies its jerky progress. A
sense of comic physical movement is conveyed by the sound of
the slide whistle because it is one of television's familiar conventions, and children snap back to attention. They continue
to pay attention to the peregrinations of the magic line and the
accompanying slide whistle.[9] Carrying the synchronizing of

[7] Goulet and Stearns, 1970; Lumsdaine, 1963; Rowe, 1972; Rowe and Paivio,
1971; Yamamoto, 1969.

[8] For example, Broadbent, 1958; Travers, 1964, 1970.

[9] This and several other examples of *Sesame Street* segments are taken from
a report by Samuel Gibbon and Edward Palmer prepared for the Children's
Television Workshop, entitled *Pre-reading on* Sesame Street, 1970.

sight and sound into actual production required that we learn how one modality can be used to support another, instead of canceling out or interfering with the other.

Displayable Skills

Educators have questioned the value of learning simple symbolic skills (letters, numbers, the names of common geometric forms, and so forth) on several grounds. Those who believe that the choice of symbolic skills that schools traditionally teach is arbitrary and whimsical will believe, in turn, that any early preparation for learning those skills is equally mindless. Those who believe that learning information is useless when compared with "learning to learn" will note the futility of the early acquisition of simple symbolic skills. Still others are repulsed when the adult society prescribes in an authoritarian, dictatorial manner what the younger members of the society must learn. They believe that children will never learn to guide their own behavior if such choices are made for them, and also object to the arrogance of small, often self-selected groups of adults insisting that they know what is good for all young people in this society. These good arguments are balanced against an equally good one in favor of the early learning of displayable skills: the value of an older person recognizing and admiring the real accomplishments of a young person. An older person taking visible pleasure in a child's accomplishments surely goes a long way toward making that child feel good about himself and what he is capable of learning.

Some Assumptions about Teaching

During the planning of *Sesame Street,* these ideas about learning led to some useful ideas about effective teaching by television. Our ideas were still unformed, but we assumed that through television an older person could tell a younger one

I minute of Educational T.V.!

(or perhaps even a younger person could tell an older one)—
in as interesting a way as he could contrive—what he thinks he
knows about the world and how people, ideas and events interact in it.

Entertainment and education often have been regarded as
competing for a child's attention. Entertainment is seen as
frivolous; too much entertainment is viewed as a symptom of
flabbiness and decadence. Education is seen as serious and
earnest, but awfully good for you if you have the strength of
character to persist in tedious hard work; not only does education teach, but it builds character by forcing children to work
at what is not, and should not be, much fun. In this view, entertainment can only contaminate education, robbing children
of the opportunity to learn how to do things that they really do
not want to do. How will a child learn, after all, to accept the
confinement of a job and other responsibilities if we do not
start early to teach him to accept tedium? In this view, making

education exciting is a disservice to its higher purpose of producing disciplined character. To use entertainment in the service of education is tantamount to coddling.

Since we have been maintaining this lunatic view for some time, it is not surprising that we do not know how to combine entertainment and education so as to augment each other. We have begun to acknowledge that entertainment need not be empty of educational value and that education need not be unentertaining. What we now need to discover is how to make entertainment instrumental to learning so that learning contains the excitement and joy that a child has experienced while not being "educated."

Television's Tutelage

Teachers always have known that new learning is expedited by starting from experiences that are familiar to the child and then building and extending into new and unfamiliar material. There may be occasions when a teacher will choose to confront a child with a totally novel situation, removing the props provided by previous familiarity with any elements of the new situation. The child then is forced to come up with something entirely new on his own. Under most circumstances, however, the child will learn new material most effectively if it builds upon something he already knows.

We developed several examples of using the familiar as a bridge to the unfamiliar during the planning period, illustrated by our televised episodes on letter recognition in which similarities are illustrated visually between the letter forms and the shapes of familiar objects. At the start of one animated film, an unseen narrator invites two boys to watch a story about the letter *J*. As a large upper-case *J* descends between them, one of the boys remarks that the *J* looks like a fishhook. The voice of the narrator intones, "It's not a fishhook, it's a *J*." This is followed by a rhythmic sequence in which the letter is used as part of a short story filled with *J* sounds and with words beginning with *J*. At the end of the story, the second boy says, "So that's the letter *J*." The first boy replies, "It still looks like a fishhook to me." Similar analogies are developed between other letters and familiar shapes. *Y*, for example, has on different occasions been compared visually with a fork in a road and a branching trunk of a tree.

Other examples of using the familiar as a bridge to the unfamiliar involve the use of the parts of a child's body. Films that encourage and guide the child to use his fingers to form letter shapes provide him with a physical analogy always available to him and adds a kinesthetic dimension to letter learning. At various times, characters on *Sesame Street* have used their fingers to make *U*, *V* and (by putting two *V*'s together) *W*. Observation of children watching these show segments suggested that most children are drawn irresistibly to imitate the performers.

Another example of a bridge from the familiar to the unfamiliar is the search for letter forms embedded in the child's real environment. In one *Sesame Street* segment, a puppet finds the letter *E* repeated in the structure of a door, and in another, *T* is discovered embedded in the railing around the basement windows of an apartment house. When such embedded letters are found, a cut-out letter is matched to the embedded letter to confirm the presence of the embedded form for the child who may not have seen it. This search for embedded letters not only teaches letter recognition but also provides practice in another essential cognitive skill, distinguishing between figure and ground by isolating relevant characteristics. In all these instances, we used the child's familiarity with his real environment as a base upon which to introduce unfamiliar concepts.

Direct and Indirect Teaching

Direct teaching involves both telling and showing the children what you intend to teach them, then telling and showing it to them, and finally telling and showing them again what you have taught them. Many of television's commercials use this direct approach: here is the product, here is what it does better than any other product, buy it (please).

Only a small part of what children learn is taught to them directly. The importance of informal learning in undirected play is beyond dispute. Most of television's messages are indirect; the message is illustrated in action but not taught directly. On commercial television's family situation comedies, father is bumbling and helpless, but lovable—doubly so if he happens to be a professor. We are not told this in words, but we watch him repeatedly bumble. On game shows, women are greedy, grasping and hysterical with gratitude when receiving a refrigerator or dishwasher for nothing. On soap operas, only bad people have sexual impulses; good peoples' sex is apologetic and engaged in solely for purposes of reproduction. Good children are respectful and reverent, dogs are heroic and loyal, fish are clever (dolphins) or vicious (sharks). The stereotypes abound, but are communicated indirectly through action.

Indirect teaching on television indeed can be extremely effective. Recall the long list of behaviors that children can learn by modeling the behavior of others, without any direct reinforcement, deliberate teaching or overt practice, ranging from self-sacrifice to aggression and back to altruism. *Sesame Street* uses direct methods to teach basic intellectual skills, but adopts indirect teaching methods to display certain social attitudes, such as people treating each other with kindness and courtesy, respect for racial differences, taking another person's point of view, modes of conflict resolution, and accepting rules of justice and fair play. Indeed, almost all the aspects of social development that *Sesame Street* experiments with are approached in this way. During planning, we tried to test a full range of direct and indirect teaching methods on television, seeking to fit the approach to what we were trying to teach.

Showing the World

One of television's great powers is its capacity to transport, to show the world to children—to display people, events, and ideas that they have never encountered before and are unlikely ever to have the opportunity to confront in person. But what parts of the world, and what events and experiences? If a child lives in a city ghetto, what do we gain in using television to depict its harsh realities? What does the child gain if instead we show the brighter and gentler—indeed, the sweeter—side of how things are and what they could be? In our earliest planning of *Sesame Street*, we tried to keep the full range of options open on these questions, but as we went along, our drift toward the sweeter side of life emerged. We knew that if we

"You see, son, I'm afraid the real world out there isn't much like 'Sesame Street.'"

Drawing by D. Reilly; © 1971
The New Yorker Magazine, Inc.

persisted in this drift, we would be criticized for sugar-coating and distorting the unpleasant realities, and for abdicating the responsibility to show conditions that children must learn to change rather than tolerate passively. Our judgment, however, was that in order to depict reality, *Sesame Street* should not add more stridency and bitterness to the harshness already present in the child's environment. The drift toward showing the warmth and kindness that might exist continued. With all its raucousness and slapstick humor, *Sesame Street* became a sweet show, and its staff maintains that there is nothing wrong in that.

The issue of showing the world as it is or as it might be centers on how to depict the difficulties of urban living. *Sesame Street* has taken children visually to an automobile assembly plant, a fishing ship, the back of a bakery, an African play area for children, a farm, a junkyard, several zoos, down a mail chute, and to many other places that they could not visit on their own. Once *Sesame Street* took children on a bus ride around town, showing them what the driver does and how the passengers handle things. Now, we all know that a bus driver is often not our best example of someone who is courteous and civil. But on *Sesame Street*'s bus trip, the driver responds to his passengers' hellos and thank-yous, tells a child who cannot locate his money, "That's all right, you can pay me tomorrow," and upon seeing a young woman running after his bus just as it has left the curb, actually stops to let her on. Why present to gullible little children such an outrageous misrepresentation of the realities of a city transportation system? We wanted to show the child what the world is like when people treat each other with decency and consideration. Our act of faith—supported by some evidence on the modeling of kindness and altruism—was that young children will learn such attitudes if we take the trouble to show them some examples, even if we stretch familiar reality a bit in order to do so. The harsh realities of a child's world surely exist. We lose credibility to the child if we ignore them entirely, and no effort to teach can afford this. But, even at the risk of sugar-coating these realities, perhaps we can suggest the vision of better things.

No Preaching

Preaching at children often works. If adults are committed enough to their version of what is right and true, and if they have a strong enough hold over children to keep them captive, the children cannot escape. What children should learn through being preached at has been changing through the centuries, but the accepted virtues are always couched in fine, spiritually enriching phrases. Starting with Aristotle's "temperance" and "good temper," we have progressed historically through self-sacrifice and service, renunciation and self-control, loyalty and patriotism, honesty and responsibility and diligence, cleanliness and Godliness, and most recently, respect for law and order. Without question, preaching to children—hard enough and long enough—succeeds.

> There is no absurdity so palpable but that it may be firmly planted in the human mind if you only begin to inculcate it before the age of five, by constantly repeating it with an air of great solemnity. [Schopenhauer, *Essays*]

We finally have developed some qualms about this. Many of us still believe we know what is right for others, especially for children, but we are not quite so sure any more; we have begun to wonder about the justice of preventing children from struggling to reach their own conclusions about virtue and morality. Beyond general reservations about preaching, we know that preaching on television, in particular, simply does not work. Maybe preaching demands a captive audience, and television's audience exercises free choice. Maybe the difference between preaching and what people have come to expect from television is too great. In designing *Sesame Street*, we never did consider preaching to children, but we did give considerable thought to the various forms that preaching on television has taken in order to avoid slipping into them. Others before us had done so. Our assumption about teaching by television was that children abhor preaching and that our first inadvertent excursion into it would be the last time that many children would watch the program.

No Trivializing

For some reason, when adults on television speak to children, their voices often assume a strange "talking to children" quality, rising a few tones, lisping a little, and singsonging along. Perhaps this happens whenever adults speak to children they do not know as individuals. On television, this nonhuman quality of adult speech somehow seems especially chilling. Although we have no evidence of how children perceive the "voice talking down," its unctuousness seems inescapable and as belittling as any other continual undeserved punishment.

Equally unctuous is the common practice on children's television of trivializing or reducing a topic in the misguided effort to present it at the child's level of understanding. It is often quite necessary to simplify material for children, extracting the essence of the message and presenting it without distracting irrelevancies. But simplifying and trivializing are not synonymous and children probably know the difference when they see it.

Numerous commercial television programs display the ulti-

mate in condescension toward children. Take a locally syndi-
cated Bozo the Clown's treatment of birthdays—special occasions full of important personal meanings for most children. A
group of roughly fifty children is assembled and seated in a
grandstand, each with a funny hat propped on his head, each
having a worked-up, frenzied good time. Bozo is introduced by
a ringmaster with a "funny" German accent who tells the children that Bozo is "flown in at great expense, straight from the
Klingenstein Pavilion." The pavilion is part of a hospital in
New York City. One of the more repellent habits of adults on
children's shows is to needle and amuse each other, totally ob-
livious to the presence and understanding of the children in the
studio or in the viewing audience. It would seem that children
do not really count. They are simply props, and since adults are
not likely to be watching Bozo the Clown, the adult performers
can get away with anything for their own pathetic amusement.

Bozo now rallies the props in the grandstand to accompany
him in a rendition of "Happy Birthday," picking the name
"Joanna Ruth" at random. There is no "Joanna Ruth" in the
studio; the props have no idea to whom they are paying such
homage, but they sing away anyway. Singing to an unknown
child may seem like harmless fun, but can children really be
unaware of how they are being treated and how these adults
must regard them?

Such blatant abuse seems so heartless that one wonders how
it is allowed to continue. The answer: No one cares.

Chapter Five

Production

Television directors developed their styles working with thin, one-dimensional characters and situations, almost continuous dialogue, sharp visual contrasts, quick jabs at the emotions, and lots of climaxes. They tried to be "effective." Some of them got pretty good at it.

Pauline Kael,
The New Yorker,
January 27, 1968

The creative staff of the Children's Television Workshop made several decisions during the planning period that contributed greatly to *Sesame Street*'s success. They decided to develop a magazine format for the show that would allow a mixture of different styles, paces, and characters. Depending upon a single star character in a series is very risky. If the star is wrong, so is the entire series. The magazine format permitted enormous flexibility, allowing segments to be dropped, modified or added. It is unlikely that any other approach would have provided enough room to present material on the wide range of goals we had selected.

To be useful to the producers and writers, the exact meaning and intent of each goal had to be clear. The creative staff already had achieved considerable understanding in the seminars by constantly pressing the educators there to define the suggested goals. Another way to make the goals concrete is to state them as "behavioral objectives"—that is, what a child would actually be able to do, what behavior an observer would see, if the child had mastered the skill. For example, one of our few social goals is the ability to take another person's point of view—to understand that another person may see and feel things differently from the way you do, and then to be able to imagine yourself in that person's place. Although some psychologists (for example, Piaget) estimate that this is an advanced skill that cannot be acquired before roughly age seven, we decided to experiment with it for several reasons: It seemed especially suitable to a visual medium, its importance for school preparation was clear, and it appeared to be a general skill that could help a child to acquire other specific skills. The Workshop's researchers undertook to translate this and other goals into behavioral terms. For example:

> Social interactions.
>> Differences in perspective
>>> The child recognizes that a single event may be seen and interpreted differently by different individuals. *Ex.* Given a picture showing one boy in a bathing suit and another boy in a snowsuit, the child can express the feelings of both boys in the event of snow.

To further clarify the meaning of this goal, some general teaching strategies also were proposed:

> (1) Start with the child's point of view and then present the opposing point of view in juxtaposition with his. (2) Have the child pretend he is someone whose point of view is obviously different from his own. (3) Start with a two-person situation where one person is totally oblivious to another's point of view and develop a need for communication. (4) Keep the situation constant and have several characters enter, in turn, and react differently in the same situation. [Reeves, 1970, p. 4]

Even with these clarifications, the producers still needed some indication of where to begin. They obviously needed to know the range of competence of their three-to-five-year-old audience and how high these children might be expected to reach. Estimates of initial competence for most of our goals were not available, particularly for urban disadvantaged children, and therefore the Workshop's research staff set about the impossible task of collecting them (Reeves, 1970). During this planning period, the research group was composed of about six people, and they were attempting to do what all the psychologists and educators in the world had not done previously. Some estimates of the levels at which production should aim were necessary, however, and the researchers collected what data they could.

The research staff also developed another resource for the producers and writers, the Writer's Notebook, which suggests several situations familiar to young children in which each goal could be played out. Without expecting that all the ideas in the notebook would be used by the producers, the researchers prepared it to serve as another bridge between the goals statement and script development. Script writing then is tied to the statement of goals, the translations of these goals into behavioral terms, the data on competence levels, and the suggestions for familiar situations contained in the Writer's Notebook. No effort is made to sequence material from show to show, but within each one-hour program, a specific amount of time is allocated for each goal in the curriculum. To be certain that some balance is retained among goals over the full broadcast year, an assignment sheet is prepared for the writer in advance of each show, suggesting roughly how much time to allocate in that show to each topic.

Lists of procedures do not create television programs. Creative people do, following their instincts and intuitions along with anything that observations of children can tell them. Knowing that they would need to catch, focus and sustain the children's attention to what was being taught, the producers and writers developed many different production approaches; then the Workshop's research staff began testing these materials with children, observing them individually or in small groups, in homes, day-care centers and nursery schools. What would it take to get children to watch an "educational" program instead of something else?

Catching Children's Attention

Children are accustomed to watching television that is expensively produced, with high quality in visual appearance and form if not in content. The primary exceptions are the inexpensive, locally produced children's shows (*Bozo the Clown, Romper Room* and many others) and the instructional television programs that are created locally for in-school use. Neither example of inexpensive production seems to elicit much attention from children; the programs simply do not resemble the expensive look of the television that is most familiar to them. Indeed, instructional television produced for school use (showing teachers lecturing in front of blackboards and science instructors demonstrating experiments from behind laboratory tables) is really not regarded by some children as television at all.

Training the child to attend (focussing on the problem and on data collection skills)

No matter what we think of the commercial television programs that children are exposed to, lots of money is spent to produce them. Commercial advertisements use animation and appealing music and sound effects, all designed to get the viewer's attention quickly and to hold it tightly for the commercial's short duration. The situation comedies that the child knows so well use skillful professional actors, attractive and realistic settings, and a variety of camera techniques. Science-fiction shows are full of visual gimmicks, often slickly contrived and convincing in appearance. The young viewer's attention will not be diverted to an educational program by its good intentions. Any open-circuit show must compete for his attention with others that spend large amounts of money on professional, high quality production.

Music and Sound Effects

Music in films and television often is called "background," and perhaps for adults its primary function is to accompany the action and dialogue. But for children, music and sound effects serve a remarkably wide range of functions, demonstrating the children's abilities to find meaning in many different musical forms and styles.

Music's most obvious use on television is to regain a child's lost attention by signaling the entrance of a familiar, appealing character or episode. In viewing television, young children tend to drift in and out of visual attention. As this happens, the dual-attention abilities of many young children allow them to listen without quite listening, even when they are not actively watching. Auditory cues, usually in the form of music or sound effects, then signal them that an uninteresting sequence has ended and that a new character or episode, recognized by a consistent musical signature, has begun.

Equally obvious is music's function as an aid to memory in learning material in sequence. Almost any child can more easily sing the alphabet than recite it, and the learning of other sequenced materials, such as counting or recalling the order of the days of the week and months of the year, seems easier for young children when put in rhythmic and musical form.

Music and sound effects also provide a direct means of teaching basic skills. For example, *Sesame Street*'s curriculum includes "auditory discrimination," one subcategory being "sound identification: the child can associate sounds with familiar objects or animals, *ex.*, car horn, wood saw, moo of a cow." Here sound effects can provide a direct teaching device. For example, one puppet character, dressed in hat and overcoat, comes to the door of another puppet's house asking if he may use the telephone to call an auto repair shop for help. The puppet making the request looks and acts perfectly normal and explains that when he stopped his car to wait for a train to go by, his car stalled and he was unable to get it started again. As he talks, however, he displays one unusual characteristic: most of his description is provided in words, but whenever he arrives at a key phrase in his narrative (for example, car driving, train going by, car stalling), he utters the sound effect representing what he is describing. His story involves a baby's crying, a cow's moo and other distinctive sounds, all of this delivered with accompanying sound effects as the other puppet listens in increasing amazement. When the other puppet then tries to repeat the message to see if he has heard it correctly, he finds to his own surprise that he also speaks in the same sound effects.

The use of sound effects in direct teaching can also be more subtle. For example, in one of our efforts to communicate a basic reasoning and problem-solving skill, we prompt children not to act upon the first problem solution that occurs to them. Instead, we show them that they can try out different possible solutions, pretesting them in their minds before choosing one to act upon. In one episode involving the puppets, Ernie approaches Bert to ask his advice on where to place a large vase. Ernie has to decide among several different-sized shelves, only the largest being big enough to hold it. Bert, engrossed in reading his newspaper, tells Ernie to "figure it out for yourself." Ernie then imagines what would happen if he were to place the vase on the small shelf. We see no action; all we see is Ernie's face as he thinks about possible consequences. But as we watch

Ernie thinking we hear in turn the vase falling (a slide-whistle sound effect) and breaking (crashing sound effect), and Ernie being ejected from the house (Bert's angry voice, door slamming). Having pretested this option in his mind and rejected it, Ernie then projects the likely consequences of placing the vase on the shelf of correct size; sound effects again play out the placing of the vase, exaggerated congratulatory voices, a trumpet signaling success, and finally a magnificent fanfare. Having imagined the consequences of this option, Ernie proceeds to act it out successfully in reality.

The striking range of functions of music for young children is displayed by the following musical forms, each readily discernible to most young children and each used in *Sesame Street* episodes.

- magical-occurrence music
- emotional-state music
  - joy
  - sadness
  - anger
  - fright
  - threat
- denouement music
- solemn music
- detective music
- wishing music
- animal-movement music
  - snakes slithering
  - kangaroos bounding
  - turtles strolling
  - horses galloping
  - penguins strutting
  - birds flying
  - elephants swaying
  - gorillas swinging
- danger music
- trying-hard music
- sneaking-up music
- frustration music

- racing music
- escape music
- chasing music
- colliding music
- near-miss music
- reverie music
- graceful-movement music
- awkward-movement music
- thinking music
- imagining music
- resolved-frustration music
- mischief music
- making-a-mistake music
- fast-motion music
- slow-motion music
- calliope music
- jungle music
- cavalry-charging music
- gathering-storm music
- start-of-a-long-journey music
- end-of-a-long-journey music
- being-hot-in-the-sun music
- being-cold-in-the-snow music

Each musical form by itself can convey its meaning to young children, but when two or more forms are contrasted within an episode, their impact is heightened. For example, within a single segment showing the movements of several animals, the playful and whimsical music accompanying the activities of penguins and small monkeys changes abruptly to ominous and powerful music when gorillas are shown.

One reason for music's great impact with young children is that it evokes physical participation, with variations in musical style evoking different forms of participation. Young viewers tend to rock and sway to simple melodies. The bouncier the tune, the more intense the physical reaction. With some songs the child almost seems compelled to get up and dance. When the child knows the words to a song, his response will be verbal as well as physical. Thus a child might first dance to a song with a bouncy melody; then as he becomes more familiar with it, he is more likely to rock back and forth in his chair while singing along.

Our observations of children indicate that in order to be effective, music and sound effects must be integrated carefully with visual movement. Children's attention will be lost if the music is associated with static visual material. If the visual elements are static (e.g., a seated orchestra playing, a stationary folk singer accompanying himself on his guitar), the music—no matter how appealing in itself—will not attract or hold the children's attention. A static visual presentation apparently stymies physical participation and violates the children's expectation that televised visual action will accompany what they hear.

Repetition

Repetition is another factor in eliciting attention. It is impossible to produce television material that is new and unfamiliar to all children, and our observations of children suggest that they would not like such material very much even if it could be produced. The reappearance of a familiar character, episode or format will often recapture a child whose attention has drifted away. Repetition also provides opportunities to practice tasks as they become increasingly familiar, teaches the television formats and conventions that facilitate learning, and provides the bridge from familiar to new and unfamiliar concepts.

Children seem to like certain pieces of televised material better after they have seen them several times. This seems especially true of short films or animation that build step by step to a humorous or incongruous outcome. This progression permits a child to anticipate each step in turn, saving the humorous outcome for the end but giving the child the safety of knowing that it indeed will occur after he has followed the episode through its earlier steps. The child's initial reaction to a televised segment also determines its increasing appeal with repetition. If this first viewing contains some surprise for him and also contains more elements than he can grasp in a single viewing, repetition permits the child to confront the grounds for his surprise and to sort out some of the complexities. Repetition thus offers opportunities to teach the relatively complex concepts or situations which a child cannot easily understand fully from a single exposure. Far from being merely a vehicle for simple, rote or memorizable material (although it certainly accomplishes that purpose very well), the repeated segment can act as a mind-stretcher, permitting the child to return repeatedly to a subject incompletely explored during its first presentation. A child may experience even exact repetition of a segment differently each time, and thus explore its several facets.

As important as exact repetition, but serving a different purpose, is repetition that includes variation of either format or content. On *Sesame Street* the common variation has been to keep the content constant while varying the formats in which that content appears. For example, teaching recognition of the letter *W* was the subject of three different animated films, four different segments videotaped for repetition, and a number of incidents using the live characters on *Sesame Street*. The letter *W* appears sometimes as a three-dimensional object, sometimes as a line drawing, sometimes as a cardboard cut-out, and so forth, but it always retains its distinctive features as a letter despite its different surroundings. Almost every curriculum objective is presented in different formats so that the child learns to generalize what he has learned across several different forms of appearance.

Another variation in repeated segments is to keep the format constant while varying the content. For example, the speech-balloon format is used in teaching recognition of all the letters of the alphabet except Q (which never appears, of course, unaccompanied by a U). In each of these ten-to-fifteen-second animated films, the figure of a character, different for each letter, appears against a plain white background. This character pronounces the name of the letter, a word beginning with that letter, and the name of the letter again. As the letter name is spoken, a balloon emerges rapidly from the character's mouth and that lower-case letter appears within the balloon. As the word is spoken, its remaining letters also appear in the balloon. The balloon then assumes a life independent of the character who produced it, who now is helpless to control the action that takes place within it. Within the balloon, the word forms the object it names or dissolves into a scene illustrating the use of the word. A quick visual joke ensues, generally involving the original character, and the scene within the balloon then dissolves back to the letter as the character pronounces it a second time. The word used to illustrate the use of the letter a, for example, is "ape." The printed word dissolves into an animated ape, who strums a ukulele and sings in a high falsetto voice the first phrase of "Tiptoe Through the Tulips." The ape disappears, a reappears, and the original character, who has been observing the spectacle, turns to the camera with a quizzical expression and says, "a?" Brief episodes of different content, but each following the same general format, are designed for each letter of the alphabet except Q, and are illustrated in the photo insert section.

As with most other production and writing methods, the use of repetition has its limitations and must be used judiciously. Some material suffers badly when repeated. For example, interest in slowly paced or long segments tends to decline with repetition. Repetition will hold attention only until the different facets of a complex segment have been explored.

Directing Attention

How do we take advantage of attention to the television screen once we have captured it? Are there methods that will help the child direct his attention to the salient and distinctive features of the material to be learned? During the planning period, the producers experimented with several techniques, including the use of surprise and incongruity, animation and pixilation, and the meshing of the instructional message into the televised action.

Surprise and Incongruity

Children will direct their attention to what surprises them, to an image or event that violates their established expectations about the order of their world. They focus upon these deviations because these pose a puzzle that must be unraveled in order to reestablish a sense of order and regularity. Did the child actually see the surprising event correctly? If so, how could it have happened? Few people can let such violations of expectation rest without working hard to resolve them, and this motivation is a powerful one for children, apparently operating as early as the first year of life.[1]

Television provides several means of confronting children with surprises and incongruities. Slow-motion and fast-action show people and objects moving at unaccustomed speeds; one of the most appealing devices for children is the pixilation technique that produces a kind of speeded-up comic movement like

---

[1] Berlyne, 1960; Charlesworth, 1969; Day and Berlyne, 1971; Kagan, 1970, 1971; Piaget, 1952.

the Keystone Kop chases in the days of silent movies. Stop-action, for example, can suspend a horse's jump in midair, giving the child an opportunity to observe more closely the characteristics of the jumping horse, but also surprising the child through the novel experience of watching an animal in flight suddenly fixed in space. Playing videotape backwards provides other strange and unexpected visual experiences— for example, water flowing forward in a stream is suddenly stopped, and then magically flows backward into its source. Other camera and editing techniques permit appearances and disappearances to occur far more suddenly than they do in the child's normal experience, the abruptness catching and directing attention. Close-up shots show unexpected charac-teristics of common objects; looking really closely at the skin of an orange or the surface of an automobile tire reveals un-anticipated properties of these objects. Long shots, allowing views from unusually great distances, are another source of dis-crepancy. Who has not been stunned by the view of the earth from the astronaut's perch on the moon? Sound effects and music also bring their share of surprise to the viewing child. The puppet who speaks in sound effects while describing his misadventures brings an incongruity that captures attention through novelty.

Since adults spend a lot of time trying to convince children of adult infallibility, one of the most remarkable and pleasing novelties for children is to observe adults making errors that children easily identify. In one series of segments on *Sesame Street*, two adults, Buddy and Jim, confront a series of simple problems, but can never seem to solve them. They attempt to place a picture on a wall by hammering the blunt end of the nail into the wall, fail to observe that the nail should be turned around, and then conclude that they must walk to the wall on the opposite side of the room in order to point the nailhead into the wall. In another segment they conclude that making a peanut-butter-and-jelly sandwich is an impossibly sloppy undertaking because both the peanut butter and the jelly al-ways seem to end up on the outside of their sandwich. Here the incongruity and surprise are augmented by the special appeal to the child in knowing that for once he knows more than the adults know. These devices have a long history in children's programs; Laurel and Hardy and The Three Stooges traded on the same combination of incongruity and the child's occasional thrill of finding that he knows more than an adult.

As usual, there are cautions to be observed in using this "one-up-on-adults" approach. Children are accustomed to adults who really do know more than they do, but who pretend ignorance, in a semi-amused way, in order to bait them. Children usually disdain this falseness. If, however, ignorance is actually inherent in the exaggerated characters, such as Buddy and Jim, it is not regarded as a false and contrived maneuver. Children apparently can distinguish between adults who feign the need for enlightenment from children and those whose characters are consistent with being truly less informed than children are.

The producers experimented with other devices for surprising the child. Using the television screen as a magical drawing board creates the same kind of surprise as when an adult makes a mistake, adding to it the opportunity for the viewer to observe children correcting mistakes. For example, the viewing child sees the beginnings of a line drawing being formed on the screen, representing the familiar form of an animal or an object. A group of unseen children is heard giving instructions in how to draw the object. In effect, the artist is the television set, since the lines appear as if of their own accord. As the line drawing is formed, however, certain lines are drawn incorrectly, and the viewing child hears children's voices spontaneously commenting on the composition of the drawing and correcting mistakes as they appear.

Animation

Animation is another production technique for creating incongruity. In the animated cartoons that flood children's television, animation is used primarily for its reversibility, producing endless cycles of annihilations and resurrections. But animation can generate many other illogical surprises that fascinate young children.

> In animation, anything can turn magically into anything else, and children love it for the illogic that is a visual equivalent of their nursery rhymes and jingles and word games. [Pauline Kael, 1970, p. 229]

On *Sesame Street* several forms of animation are used to teach letter recognition. The speech-balloon format is one style. Another shows a ball thrown by a little girl as it bounces between ruled lines drawn across the screen, leaving a visible path in the form of the letter M. Also, the animation technique of pixilation is used in teaching letter recognition. This pixilated effect is achieved by placing the actors on the set, clicking off several frames of film, moving the actors minutely and clicking off several more frames, etc. When the film is run in fast action, the actors move in the choppy, exaggerated style that children find unnatural and amusing. In one use of pixilation, two live actors appear, each carrying a part of a huge three-dimensional letter. Through grotesquely inaccurate trial and error, accompanied by silent-movie chase music, they discover the parts fit together correctly to form the letter. Watching the comically incorrect efforts and the final correct arrangement helps the viewer fix in mind the correct letter form.

Certain animation techniques exert their magic by giving abstract symbols life and movement, permitting them to become part of the dramatic action. For example, in producing "clay animation," clay is molded in successive stages, each photographed on a single frame of motion-picture film. When the film is projected, the clay appears to form itself into a succession of shapes. In a typical segment, a small blob separates itself from a larger narrator blob and forms into the letter E. Next, two G's are rapidly produced from the clay E, and the three letters are aligned to spell *EGG*. A clay egg forms behind the word and hatches to produce a baby eagle. The word *EGG* changes to *EAGLE*, and the eagle eats the word.

Action

Children direct their attention to visual action on television, ignoring whatever is not functionally related to that action. By animating abstract symbols (and even concepts, if put in concrete visual form), these elements can participate as actors instead of being superimposed on the dramatic action as stationary bystanders.

Animation is only one way of directing attention by making the material to be learned a part of visual action. All forms of television production for children must find functional ways to bind educational content and visual events. If the content remains superimposed or peripheral to the visual action that children expect from television, it surely will be ignored.

Instructional content can be engaged directly in the visual events instead of being imposed upon them superfluously. For example, as Big Bird (the eight-foot-tall puppet who is clumsy and not very bright but charming and lovable) enters *Sesame Street* from the right, a small letter *h* enters from the left. Big Bird greets the *h* amiably and then decides that since he is tired, the *h* looks like a comfortable place to sit. As Big Bird tries to sit on the *h*, it moves offscreen, the accompanying sound effect communicating that the *h* considers Big Bird too large and heavy to sit on it. Jointly, Big Bird and the letter decide that given their relative sizes, the *h* should sit on Big Bird instead of the reverse. Here, the *h* is an essential part of the action and inevitably draws the children's attention.

In another example, Kermit, the saturnine but gentlemanly puppet frog, involves the letter *W* in the action accompanying his lecture describing the letter's attributes. Indeed, in this instance, all the action is initiated by the *W* itself, and Kermit becomes more and more perplexed by the letter's antics. In the first segment, the *W* deteriorates into its component parts (*W* to *N* to *V* and so forth) as a consequence of the Cookie Monster's voracious appetite, with Kermit desperately trying to retain his composure and continue his lecture. In the second segment (illustrated by some episodes in the photo insert section), the *W* comes to life as Kermit names selected words beginning with W, and the W itself acts them out. After such words as "walk" and "wander," the W engages Kermit in mock battle while Kermit continues with such words as "war," "weakening" and "Woe is me!"

Puppets also appear in another example of making symbols the focus of dramatic action. Two puppets—Bert and Ernie—become involved in a dispute over who has access to a cabinet containing cookies. Bert, in an effort to establish his exclusive right to the cabinet, has painted a B for Bert on the front doors of the cabinet. Ernie has noticed that the letter spans the division between the doors. In apparently innocent elaboration, Ernie establishes that the initial on the door designates the name of the person who is allowed to enter the cabinet for cookies, and Bert impatiently confirms the rule. Ernie then matter-of-factly opens wide the right-hand cabinet door, removing from sight the bumps on the B and leaving a skinny but discriminable E for Ernie, who helps himself to a snack.

Children almost always ignore certain familiar forms of televised inaction. Most common is the "message monologue," where a single character appears on the screen, facing the camera from a more or less stationary position and telling the audience something. (Due to insufficient funding, most in-school instructional television is forced to take this form; its failure to attract children's attention is now legendary.) Adding another stationary character to give the first stationary character someone to talk with does not help much. Such segments remain heavily laden with words that are not integrated into visual action. Soap operas generally follow this format, with, for example, two women seated on a living-room sofa, sipping coffee (which often is the extent of the action) while discussing their misadventures or the unseen misadventures of their unseen acquaintances. These soap operas are not designed for children, and the tolerance of most adults for sheer secondhand gossip far exceeds that of children, but the static quality of their visual conventions is an excellent example of televised inaction that will not hold children's attention.

Similar inaction appears on programs intended for children when the adult hosts, in such programs as *Bozo the Clown*, play to each other for their own amusement, ignoring both the viewing children and those in the studio audience. These verbal exchanges between adults exclude children, who respond with appropriate inattention. Another example of inaction common in children's programs is the verbal gag, which television writers often come up with to break the monotony of their work. These short verbal jokes or puns are simply added to the physical action, not integrated into it, and usually do not register with young children. A final example is the reading of storybooks on television. There are good reasons for books to be read on children's television: to convey the pleasure of reading; to provide opportunities to point out the relationship between the written and spoken words; and to show adults interacting warmly with young children during storytelling. However, book reading on television simply does not work because of its static visual quality and its total reliance on still pictures and spoken words.

Action, then, is a key ingredient in children's television, and it assumes many forms and styles. One of its most familiar forms is perhaps the most criticized: zany, slapstick comedy that often also displays one person harming another. During

the planning period, we worked hard to clarify our ideas about the use of slapstick, concluding that the elements of zaniness and harm are separable, and that absurd comedy, even when the elements of harm are extracted from it, will retain its great appeal for children. We came to believe that slapstick's appeal lies mostly in its incongruity and surprise, not in its harmful outcomes. Thus from time to time action on *Sesame Street* is as nonsensically slapstick as the real world can be. We aim for wit, whimsy and useful knowledge; but small doses of good, honest, forthright silliness can only make us more credible to our children, who, after all, know as well as we do how absurd life sometimes can be.

Sustaining Attention

To teach effectively, the child's attention must not only be caught and focused, but also sustained. Often children's attention is caught momentarily, but they do not hold still long enough to persist in completing the task at hand. This notion of attention span is contained in the common complaint of teachers and parents that "I just can't get him (her) to pay attention!"

Humor

Humor is an obvious and appealing device for holding attention. Since traditionally we have regarded humor as a slightly disreputable diversion from the hard, serious work of education, and since we have often accused teachers who indulge in it of coddling or currying favor with their students, we know virtually nothing about how to make humor instrumental to learning. Perhaps education that relies upon captive students can survive without such knowledge, but the televised teaching of children is so completely dependent upon the effective use of humor that we must begin to understand it. Humor is probably as much a matter of individual taste in children as it is in adults, and therefore seems to defy generalization.

Several sources of humor contain the same surprising and farcical incongruities I described earlier. Slapstick comedy is a favorite with preschoolers; they find it more amusing than any other comedy form we have observed. They laugh when Ernie outsmarts Bert, when Bert retaliates, when the Cookie Monster foils one of Kermit's lectures, and when a chef falls down with his cakes and pies. The exaggerated physical action of slapstick seems related to its success with children. Although there are some forms of play with words that young children do find amusing, what seems funny to them tends to be physical rather than verbal. Stand-up comedians attract little attention until they fall down, not necessarily because falling down is injurious but because it is unexpected.

Trickery always has been essential in slapstick comedy, where one person takes advantage of another through guile. But today a more advanced level of morality seems to characterize the slapstick comedy that amuses young children: the underdog-turns-the-tables form of justice. Here the person who attempts to take advantage of another through trickery ends up at a disadvantage himself—being tricked through his own guile or cunning. For example, on *Sesame Street,* Ernie (innocent and guileless in this episode) encounters a shifty Salesman puppet dressed in trench coat and slouch hat, who tries to sell Ernie a cut-out number 8. The Salesman's manner is insidious and fraudulent; he flatters Ernie, agrees with everything Ernie says through a soothing "Riiiiiight," and engages in other forms of persuasion that clearly communicate his belief that Ernie is an easy mark. In earlier days of slapstick comedy, the episode might have ended with the Salesman's successful sale. But *Sesame Street*'s episode results in Ernie gently frustrating the Salesman by having already acquired a large stock of cut-out numbers, although he has no 8's. Explaining that he has no money, Ernie offers to exchange his own number collection for the Salesman's 8. Realizing there will be no profit in this exchange, the disgruntled Salesman stomps away. The innocent Ernie has turned the tables. Although *Sesame Street*'s producers and writers had some early misgivings about how well young children would understand the intended salesman characterization and the justice represented in the "worm-turning" outcome, young children understood and were entertained by this and similar episodes.

Another source of amusement for young children is the incongruity of adults making obvious errors and the humor derived from personal idiosyncracies: A puppet named Professor Hastings gives comically confused lectures about such diverse matters as the shapes of letters and the benefits of physical exercise, interrupting each lecture at unpredictable occasions for short naps. Kermit the Frog acts as introducer and assistant to the Professor, doggedly unraveling the Professor's confusions and gently awakening him from his naps so that the lectures can continue. Amidst the Professor's rambling confusions, he is sporadically capable of remarkably clear insights. Suddenly discovering that his assistant Kermit, whom the Professor has been perceiving and addressing as "young man," is really a frog, he says, "Young man, do you realize that you are a frog?" Or while failing to rise from a deep knee bend while lecturing on the benefits of physical exercise, the Professor observes Kermit's feet and remarks, "Young man, do you realize that you have webbed feet?"

Humor for children also stems from the suspense of waiting for the incongruous to occur. Viewing children cannot predict the exact outcome, but they know that a particular format will follow a predictable sequence in its early stages and then proceed to an unexpected conclusion. For example, a series of short animated films is designed to teach counting backwards from ten. In these films, an identical situation—a countdown to a rocket blast-off—results in a variety of comic endings. The launch director solemnly counts off the seconds as surrounding dignitaries wait expectantly. The numbers appear at the top of the screen as the countdown progresses. In every film but one, something catastrophic happens to embarrass the launch director: the rocket blasts off prematurely, leaving the charred launch director sheepishly completing the countdown for his disgruntled audience; the rocket blasts off at the right moment but in the wrong direction, disappearing into the ground; the launch director himself blasts off, his panic-stricken count of *Oooooone* fading in the distance; and so on. The naturally suspenseful situation of the rocket countdown is enhanced by the additional suspense of waiting for a particular form of disastrous payoff, with the child's attention being drawn to the number sequence. The one exception to the consistently catastrophic launches is a successful launch which is greeted with cheers and waving of banners. This straight version itself becomes comic. The viewer who has come to expect incongruous disaster, in what precise form he cannot anticipate, now is further surprised by incongruous success.

Language can be another source of humor for children. Although word play divorced from action must be used cautiously, most children do take pleasure in playing with language; certain emphases on verbal humor on *Sesame Street* are designed to promote this pleasure. Several catch phrases used repeatedly for comic effect have been widely recognized and repeated by viewing children as part of their spontaneous play away from the set: for example, "Cookie!" repeated in guttural tones by the voracious monster puppet who plagues Ernie and Kermit the Frog; or the insidiously soothing "Riiiiight!" uttered by the mysterious salesman puppet. Children also enjoy certain large words and nonsense words that seem to roll around on the tongue: "Bubble," "vigilante," "ukulele," "propeller," and "mumps" all seem to possess this magic.

Although young children seem to enjoy word play, they do not respond well to puns and other plays on words. Puns inevitably depend upon the double meanings of words and phrases, and perhaps because young children do not possess enough verbal sophistication or because puns generally are unrelated to television's visual action, they do not seem to interest or amuse young children. Another limitation in using humor is that it may compete with the intended instruction. Comedy has been most successfully used when the comic moment coincides perfectly with the critical learning opportunity. Otherwise, the child may learn the joke but not the lesson.

In addition to sustaining the attention of young viewers,

humor serves the function on *Sesame Street* of enticing parents and older siblings to share the young children's viewing. To capture the interest of older family members, several forms of humor are used: verbal humor, spoofs on familiar television game shows and soap operas, the use of guest celebrities, and so forth. Parent and sibling involvement, however, has its upper limit. Although every effort is made to induce family involvement instead of using *Sesame Street* as the traditional baby-sitter, nothing is included in the program solely to attract this older audience and nothing is made to depend entirely upon their participation with the young child.

The use of humor is one way to get parents and older siblings to watch with younger children. The appearance of well-known guest celebrities is another. Some celebrities such as Batman and Robin are enlisted because of their unassailable authority with four-year-olds. But others not so familiar to the pre-schooler—as, for example, Burt Lancaster, Carol Burnett and Odetta—are used for their appeal to the older members of the family. James Earl Jones was one of the first celebrities to offer to help by appearing on *Sesame Street*, and his performance yielded some unexpected returns in developing production methods.

We asked Mr. Jones, a stage and motion-picture actor of imposing voice and appearance, to recite the alphabet in any manner he desired, so long as he paused long enough between letters to permit editing of the videotape. Mr. Jones's recitation of the alphabet takes a full minute and a half. He stares compellingly at the camera throughout. At the time the sequence was made, his head was shaved for his role of Jack Johnson in *The Great White Hope*, and it gleams in the close-up. His immense hollow voice booms the letter names ominously. His lip movements are so exaggerated that they can easily be read without the sound. The performance should be seen by every actor who ever complained about his lines.

As Mr. Jones recites the letters, they appear beside his head. Each letter appears visually for a moment before it is named. Once named, the letter disappears, and another brief pause ensues before the next letter appears and is named. So powerful is Mr. Jones's presence that we were concerned that very young children might be frightened, but observation of viewing children established the contrary, and still further observation confirmed the presence of the James Earl Jones Effect.[2]

The effect appears in stages. The first time a child sees the Jones performance, he begins almost at once to respond to the implicit invitation to say the alphabet along with the performer. On somewhat later repetitions, the child begins to name the letter as soon as it appears, before Mr. Jones has named it; Mr. Jones's naming of the letter then confirms or corrects the child's identification of it. With still further repetition, the child begins to anticipate the printed symbol. As soon as the preceding letter disappears, the viewer names the next, saying the letter before Mr. Jones does. Even without two-way interaction between television and the viewer, the child progresses from following the instructional message to anticipating it.

Anticipation

The apparent value of anticipation in the James Earl Jones sequence led us to try to induce anticipation deliberately. When Pat Paulsen volunteered to perform, he was asked to recite the alphabet and the sequence of numbers with hesitations, as if he were unable to recall the correct sequence. His timing is roughly the same as Mr. Jones's—the letter appears, pause, letter is named, pause, letter disappears, pause, next letter appears, pause, and so forth—until Mr. Paulsen falters. At this point, the letter appearing next to his head flashes several times as if to remind him or to induce him to think hard; Mr. Paulsen sneaks a quick look at the letter, names it in happy relief, and goes on. The pace allows children to anticipate, to respond, and then to have their responses checked against the letter's or number's actual appearance.

This anticipation effect, discovered by accident but apparently powerful in sustaining attention, now appears in a num-

[2] Gibbon and Palmer, 1970.

ber of forms on *Sesame Street*. For example, to teach the contrasting meanings of the relational words "around," "through" and "over," five children appear in a three-minute, live-action film playing "Follow the Leader." The children shout out each of the words and then demonstrate its meaning by going *around* a clothesline in a backyard, *through* a large pipe in a junkyard, and then *over* a sawhorse in a lumberyard. *Our Gang* comedy music accompanies their activity. One child fails to negotiate the going around, through, and over on his first try, but remains cheerfully willing to try again and is helped by the other children until he succeeds. At this point, the anticipation effect appears: After establishing the meaning of words by showing the children acting them out while labeling them, the film is run in reverse action, with the children moving backward physically although still moving over, through, and around. This provides an opportunity to rehearse the meaning of these words. The children are seen jumping over the sawhorse backwards (a visually surprising spectacle, as each child jumps high, but in a backward direction); then they shout "Over!" While watching the reversed action the viewer has had time to anticipate the word "over"; while watching the children demonstrate going "through" the pipe in reverse, the viewer can anticipate that label before the children supply it, and the film ends with a similar opportunity to anticipate the word "around."

This segment also illustrates the effort made on *Sesame Street* to build into each episode whatever additional values can be introduced without distraction from its central message. Although the film is primarily designed to teach the contrasting meanings of the words "around," "through," and "over," the child who often fails on his first efforts to perform these activities maintains a cheerful, undefeated attitude in the face of his failure and persists until he succeeds. The other children do not deride his failures, but take commiserating notice of them and then help him.

Another effort we made to induce active participation is illustrated by our teaching children to recite the alphabet. Although this is regarded by many as a relatively trivial skill, we had several reasons for including it on *Sesame Street:* it can become a badge of competence for the very young child, an important displayable skill; it seemed important to include in each *Sesame Street* program all of the letters of the alphabet, lest any viewer be misled into believing that the few letters stressed in each show were the complete list; by presenting the letters visually as their names are rehearsed, alphabet recitation constitutes a review of letters already learned and a preview of those yet to be taught; presentation of the full alphabet may provide an opportunity to discriminate between visually or orally confusable letters; and reciting the alphabet is a natural occasion for the type of overt participation that we sought in response to the program.

The traditional alphabet song is sung by adults on *Sesame Street* on several occasions, usually with children on the set joining in. On these occasions, the child at home is asked to sing along. The same traditional song has been used with less success in an animated film. This film shows a little girl who walks out onto a stage, apparently for an audition. An off-camera voice, presumably that of her mother, tells her when to sing and corrects her delivery during the song. The letters appear on the screen as the child sings. The film seemed amusing to the Workshop staff, and during the planning period it tested well for appeal with children. But we also observed that the film frustrated many children. Those who had already learned the alphabet song and wanted to sing along found the interruptions confusing. The rhythm of the song was broken and the offstage comments were distracting. Those who were still struggling to learn the song found the film difficult for the same reasons. Here is an instance where the intended humor of the mother's remarks and the child's reaction to them apparently interferes with the intended instructional message.

Some educational situations demand children's participation, whether they willingly offer it or not. In response to televised invitations to participate, however, certain children will not display an active verbal or physical response no matter how compelling the inducement may be. This is part of television's nonpunitiveness; the child may respond less energetically and enthusiastically than we hope, but each child is free to decline the invitation without fear of punishment or of attention of any kind. Since television actors cannot know whether the children have participated, congratulating the unseen audience may confuse the child who has not found the solution or who has confidently chosen an incorrect solution. It also may confuse the child who had declined to participate at all.

Diversity of Program Elements

A final consideration in sustaining children's attention is the use of a diversity of program elements. Children lose interest when the program dwells too long on one subject or remains too long at one pace or in one style. This feeling of sameness appears in several guises and always loses the children's attention.

In television production, it is sometimes assumed that a "theme" within a program will link together its elements and help to sustain attention. This proved wrong,[3] producing instead a feeling of sameness. The research staff's brief reports on two shows contain these observations:

> Pet Show: The children were very interested in this theme at the beginning. They were attentive, responsive, and loved Slimy the Worm. But by the time first prize was awarded, the children were restless and inattentive.

> Ice Cream Machine: Much of the street action revolved around the installation of an ice cream machine on Sesame Street. By the time the ice cream man quit, hardly any children were still watching these segments. [Reeves, 1971, p. 2]

Also, a program tends to have the feeling of sameness if too many programing elements within it are similar in characters

---

[3] Our experience here, that young children do not easily tie together the sequence of events in a story line, is confirmed by several research studies, including Leifer et al. (1971) and Collins (1973).

(no matter how attractive the performers may be), content, style or pace.

> Folk Singer: Nearly half of this program revolved around the folk singer. This included his singing of six complete songs and snatches of several others. By the end of the program, only three of the six viewing groups were still intact and few of the children in these groups were watching anything.

> Animal Films: In this program, five animal films were programmed into the last half of the show: Mandrill Mother and Baby, Tree Kangaroo and Baby, Baby Reindeer, Animal Coverings, and Koala. In such a case, it is difficult to judge how attentive the children might have been to the individual films had they not occurred in the same program. [Reeves, 1971, p. 3]

No production or writing technique ever works effectively if the characters shown (adults, children, puppets, animated figures, animals, etc.) are not appealing to children or do not include a variety of distinctive and reliable personalities. Among the earliest inhabitants of *Sesame Street* were several distinctive adult characters: Gordon, a strong black male-identification figure; Susan, Gordon's wife, but an independent female-identification figure as well; Bob, amiable, low-keyed, helpful; Mr. Hooper, slightly mean and abrasive but with a poorly hidden nice streak; Buddy and Jim, two adult blunderers who confront a series of simple problems (easy enough to be solved by the viewing child), but who can never seem to get the obvious solutions quite right. Among the earliest animated figures was, for example, Baby Alice Braitewaithe Goodyshoes, an arrogant, sanctimonious know-it-all (her standard introduction of herself is "Hello. This is Alice Braitewaithe Goodyshoes, the smartest girl in the whole world!") whose cockiness and composure dissolves only slightly when her expertness is called into question. Although all these and other *Sesame Street* characters are designed to be distinctive, the range of personalities among Jim Henson's Muppet characters perhaps best illustrates the needed diversity of characters in television for children. These puppets generally remain reliably in character across different episodes (a strong preference of young viewers) and can portray more exaggerated and therefore clearer roles and functions than human figures. The Muppets appear in the photo insert section.

> *Oscar the Grouch:* firmly and insistently contrary; from personal preference, he despises the standard virtues (friendliness, cleanliness, consideration for others, gregariousness, etc.) and thrives on what others reject (disorder, dirt, surliness in dealing with others, total privacy, etc.).

> *Big Bird:* naïve; easily flustered and confused; prone to making obvious mistakes while remaining cheerfully undefeated; accepted (but not patronized) by others around him.

> *Kermit the Frog:* half pitchman, half courtly gentleman; tries hard to remain cool in the face of gathering chaos and usually succeeds with only minor but visible cracks in his composure.

> *Ernie* (most often, but not always, appearing in *Bert's* company): an appealing tease; often trapped by his own craftiness and cunning; retains a true sympathy and fondness for his would-be victims.

> *Bert:* usually Ernie's straight man, but more intelligent and less innocent than most straight men; long-suffering and put-upon but retains a personal integrity and refinement that allows him to confront the intrigue and chaos gracefully; capable of delicate double-take and slow-burn acting.

> *Cookie Monster:* voracious; sly in satisfying his incessant appetite yet aware of others and willing to understand their reasons for frustrating him; usually succeeds despite their efforts.

> *Grover:* cordial and accommodating in a slightly gruff way; seeks opportunities to be helpful even when this places great physical and mental burdens upon him; often ends up in total exhaustion as he amiably extends himself to the utmost to cooperate.

> *Herbert Birdsfoot* (often appearing in *Grover's* company): a careful and knowledgeable pedant; courteously accepts Grover's offers to assist in demonstrating Herbert's lectures by ma-

nipulating physical materials, visibly resulting in Grover's overworking and consequent exhaustion.

Roosevelt Franklin: an agile, quick-witted and quick-moving, street-language-articulate black-child puppet; knows a lot, likes to learn more and to show what he knows and can do; a learning addict.

Roosevelt Franklin's Mother: nags and pushes Roosevelt a little (this does not seem to bother him much), but takes obvious pride in his knowledge and achievements: "Roosevelt Franklin —he sure does know his numbers!!"

Professor Hastings: verging on senility; gives comically confused lectures, interrupting each at unpredictable occasions for short naps; sporadically capable of remarkably clear insights that stand in marked contrast to his general muddlement.

Sherlock Hemlock: a not-quite-competent detective who constantly searches for crimes to solve and prides himself on his detecting prowess; succeeds in deciphering certain clues, but never quite arrives at a crime's final solution without assistance.

The Salesman: archetypical trickster who trades on the vanity and greed of others; often ends up as victim of his own avarice.

Count von Count: looks just like Dracula, but his real fetish is anything to do with numbers.

In addition to these distinctive puppets, an infinitely expandable troupe of Anything Muppets comes in all sizes, shapes and appearances and can play any role from local grocer or postman, to members of a group of small boys and girls, to varied forms of monsters, to a hip but somewhat seedy and disheveled musical group.

According to our research, beyond responding to puppets and animated figures, children generally prefer watching and listening to other children rather than to adults. If the televised children are involved in some activity, especially when they are trying to solve a problem that the viewer can work through with them, attention proved to be especially strong. Also, our viewers particularly enjoy hearing other children's voices; several films that originally evoked only mild interest worked much better when children's voices were added to the sound track.

Televised children are most effective when they display distinctive and reliable personalities, but this is difficult to achieve. On *Sesame Street*, it seems especially important that the televised children be spontaneous and unrehearsed; nothing is more stilted and unnatural than child actors reciting lines from a prepared script. But when the televised children do respond freely and spontaneously, their behavior often is unpredictable and difficult to construct into a set of distinctive personalities. Distinctiveness of character often must be sacrificed for spontaneity and naturalness. If unpredictable behavior by children raises problems for teachers within the classroom and parents within the home, this same unpredictability presents continuous, unplanned crises for the on-screen *Sesame Street* cast. Since these cast members are not professional educators, the televised children's spontaneity poses a constant threat of embarrassment. The adult cast's early reaction was to restrain children by restricting their opportunities to initiate or respond —much like the inexperienced university instructor who does not call upon students who threaten to interrupt his lectures with questions or comments. Slowly, some relaxation is being achieved as the cast learns to respond to the children's spontaneity with spontaneity of their own, even when this forces a radical departure from the planned televised lesson.

Watching adults or listening to them talk—especially when they are presenting "message monologues"—is much less appealing to children than watching other children. For example, in the early planning of *Sesame Street*, we developed a continuing series of episodes called "The Man from Alphabet," featuring a bumbling adult detective hero and a super-reasoning child who unravels the clues and solves the crimes. They never held the attention of young children and the approach was dropped. Apparently, "The Man from Alphabet" simply talked too much.

Children will pay some attention to adults if instead of showing the adult speaker on the screen, the camera shows what he is speaking about; or if the adult shares the screen with children, directing his talk to them; or if the adult makes mistakes, providing opportunities to be corrected by children. In these instances, the adult seems to use language that the child viewer can understand because he is talking directly to a child. When an adult is on the screen by himself, however, children interpret this as part of adult television, not intended to be understood by them.

Presenting a diversity of distinctive characters inevitably means presenting the diversity of dialects natural to them. Although there were some misgivings during the early planning of *Sesame Street* about presenting any other language models than "correct" standard English, we do present the full range of dialects, accents and informal street language appropriate to the range of characters on *Sesame Street*. We have found no evidence that children are confused by this or learn "incorrect" language practices. The natural diversity of language simply reflects the natural diversity of characters. For example, Roosevelt Franklin, the black child puppet, speaks a black English dialect; Gordon—the adult black male-identification figure—speaks both standard English and black English on different occasions or even changes his speech within a single segment, depending upon the situation and the other characters he is with.

The mixing of several visual styles also helps to sustain attention or to retrieve it when it is lost. *Sesame Street* mixes four main ingredients: puppets; the cast of live adults and children on the set; animation and pixilation; and live-action films. All these styles are accompanied by appropriate music and sound effects, and are supplemented with the appearance of guest celebrities, "mystery drawings," spoofs of game shows and soap operas, skywriting, stop-action techniques, and so forth. This variety of style permits the mixing of fantasy (puppets, monsters, animated figures, etc.) and reality (live adults and children, live-action film, etc.). Some early misgivings that combining fantasy and reality might create confusion between them did not materialize. For example, when the puppet characters Oscar the Grouch, Big Bird, and Bert and Ernie joined the adults and children as inhabitants of *Sesame Street*, viewers

"Look, Cornelius, where the hell is Sesame Street?"

took this as one natural expression of the magical incongruity created by television. This mixing of fantasy and reality holds considerable appeal for young children, an appeal apparently shared by some adult cartoonists as well.

Beyond these useful diversities in characters, content and style, varied pace and mood are critical in sustaining attention. The appeal of any single segment is tied closely to the contrasts provided by the episodes preceding and following it. Both fast-paced and slow-paced material will hold children's attention (the common criticism that *Sesame Street* is continuously frenetic is simply inaccurate), but a slow, peaceful episode is more appealing when surrounded by fast-moving episodes than when it follows another slow, quiet piece. Interest in any particular episode is higher if it creates a pace and mood that looks, sounds and feels different from the one that preceded it. The observation that visual action appeals to young children need not mean that the action always must be rapid or frenetic to be effective; instead, its pace should be varied.

Observations of dramatic improvements in intellectual skills around ages five to seven[4]—including the ability to sustain attention[5]—suggest that for children below these ages only television programs of short duration would be suitable. But on the premise that only a program of sufficient total length would stand any chance of providing educational benefit, *Sesame Street* was designed to be one hour in length. The most common misgiving of educators was that this would be too long to hold young children's attention. This misgiving turns out to be wrong. When the segments within a program are varied in character, content, style, pace and mood, young children's attention holds up well over a one-hour period.

During this early planning period, all these production possibilities seemed worth trying. The research team had been observing children reacting to these different techniques and styles and had been feeding their conclusions to the producers and writers. We expected this collaboration between researchers and creative staff to develop slowly. Instead it emerged quickly and was reinforced as programs were designed and tested. In the long run, it was essential to *Sesame Street*'s success.

[4] Sheldon White, 1965.
[5] Kagan and Kogan, 1970.

Chapter Six

Research Planning

The bird that I'm going to write about is the Owl. The Owl cannot see at all by day and at night is blind as a Bat.

Excerpt from a research report
by a ten-year-old, quoted by
Edward Weeks, *Atlantic Monthly*

During the planning period, we were experimenting with many different production techniques and had only just begun to produce bits and pieces of what was later to become *Sesame Street*. Although we had little televised material in hand and only a few ideas about what the producers would eventually come up with, we knew that we would need to begin planning our research at the earliest possible time. Research would be needed to tell us how well children liked what we did and how we could make the programs more appealing to them. It also would be needed eventually to tell the public and our financial backers what the programs had accomplished in reaching large numbers of children nationally and in teaching them effectively. We knew that these jobs would be expensive: roughly 10 to 15 percent of the Workshop's initial two-year budget of eight million was allocated for research. We also knew that these were complex jobs with few precedents to guide us. Certainly no commercial television programs for children had attempted them.

Research on how well we appealed to children would be of no value unless it was used to continuously improve the pro-

The original cast, the Muppets, Big Bird, Oscar the Grouch,
and visiting children gather on *Sesame Street*.

Scenes from Kermit the Frog's lecture on the letter W.

a. Kermit the Frog delivering his lecture on the letter W.
As Kermit says that the letter W is used in the words
"Walk" and "Wander," the W approaches him.

b. Kermit is surprised by the letter's behavior.

c. The letter begins to pummel Kermit.

d. Kermit, about to succumb to the *W*'s attack, sighs,
"W is for weakening. Woe is me!"

J

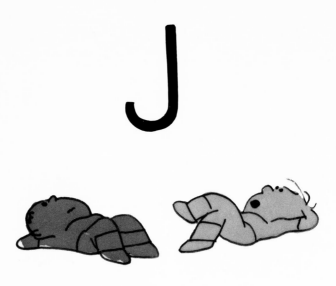

Scenes from the J commercial.

Junebug

J_{ig}

a. The animated character pronounces the letter *f*, which then appears in a speech balloon.

b. The letter *f* and the balloon grow in size.

c. The word "fly" then appears in the balloon; a fly enters the balloon, its flight gradually erasing the word.

d. Escaping from the balloon, the fly lights on the character's nose, and he prepares to dislodge it with the fly swatter.

The Muppets

grams. This would demand close collaboration between researchers and the creative staff; yet traditionally producers have relied exclusively on their own instincts, rarely seeking the reactions of children. Television producers have not only ignored this source of information, but often have vigorously rejected it, almost as if checking with children were a sign of cowardice—an admission that they did not trust their own intuitions. Yet without research on the children themselves, producers and writers simply cannot know, in time to permit changes, if they have hit upon an appealing approach, how to build on it, or when to abandon it and start over. The value of child-testing seems so obvious that one would expect it to be routine. Actually it is almost never done.

We eventually assigned our highest research priority to observing children's responses to our televised segments as they were being developed, and modifying them according to the children's reactions. Although we knew that problems between researchers and producers might arise, we also knew that child-watching research was essential.

Collaboration between Production and Research

As our producers and researchers looked for ways to collaborate, the producers expressed doubt that it could be done. Perhaps there were very good reasons why it had never been done before. David D. Connell, the Workshop's vice-president for production, describes his early skepticism:

> My background was in commercial television, where we felt we had developed a pretty good set of instincts about what kind of show would appeal to children at any given age. I frankly was skeptical about the idea of researching every moment of a television show, and certainly of being told how to design it. There was the risk of intellectualizing the material to death and ending up with a program most notable for its monumental boredom. It would be like trying to analyze the ele-

ments of a joke, only to find that when we had isolated all the pieces, there was nothing learned and nothing to laugh about. But if *Sesame Street* was an experiment—and it very definitely continues to be one—this notion of broadcaster/researcher cooperation was the most bold experiment within it. I kept thinking of the biologists who cross-bred a crocodile with an abalone in hopes of getting an abadile. Only something went wrong and they ended up with a crocablone. Nothing like this had ever been attempted before. [Connell and Palmer, 1971, p. 67]

Collaboration placed unfamiliar demands upon both producers and researchers. The producers felt that it threatened their autonomy. Accustomed to full creative control, they faced the prospect that the researchers, with the weight of observations of children behind them, would share that authority. In addition, for the producers merely to understand what the researchers were reporting about their child-watching, they would need to take a new and different perspective on children.

Connell's concern about "intellectualizing the material to death" and thus destroying its life and spontaneity contained a more direct threat. A good producer trusts his instincts and draws freely upon feelings and personal experiences. Deliberate observation of children's reactions would be one more constraint upon the free use of that intuition. Several constraints already were operating. Our intention to find ways to make entertainment educational (or to make education entertaining) was one of these, and the methodical process of arriving at our educational goals had been another. In addition, a stream of observations of children was now superimposed on the producer's creative instincts. It was a heavy and unaccustomed burden.

The researchers experienced burdens of collaboration that were no lighter. Research in child development is encrusted with traditions. If collaboration was going to work, the researcher would have to modify, abandon or even violate several parts of his standard paraphernalia. The researcher's most familiar role in education is to police programs after they have been completed, evaluating how well they have met their professed goals. Without this evaluation, our only grounds for judgment are public-relations claims and the persuasiveness of the programs' proponents. But deciding how well a program has done after it is over does not contribute to making it better in the first place. To collaborate with producers, the researchers first had to give up the role of policeman; then they had to find ways to work with producers to improve the programs before broadcasting began.

Other research traditions surround its pace and timing. Arriving at sound knowledge about child development takes time, and researchers do not rush the process if they can avoid it. Merely developing a clear and workable idea about what to study often takes years, sometimes a full career of years. Methods must then be developed and tested, subjects selected and located, data collected and analyzed with a minimum of error, and reasonable generalizations extracted. To really be sure of the findings, researchers must then repeat their studies to see if the findings stand up over several tests.

Research rarely goes smoothly, and even when it does, it seems to take forever. Published reports look neat and logical, but what goes on in reality is messy and confused—a series of crablike moves, each selected through the researcher's faith that it may push him a small step ahead. Keeping to a plan is almost unheard of. Knowing this, researchers never promise to deliver knowledge on schedule, and when they are forced to, they know that only uncommon good fortune can rescue them. But television shows go on when scheduled, ready or not, with no room for uncertainty or delay. Failures to learn what was needed from research cannot be passed off with jokes about impractical, absent-minded scientists.

Other research traditions would also have to be suspended:

• Researchers usually want to observe enough children to justify general conclusions; but in order to collaborate in production, and because he is not trying to generalize but instead to offer recommendations about specific program materials, a researcher often must try to extract useful information from observations of only a few children, and must therefore accept greater risks of being wrong.

• Researchers usually like to apply uniform procedures to all children in a study to exercise a certain amount of control; but to collaborate, a researcher often must change his procedures from child to child, building up to a conclusion that a producer will find useful.

• Researchers often work in laboratory settings; but to collaborate in television production, a researcher must observe under conditions that are as natural for the child as possible.

• Researchers aim their publications to those who share their professional language and who usually are not physically present when their findings are reported (and therefore cannot immediately accuse them of stupidity in person); but to collaborate, the researcher's audience is sometimes as small as a single producer or writer who does not share his professional language, and who by being physically present can confront him directly.

Beyond these unfamiliar demands, the researchers have to resist some alluring temptations. The Workshop's researchers found themselves out of academe and its laboratories and into "show biz." Like other people, they had watched television a great deal and harbored the feeling that they could easily become instant experts in television production. Yet if they tried, their usefulness to production would be lost. While understanding the producer's activities and perspective, they had to remain in their own role and do what they know how to do—observe children accurately and convey the meaning of these observations to producers in a usable form.

Another pitfall is more hidden. The success of *Sesame Street* ultimately rested as much with the researchers at the Workshop as the producers. As programs were born and grew, the researchers came to regard them as their offspring. All researchers are tempted to abandon dispassionate detachment from their studies and to become advocates, but for the researcher collaborating in television production, the temptation is almost beyond resisting. Clearly, *Sesame Street's* researchers were as proud of their programs' accomplishments as anyone on the staff; this is the special danger—if the researcher allows his enthusiasm to color his observations of children, his advice becomes useless and even misleading.

Selecting Functions for Research

Gathering observations of children watching television is only one of several useful functions that research could perform in the development of *Sesame Street*. Since we did not have unlimited personnel and financing for all these functions, we had to make choices. In selecting educational goals, we had prepared a full inventory of possibilities and then selected priorities among them. Now, in selecting functions for research, we again made an inventory of possibilities and selected priorities among them. Some of these research activities assisted the program planning that preceded broadcasting; others took place during and after *Sesame Street* went on the air.

Before Broadcasting

ESTIMATING INITIAL COMPETENCE

Our educational goals told the producers and writers what to teach but not the level of instruction to aim for. If most children have already learned certain skills by preschool age, there was no point in our developing programs to teach them. If other skills and concepts were so complex that we could not find any preschoolers who had learned them, they were likely to be beyond the reach of televised instruction for this audience. We needed precise information about what children already know.

Unfortunately, after decades of child-development research, little information is available about the range of competencies among different age groups. The evidence that does exist is not organized in any systematic way, and compiling the fragments would require an exhaustive and time-consuming search. We could conduct our own testing of children in the many goal areas in our curriculum, but since this demands careful test construction and administration, valid sampling methods, and extensive data analysis, it is also expensive and time-consuming. But since some estimates of the range of existing competencies were absolutely essential to production, we got what information we could by searching through the existing research and also by conducting some tests of our own. When we got beyond our time and money, we drew upon our general knowledge of child-development research and our informal observations of children.

ESTIMATING THE APPEAL OF EXISTING MATERIALS

Through research, we also hoped to anticipate the television preferences of our audience by testing their reactions to existing programs. Since few television programs have even tried to combine education and entertainment, and certainly none had discovered the secret formula for the merger, we knew that the yield would be limited. But other programs would be only a switch of the dial away from ours (a switch that young children learn to make early in their lives), and there might be some value in learning from their successes and failures.

Ed Palmer and his research group devised an experiment to measure children's interest by continuously recording whether their eyes were toward or away from the television screen. We knew that this measure of appeal is imprecise: simply observing whether or not children are facing the screen does not tell what is going on in their minds. We might have gotten more precise estimates of attention by using measures of eye movements; when children are not only facing the screen but scanning it systematically, there is greater reason to believe that they are mentally processing what they see.[1] However, eye-movement research is expensive and places children in unnatural viewing conditions because of the recording equipment used. Whether or not the child is watching the screen would

---

[1] Guba, 1964; O'Bryan, 1972; O'Bryan and Boersma, 1971.

give us a rough but useful index of the relative appeal of different programs. In addition, graphing the fluctuations in visual attention within a program would permit the researchers and producers to see from moment to moment the elements that hold attention and those that fail.

These estimates of appeal of existing television programs are relatively inexpensive to gather. During the early planning of *Sesame Street*, they gave us some idea of the television preferences of our audience. We watched children's reactions to over thirty existing programs, including *Yogi Bear, Misteroger's Neighborhood, Huckleberry Hound, Captain Kangaroo, The Monkees, The Flintstones, Lost in Space, Rowan and Martin's Laugh-In,* and *Roger Ramjet.* Most of our observations simply confirmed that preschoolers are attentive to fast-paced action, novel or incongruous situations, variety in format and content, animation, puppets, other young children, animals, slapstick comedy and commercials. Other observations were more instructive to us: their attentiveness to the sound track and to different forms of music, their fascination with nonsense words that sound funny to them, their confusion when familiar characters appear in an unfamiliar context, their preference for what may seem to an adult to be endless repetition.

The attractiveness of pixilation was discovered in a film called *Neighbors*, done by Norman McLaren for the National Film Board of Canada. *Neighbors* drew very high attention levels among children. It contains considerable violence, and at first we thought that this was why the children watched so carefully. However, it also contains pixilation, and after watching many children responding to the film, we decided that it was this technique—not the film's violence—that had held the children's attention.

PILOT TESTING OF EARLY SESAME STREET PRODUCTION

Our early observations of children were made on individual segments of *Sesame Street* as the producers developed them. These observations underscored the importance of variety within a program for preschoolers,[2] and the producers decided that a magazine format would leave room for this variety. It also had the advantage of allowing unsuccessful segments to be dropped without changing the overall appearance of the show. We also expected that when the individual segments were produced and assembled, the appeal that each episode carried on its own might change either for better or for worse, depending, for example, upon its contrast with the segments preceding or following it. Thus, another function for research was to test several full one-hour shows, giving the producer a dry-run estimate of the format's appeal before national broadcasting began. Other research was planned for the time when we actually went on the air.

During the Early Broadcast Period

AUDIENCE SURVEYS

When broadcasting began, would the children watch? Even our noncommercial national programing had an obligation to reach a large enough audience to justify its expense. Before broadcasting began, we were feeling intimidated that we would be judged on two criteria simultaneously. As a national program, we would need to attract a large audience. As a program with serious instructional purposes, we also would be judged by how well we taught these children. When broadcasting began, *Sesame Street* would be asked to do both. Anticipating this, we stressed the teaching criterion and simply hoped for the best on the size of our audience: "The show's justification clearly must lie more in its achievement of its instructional objectives than its ability to capture a large audience."[3] Despite our protestations, we knew that "cost-effectiveness" questions would be raised; surveys of the size of our audience would be necessary to answer them.

Such surveys have been common in commercial television,

[2] Reeves, 1970.
[3] Samuels, 1970.

estimating how many viewers are delivered for each commercial dollar invested. Market research is less interested in why people watch or do not watch, and in what the benefits and damages are. It does a good job of measuring the size of the market delivered, but does not probe much into underlying motives.

Audience measurement also effectively estimates selected portions of the total market, focusing for obvious reasons on people who have money to spend and ignoring those who do not. For *Sesame Street*, we would be interested in how many three-, four- and five-year-olds we were reaching, both from poor and well-to-do families. Among these families we would need to know not only how well *Sesame Street* was accepted by the young children but also whether the parents and older siblings in the low-income families were interested in encouraging the young children to watch and perhaps in watching with them. Since audience surveys have not traditionally asked about young children and inner-city families, we knew that they would be difficult to conduct.

COMMUNITY USE

No television series by itself will produce important effects upon children unless it is reinforced by other influences in their lives. We believed that the more we could involve the parents, older siblings and others in the child's viewing experiences, the better the effects of the series would be. Primarily, we believed firmly in the value for a young child's self-concept of an older person admiring his real accomplishments. Creating this appetite for learning might be of far greater importance than teaching any particular set of skills. We also anticipated that when parents, older siblings and others have an opportunity to watch a child respond and learn, they develop more constructive expectations for him, expectations that in turn have powerful consequences for the child's expectations for himself.

This reasoning led us to identify another fruitful research function, the search for ways to help parents, older siblings and others to use the show effectively with young children. For example, when *Sesame Street* began broadcasting, we planned to observe what happens naturally when people spontaneously look for ways to increase the program's value for their children. Do they bother on their own, and if they do, what means do they use? The Workshop would also try to develop new procedures that individuals and organizations could use to build upon the children's viewing experience. For example, viewing groups could be formed in day-care centers, neighborhood organizations and homes; or parent workshops could be organized to promote parent-child activities; or adolescents could be enlisted to work with small groups of young children; or other volunteer groups could be established at the local level. The researchers would need to test the acceptance and value of these experiences for the young children.

PERIODIC PROGRESS TESTING

We would have to await the end of the first broadcast year before the effects of the full series could be assessed. However, twenty-six weeks would go by before the series of 130 programs was over. If *Sesame Street* were producing little or no effect, it would take the full year before this was discovered, too long a delay to permit corrections. However, if we knew that a group of children had watched consistently for six weeks (30 shows) of the twenty-six-week broadcast year (130 shows) and had failed to show any significant learning, the producers would be well-advised to make adjustments rather than to hope for a sudden, belated explosion of learning. Research thus could guide midcourse correction.

We also intended to trace cumulative learning over the course of the series. Perhaps most learning would occur during the first few programs, in response to their novelty; after an initial burst, learning might level off with no significant gains added. Perhaps the series would have to catch on before any significant learning began; familiarity with the characters, style and format might be needed. Or learning might begin immediately and then progress in a steady course over the full broadcast year. If we tested viewing children, for example, after every three-weeks of the twenty-six week broadcast period, which of these forms would cumulative learning take? Estimating progressive changes over time was of high priority for research, but to reduce the expense of frequent testing, we decided to conduct only spot checks, after three weeks (fifteen programs), six weeks (thirty programs), and three months (roughly one-half of the full broadcast year).

Estimating Overall Effects

In the early planning stage, we still had no idea of what *Sesame Street* would eventually look like, but we had to begin planning the research that would tell the public and our financial backers if *Sesame Street* made a difference when it went on the air. For the programs to be considered effective, the children who would watch must learn more than children who did not. These differences would be estimated through "summative evaluation," conducted independently of the Workshop to avoid bias. Although a few months remained before *Sesame Street* began broadcasting, we needed to plan the research immediately. Tests had to be developed, representative groups of children located nationally, and the tests administered before broadcasting began so that comparisons could later be made after the broadcast period ended.

A program's chances of survival are only partially determined by its measured effectiveness. All sorts of political, economic and social forces determine which programs are born, survive or die. Interest in the education of gifted children bloomed when the Russians launched Sputnik in 1958. Interest in day care blossomed when women's liberation became a significant social force. Community schools emerged from the pressures of minority groups for equal educational opportunity. Compared to the power of these political and economic forces, the results of objective evaluations of programs pale in importance.

Although summative evaluation rarely supersedes these other

determinants of an educational program's survival, it can affect a program's chances; consequently, research acquires its policeman image. It tells how well the program works, sometimes to its benefit but more often to its detriment. Because our educational programs are weak and our evaluation techniques imprecise, summative evaluations more often offer testimony to failure than success. Unfortunately program developers often view program assessment as punitive; actually it serves a crucial purpose in telling them whether their programs really make a difference.

To be useful, summative evaluation must fulfill at least two conditions: progress of both participants and nonparticipants (in television's case, viewers and nonviewers) must be compared, and assessments must be made both before and after the educational experience. The gain of the participants as compared to the gain of nonparticipants (while taking into account conditions other than degree of viewing that might have produced such differences) reflects a program's effectiveness.

These are minimum conditions necessary to answer the question of whether or not an educational program works. The simple question "Does it work?" is a tempting one to ask because of its decisive, unhedging sound, but it is inadequate because it implies a simplistic search for the single best program for all children. A more rational approach would be to explore the idea of creating different educational options and to look at program effects on different children and under different conditions. For whom does *Sesame Street* work and for whom does it fail? Under what conditions is *Sesame Street* effective or ineffective? Summative evaluation must go beyond assessing simple overall effects on all children ("Does it work?") and attempt also to answer these more meaningful questions ("For whom and under what conditions does it work?").

Only a few clues exist about the differential effects of television upon different children. For example, televised instruction seems more effective than live conventional instruction for children at both high and low intelligence levels, with no differences appearing for children in the middle range of intelligence.[4] Television's success among students with low IQ's apparently rests on its narrow-focusing capacity, its focusing attention on salient content while eliminating distractions. For students with higher IQ's, television seems able to present more information *per* time unit than conventional instruction, fitting better their preferred rate of learning. In evaluating *Sesame Street,* we were aware that no single form of instruction will work equally well for all children and that learning from television would be an excellent way for many children and a poor way for others. We felt it important, in our evaluations, to differentiate those for whom the medium works and those for whom it fails.

Given *Sesame Street*'s educational purposes, we were particularly interested in the possible difference in response of children from poor and well-to-do families. Since *Sesame Street* would be broadcast nationally, our first priority was to attract three-through-five-year-old children from all social-class, cultural, and geographic backgrounds in order to gain the largest possible national audience. But we also had decided that if we failed to attract and teach inner-city children in particular, we would have failed. By announcing our intention to reach a national audience, we had ruled out the possibility that poor children would watch more than middle-class children; we hoped that every child in the country would be attracted. We did hope to make the series so appealing to inner-city children that they would learn as much as middle-class children, who have a wider range of early educational experiences, but we could not reasonably expect that poor children would learn significantly more from the same or less viewing. But to test the expectation that both poor and middle-class children were learning from viewing, research had to include both groups. Since these data could be misused to make invidious comparisons between groups, we debated the wisdom of conducting simultaneous evaluations of children identifiable by social class or ethnic background. Certainly research had supplied enough

[4] Schramm, 1962; Snow and Salomon, 1968; Westley and Barrow, 1959.

invidious comparisons among ethnic groups to generate strong reservations.[5] Granting the possible misuses of data gathered simultaneously on poor and middle-class children, however, we felt it crucial to know if *Sesame Street* would reach and teach both groups effectively, as stated in ETS's plan for the summative evaluation of *Sesame Street:*

> No mention has been made of direct comparisons between lower SES (socioeconomic status) and middle SES subjects, between black subjects and white subjects, or between Spanish-speaking and English-speaking subjects. Such comparisons are not of interest to the Children's Television Workshop. The purpose of the show is to benefit all children regardless of language background, SES, and race. Major statistical comparisons will be made within groups rather than between groups. That is, CTW is more concerned with whether lower SES viewers learn more than lower SES non-viewers than with whether lower SES viewers learn more than middle SES viewers. [Educational Testing Service, 1969, p. 16]

We were also eager to know how *Sesame Street*'s effectiveness was affected by different viewing conditions. For example, we banked heavily on the value of parents and older siblings sharing the young child's viewing experience, but only research could tell us whether this really mattered as much as we anticipated. Also, we might discover different benefits when children view individually or in groups, either in large in-school groups or smaller neighborhood ones organized by mothers or paraprofessionals. In some day-care or preschool settings all the children would be encouraged to watch in groups, while in others, each child could decide individually whether or not to watch. If our assumptions about the importance of television's nonpunitiveness are correct, we would be likely to see different benefits. We also anticipated differences in children's responses due to different mechanical conditions of viewing, such as the clearness of visual and auditory reception, transmission over

[5] For example, Jensen, 1969; Shockley, 1971.

UHF or VHF stations, and color television as compared to black-and-white reception.

At a minimum we wanted summative evaluation to estimate our success in teaching the skills we intended to teach. But we also would surely produce unintended consequences, either beneficial, harmful or both, and a complete evaluation must include these outcomes along with the intended ones. Recognizing the need to assess both types of effects, however, left the researchers a great distance from being able to do so: Since by definition unintended effects cannot be anticipated in advance, researchers inevitably did not know where to begin to look for them. Not knowing the guise in which these effects would appear, they were unable to make specific plans to look for them.

Measuring the intended outcomes sounds simpler than measuring unintended ones, but through the years researchers have not found it especially easy. What the educational program intends to accomplish is often not what the researchers know how to measure. Using available instruments, such as standardized intelligence and school-achievement tests, researchers end up measuring what they know how to measure instead of what the program developer wants to achieve. For example, an early study of Head Start's effectiveness[6] used measures of intellectual skills and concluded that no effects could be demonstrated, a conclusion interpreted by some[7] to mean that Head Start had failed. Although five of the seven stated goals of Head Start stress social and emotional benefits (self-concept, self-discipline, positive attitudes toward family and society, self-confidence, self-worth), these were ignored in the evaluation because no good measures of them are available.

In measuring unintended effects, the researcher carries the additional burden of not knowing where to look. He is not entirely helpless, however, because certain unanticipated effects will seem more likely to occur than others. One likely source of unintended effects would be episodes to which surplus elements have been deliberately added in order to make them

[6] Cicarelli et al., 1969.
[7] For example, Jensen, 1969.

more humorous, more incongruous or simply more interesting. For example, during the early planning period, we began to experiment with the speech-balloon format for teaching letter recognition. An animated character introduces a letter (for example, *a*) which then appears in a speech balloon. The letter first expands into a word beginning with that letter (for example, "alligator"), then into the animal itself. In these sequences, the animated character often ends up in some state of discomfort, ranging from being chased by an alligator to having his nose tweaked. The format is effective both in holding attention and in teaching the intended letter-recognition skills, but certain unintended lessons are suggested, some beneficial, others undesirable. Perhaps attaching letters to interesting familiar animals and objects that appear in the speech balloons will make children alert to other letters and symbols attached to familiar figures in their environment. Another possible unintended effect, however, is stimulating the dubious impulse to laugh at another's misfortune.

We considered several unintended effects which presented difficult measurement problems: When children learn basic intellectual skills, do they develop greater confidence in their ability to learn? Will parents actually watch with their young children, and if they do, will they become more interested in their children's abilities and achievements? Does watching *Sesame Street* deflect children from other constructive activities? Does it make children less likely to do things on their own or to ask questions and seek out answers for themselves? Does school become dull by comparison to *Sesame Street*, or are the two experiences unrelated in children's minds? We realized that a wide range of potential side effects might exist, and that summative evaluation must be alert to them.

It is difficult enough to do evaluation which includes both intended and unintended effects upon different children, viewing under different circumstances. But matters worsen rapidly when evaluations are asked to compare the relative "costs and benefits" among different educational approaches. Although the comparison between programs appears to be essential to any complete assessment, it currently is far beyond the reach of our evaluation techniques. Few educational programs have objectives that overlap sufficiently to permit direct comparisons. Some stress cognitive and language outcomes; others emphasize motivation, social and emotional development; still others focus on health and nutrition. Unless two programs' goals are identical—and few are—comparative cost-benefit analyses are risky.

The philosophical base for cost-benefit comparisons is even riskier. These comparisons are important only if decisions are being made to select the one, or few, educational programs to implement; then knowing the "best" or most "cost-effective" one would seem to be a basis for rational choice. But the mindlessness of searching for the "best" educational program for all children now should be obvious. In creating a range of educational options, programs do not compete but act in combination with one another. We decided to try to estimate the costs and benefits of *Sesame Street* itself, but not to compare these estimates with those of other preschool programs.

Who evaluates programs is almost as important as what is done. Evaluations should be judged on technical grounds, such as the reliability and validity of the measures, the adequacy of the sampling, and the precision of the statistical procedures. As long as the technical criteria are met, who performs the research should be irrelevant. But measurement is not yet an exact science and still leaves room for personal bias. Since the people who design a program are personally committed to its worth, more objective evaluation may be done by outsiders without this investment. Outside observers may be more willing to perceive failures as well as successes.

Even nonpartisanship, however, has its pitfalls. No outsider can ever know the program in as much detail as its designers. Those responsible for the program often feel this incomplete knowledge leads to outside evaluation that is neither fair, thorough nor accurate. One remedy is close consultation between evaluators and program designers so that they understand each other's efforts, but this opens the possibility of collusion. By and large, people do try to be nice to one another when they are working together closely, and collaboration indeed may influence the evaluators subtly and subconsciously to favor the program. Despite these problems, evaluations are rarely left in the hands of those responsible for the program itself, and this generally makes sense.

We consulted with several independent research agencies and reviewed their proposals to evaluate *Sesame Street*. The Educational Testing Service of Princeton, New Jersey, had a skilled and experienced research staff, competent testers distributed nationally, and a research plan that would take us beyond the simple question of whether *Sesame Street* worked into the analysis of for whom it worked or failed, under what conditions it was effective, and what its unintended effects were. We decided to ask them to conduct evaluations of *Sesame Street*'s effects.

Long-Term Research

The research questions described to this point were designed to learn specifically about *Sesame Street:* how to design it, improve it and judge its value. They were indispensable to producing quality television programs for national distribution. But perhaps *Sesame Street* could serve an even more important purpose: It could begin to correct our total ignorance about how children learn from the visual media.

Television's commercial origins may explain why it has never been a topic for serious study. Researchers may have feared that increased knowledge would lead only to increased commercial exploitation. Despite its commercial purposes, we know that television has opened unique opportunities to children. Because teachers in traditional classrooms can never bring the children's visual world dramatically to them, they rely upon the verbal and the abstract; some children learn well in these modes, while a great many others do not. Television provides vivid visual portrayals of the world beyond classrooms and neighborhoods, and children respond to them as they have never responded to verbal and abstract education. Yet we are ignorant about how children do learn from the visual media. This understanding certainly will come in part from experiments such as *Sesame Street,* but long-term research must extend beyond any single series of programs.

Where so little basic research exists, we can only guess at the most productive questions to ask at the outset, but each should be both descriptive and prescriptive—how does television affect our lives today, and what can we discover about how to use it intelligently?

• What effects, if any, does television have on children as young as one or two years of age? What effects could it have?

• When children begin watching television for the first time, at whatever age this occurs, how does the experience affect their perceptions of themselves and the world around them?

• How do special groups of children use television, such as the physically handicapped, the deaf, the mentally retarded, or the emotionally disturbed?

• What are the physical, physiological or medical consequences, if any, of television viewing by children?

• Can television help children to understand their own thoughts and feelings as well as the thoughts and feelings of others? If television exposes children to instances of kindness, compassion, courage, generosity and altruism—in general, to instances of caring among people—how does this affect their behavior?

• What mechanisms are involved when young children model the behaviors of televised characters? We know that extensive modeling occurs, but have little understanding of how it operates or of the mechanisms behind it.

• The model's behavior can either incite or defuse the viewer, can either increase or decrease the likelihood that the viewer will behave in the way he sees televised characters behave. What conditions lead to these contrasting effects?

• What goes on in the viewers' minds as they mentally process what they see and hear on television? Will visual representations create corresponding mental representations in children?

• How does television affect the quality of relationships among people? There are those who say that it breaks down barriers, expands the individual's world, and provides opportunities for shared experience. Others are more skeptical: "What does persistent watching do to a child's ability to relate to real people, to become self-activating, to think on the basis of his own life experience instead of in stereotypes out of shows?" (Bettelheim, 1960)

Questions as fundamental as these require long-term research, and an organization such as the Children's Television Workshop, established with the mandate to produce national television programs, cannot be expected to generate this research knowledge directly. No one is designated in our country to try to understand how children learn from television, how the visual media affect their lives now and in the future. We have no answers to these basic questions about television and, astonishingly, none are being sought.

Child-Watching

Early in the planning period, the Workshop's creative staff had produced only small segments of experimental material. But as soon as we began trying out these materials on children, we were impressed by how much we could learn about them by watching even a few children. The Workshop's director of research, Edward Palmer, had been hired specifically for his extensive experience and skill in inventing new ways to observe children's responses to television. The Workshop now gave him the opportunity to use this experience fully, and soon the creative staff found themselves, somewhat to their own surprise, relying heavily upon Ed's child-watching talents and those of his research staff.

This became the first time in television's twenty-five-year history that child-watching was systematically applied over a sustained period to the design of a televised series for children. In a few early precedents[8] for observing reactions, children were asked to press switches when they liked what they were seeing, but this seemed impossibly artificial and cumbersome

---

[8] For example, Lindsley, 1962.

for our purposes. We found no other precedents to suggest how observations could be made to adjust the shows to the reactions of children. Traditional measurement would be of no help whatever; for child-watching purposes, its techniques are precisely the wrong ones—estimating the gross effect of a large block of instructional materials, using standardized tests with their prescribed questions and predetermined correct answers, ignoring why certain outcomes appear and others do not, and disregarding how different children are affected differently. Unsurprisingly, traditional measurement is of little relevance because it asks: "Now that the program exists, how well does it work?" Child-watching asks the prior question: "What do we do to get the program to work in the first place?"

Ed Palmer and his research group designed several new approaches to observing children. When children watch television under normal conditions, they experience frequent distractions and interruptions. To simulate these conditions, Ed designed a "distractor"—a slide projector placed at a 45-degree angle to the television set and adjusted to change slides every eight seconds. The researcher depressed a push button when the child's eyes were on the set and released it when the child looked elsewhere, thus recording the proportion of each eight-second interval when the child watched our segments as opposed to looking at anything else, including the distractor. The records were prepared as graphs which the researchers and producers analyzed in detail together. Using this and other new techniques, segments produced early in the planning period were tested for their appeal and teaching value. Later, when the magazine format of *Sesame Street* began to evolve, we were able to test the segments again to see if they held up in the context of the full program.

The J commercial, for example, passed the initial test; "The Man from Alphabet" did not. The J commercial was one of several short animated cartoons designed to teach children to recognize and label the individual letters of the alphabet. Since the J commercial teaches the letter by showing the similarities between familiar objects, such as a fishhook, and the form of the letter, I described it earlier as an example of using familiar experiences as a bridge to new and unfamiliar ones. It is created along the lines of a television spot commercial, a fast-moving rhymed story filled with *J* sounds and objects whose names start with that letter—June bug, jar, judge, jury, jail, and so forth. It was the first piece of animation commissioned by the Workshop in the fall of 1968, arrived in January 1969, and was immediately subjected to extensive tests with both inner-city and middle-class children, with the most intensive work done with four-year-olds, who watched either individually or in small groups at three inner-city day-care centers in New York City.

As part of the ongoing activities in these centers, children saw the *J* commercial, interspersed with other television materials, in the presence of the distractor. As they watched individually or in small groups, careful records were taken of whether each child's attention followed the *J* commercial, the slides on the distractor, or anything else in the day-care room. Some children saw the segment once, others four times, and still others as often as ten times. Following their viewing, each child was tested individually to see if he could tell us which letter he had just seen on television, discriminate a *J* from other letters, write the letter *J*, pick out words starting with the letter *J* (both those *J* words he had just seen and other *J* words that he had not seen), and select pictures whose names begin with the letter *J*. Although very few of these day-care children could recognize or label the letter *J* before viewing the segment, the majority could do so after viewing, especially those who had watched repeated presentations.

We learned several other things from this early child-watching. When our attention measure showed that a child had watched carefully or had participated by talking or singing along, the tests given after viewing showed more learning. This connection between attention and learning is not surprising, but new techniques are always hard to create, and we were delighted to find that ours were giving consistent and sensible information. We also tested the children again four weeks after the viewing and found that almost all of them had retained what they had learned earlier.

Although the *J* commercial seemed to work well, we also discovered some ways to improve it. The segment opens with a letter *J* attached to a string dropping from the top of the screen above the heads of the two boys, who watch it with curiosity ("What's that?" "It looks like a fishhook."). A voice offscreen immediately tells them that it is the letter *J*. In the original version, the letter itself remained stationary during this action, and as the viewers watched the antics of the animated characters, they soon lost interest in the stationary *J*. The producers decided to change the segment to make the letter itself move in animation, greatly increasing its salience. The technique of animating symbols to make them actors in the visual movement soon was incorporated into other segments that attempted to teach the recognition and labeling of symbols.

Through child-watching, we also saw how easy it would be to inadvertently compete with ourselves for the children's attention. We used a strong rhyming pattern in which many *J* sounds were embedded, including "Once upon a time a guy named Joe / Noticed a June bug on his toe / Put it in a Jar and started to go / When along came a Judge and said, 'No, no, no!'" Although each *J* word appears on the screen as it is spoken, the children seemed much more aware of the rhyming pattern itself and less aware of the *J* sounds within it. Because we knew that rhyming is an excellent teaching device for young children, we decided to retain it, but we tried to shift the emphasis to make the *J* sounds within the rhyme more prominent. Here is the final script for the *J* commercial:

VIDEO	AUDIO
PICTURE OF TWO SMALL BOYS SITTING AND TALKING	FIRST BOY What's happening, man?
	SECOND BOY I don't know.
	FIRST BOY What's that?
LETTER *J* APPEARS FROM TOP OF SCREEN	
	SECOND BOY I don't know.

VIDEO	AUDIO
	FIRST BOY It looks like a fishhook.
J ENLARGES AND BOYS HUDDLE TOGETHER	MAN (*Voice over*) It's not a fishhook! It's a *J*.
	BOYS (*Together*) A what?
	MAN (*Voice over*) The letter *J*. Like to hear a story about the letter *J*, boys?
	BOYS (*Together*) Yeah!
J MOVES TO LEFT LITTLE MAN WALKS OVER TO *J* AND LIES IN HOOK—SEES BUG ON TOE GETS OFF *J*, PUTS BUG IN JAR JUDGE ENTERS FROM RIGHT	MUSIC UP—VOICE OVER Once upon a time a guy named Joe Noticed a June bug on his toe Put it in a jar and started to go But here comes the judge and said, "No, no, no."
JOE JUMPS	But Joe said, "Why?" and started to jump
JOE DANCES ON TREE STUMP	And danced a Jig on an old tree stump
JOE JOGS TO LEFT OF SCREEN	And jogged along to the city dump
JOE PUTS BUG IN TIRE PUMP	Where he jammed the June bug in a tire pump
JUDGE APPEARS AND HITS JOE ON HEAD WITH GAVEL	And the judge caught up and started to wail, Said to Joe, "Justice will prevail."
JOE IN COURTROOM	And the Jury met and set the bail

VIDEO	AUDIO
JOE BEHIND BARS	And Joe got an hour in the city jail.
	FIRST BOY
CUT BACK TO TWO BOYS SITTING	So that's the letter *J*.
THEN LIE DOWN LOOKING UP	
AT *J*	SECOND BOY
	It still looks like a fishhook.
	FIRST BOY
	You know what else we learned?
BOYS SIT UP	SECOND BOY
WORDS STARTING WITH *J* APPEAR	Yeah. Don't jive a judge by
AS THEY ARE SPOKEN	jamming a June bug.

(Scenes from the *J* commercial appear in the photo insert section.)

This early child-watching also taught us something about young children's learning of symbols. Before viewing, many middle-class children could not recognize or label the particular letter *J*, but they seemed to have some awareness that letters and other symbols existed in the world. In contrast, most inner-city children were not only unfamiliar with the letter *J* but also "seemed to have no conception of what those strange figures on the pretest cards meant. Letters seemed to be outside the realm of their experience."[9] We soon recognized that learning specific symbols was a dual task for most young inner-city children, including both the general recognition that symbols with meaning exist in the world as well as the specific recognition of what the particular symbols are. Perhaps this also should have been apparent to us from the outset, but it was only when we observed children carefully that we could see it at work.

Our child-watching with the *J* commercial was encouraging

---

[9] Ogilvie, 1969.

and instructive. In contrast, our experience with "The Man from Alphabet" was disappointing, and it was reluctantly dropped from the series. Yet in its own way, it was perhaps even more instructive.

"The Man from Alphabet" had been planned as one way to teach some of the reasoning and problem-solving skills that we had chosen as educational goals. We hoped to take advantage of the popularity of the many adventure satires on television at that time, including *Man from UNCLE, Batman,* and *Get Smart.* "The Man from Alphabet" himself would be a bumbling adult detective-spy, but the real brains behind the Alphabet Operation was a super-reasoning seven-year-old child who could solve the mysteries that confounded the man. At the Workshop, we all were convinced that the idea was excellent. It focused directly on the reasoning process, had a child as its hero, showed this child solving problems more effectively than adults, and contained a great deal of visual action and gentle whimsical humor. When four sample episodes were produced and child-watching began, several crippling faults became apparent almost immediately.

Once again, four-year-olds in day-care centers viewed individually, in pairs or in small groups. They all responded well to the visual absurdities sprinkled throughout the episodes—for example, when a chase scene was presented in pixilated action. Otherwise, the episodes were disastrous for our purposes. The central characters proved to be confusing. For example, "The Man from Alphabet" was portrayed both as a "good guy" and as a bungler, and this combination confused young children. Nor did they understand clearly the child-hero's role as the reasoner and true crime-solver. The child actor's poor diction and the stilted delivery of his lines added to this confusion. In this, our experience coincided with that of many television producers before us who had used child actors in rehearsed and scripted roles. But the major catastrophe was the one that soon began to appear so prominently elsewhere during our child-watching—too much talk unconnected with the visual action, especially from the adults.

As new televised segments were created and as our child-watching expanded during the planning period, we refined our definitions of what attributes to look for in our programs. Associated with a segment's appeal or interest value to children, Palmer and his research group[10] looked for, among other attributes:

- the effects of various forms of music.
- the optimum amount of variety.
- the optimum pacing of events.
- the optimum number of exact repetitions or repetitions with variation.
- the most and least salient or memorable characters.
- the appeal of special techniques such as pixilation, fast and slow motion, unusual camera angles.
- the relative appeal of incongruity versus predictability.

Early in the planning period, Palmer's child-watching estimated a segment's teaching value as well as its appeal. As child-watching was refined,[11] these gross estimates of teaching value were divided into several components: comprehensibility, the compatibility of entertainment and educational elements within a segment, and "activity-eliciting potential."

Since children cannot learn what they do not understand, estimates of comprehensibility were designed to see if children understood the intended meaning of what they saw and heard. For example, we looked for how well children understood certain unique conventions of television, including:

- flashback techniques.
- various camera perspectives.
- "magical" effects, such as making an object instantly appear or disappear.

10 Palmer, 1972.
11 Palmer, 1972.

- the rules of various games.

- restating a point from alternative perspectives.

- various forms of introductions and reviews.

As with estimating appeal, Palmer developed several alternative methods to estimate comprehensibility. In one approach, we presented a program by means of a video-playback system, stopping the program at predetermined points to ask viewers to explain what is happening, what led up to it and what is likely to follow. As with all research techniques, there are limitations. For example, when children know they are going to be questioned, they often attend more closely. We thus may overestimate their natural levels of comprehension.

Child-watching also helped us to estimate how well we succeeded in combining education and entertainment. When the educational message was simply tacked onto the visual action, children ignored it. But we did find that some of our segments produced early in the planning period succeeded in combining the two effectively. For example, one Muppet piece was designed to teach recognition of the letters D and R. Bert and Ernie are watching a television set that shows nothing but the capital letter D, which rhythmically pulses forward and then recedes as the announcer intones "D . . . D . . . D . . . D . . ." in synchrony with the letter's movements. Ernie complains to Bert that the set has been broken for days, constantly showing only the letter D. Bert suggests that they try to locate the cause of the problem, and Ernie then finds that the back of the set is cluttered with objects whose names begin with D: doggie, duckie, donut, dump truck, and so forth. As these objects are extracted, the appearance of D on the set now stops, only to be replaced with a pulsing R, as the announcer now intones "R . . . R . . . R . . . R . . ." Bert is disappointed to find that the set has not really been fixed, but Ernie's attention is transfixed by the appearance of the new letter and he repeats "R . . . R . . . R . . . R . . ." in rhythm with the announcer's voice. Although Bert briefly continues to complain that the set is still broken, he soon begins to share Ernie's fascination with the letter R and joins

Ernie in reciting the letter along with the announcer. This segment was of high interest to children, and yet all the visual action centers directly upon the educational content itself—the letter *D*, objects that begin with that letter, and then the letter *R*.

Heavy emphasis in child-watching also was placed on estimating "activity-eliciting potential." If viewing does not elicit either physical or mental activity, or both, learning will not occur. During and following viewing, we looked for various signs that children were acting upon what they had seen, ranging from intellectual activity to the imitation of televised models. Signs of intellectual activity, for example, included integrating separately presented items of information, anticipating upcoming events, forming new concepts, assigning motives and intentions to characters, and guessing answers to questions. One of our clearest indications that a segment has elicited a reaction is when the child relates new information from the segment to his own prior experiences or future plans.

The Personal Side of Child-Watching

Despite the high priority we gave to child-watching, good observations of children did not come easy. Not only are there no precedents, but the problems are the same baffling ones that people confront whenever they try to evaluate their own behavior or that of people in whom they have a personal interest. It always is difficult to accept the possibility that things will go wrong or that the need to seek improvements will be necessary. By setting up self-correcting devices in advance, such as child-watching, we seemed almost to invite the failures that we hoped would never occur. It is tempting to divert disaster through magical thinking: If we do not have ways to cope with problems, we will not need them; if we deliberately create these devices, we will inevitably find that we need them.

Even after the likely need for self-correction through child-watching is accepted, admitting mistakes publicly, if only among one's colleagues, never is easy. This was especially true during the early period of program development, when producers and researchers were getting to know each other and the rate of failure was greatest in producing good material. This early period also was precisely when an atmosphere of openness to self-monitoring had to be established. Fortunately, a few early acts of uncommon heroism helped to create this atmosphere. For example, after reviewing the child-watching information on "The Man from Alphabet," David Connell, who as head of the Workshop's production had commissioned the episodes, advised that they be dropped and acknowledged as "Connell's Folly." If similar acts of heroism had occurred during television's early history, we have no record of them.

Child observations cannot be used constructively if producers and researchers treat one another as adversaries. Everyone—producers and researchers alike—has his own instincts about what works for children, and observations of children can be used as weapons to defend these personal intuitions, as in "I told you so" and "Look how wrong you have been." We could not allow child-watching to become a battleground for competing preferences.

Child-watching may result in expensive modification, if not outright abandonment, of materials already produced. The budget for production can absorb changes only to a limited extent. The more successful child-watching is, the better it is in suggesting improvements, and the greater is the burden of time and money to the producers. What researchers know from their observations must be balanced against what producers can afford to know.

We acknowledged the value of child observations when program planning began, but its successful use demanded maturity, patience, diplomacy and confidence in one's professional skills. This was the first time in television's history that the children themselves would be listened to with care as a television series for them was designed and broadcast. It is a great compliment to the Workshop's producers and researchers that they made this happen.

The Role of Research Advisors

With all these possible functions for research to serve, and with each being so complex, the Workshop's fledgling research group felt the need for objective consultation with other researchers. To help set priorities and to monitor the Workshop's research activities, several experienced researchers were invited to form a Research Advisory Subcommittee.[12] As with the National Board of Advisors, this Research Subcommittee was not consti- tuted to provide window dressing or to certify the acceptability of the research. It performs as a working committee to monitor the full range of the Workshop's studies. Since its members work closely with Workshop personnel, they cannot be con- sidered totally detached, and their collaborations may some- times bias their judgments in favor of the research. However, there are also inducements toward criticism. Their assigned task is to suggest improvements. Also, whenever research au- thorities deliberate upon someone else's research, a subtle com- petition emerges among them to outdo each other in incisive analysis, more often unfavorable than favorable, and of course this critical attitude is supported by their mission to monitor the Workshop's research activities. Since tendencies both to credit and criticize operate within the subcommittee, it has provided an excellent resource for reaction and analysis.

The First On-the-air Trial

The planning period was coming to an end during the summer of 1969. The producers needed a dry run, and five one-hour

[12] The original subcommittee, with their affiliations in 1968: James S. Cole- man, Johns Hopkins; Jerome Kagan, Harvard; Francis Mechner, Institute of Behavior Technology; Samuel Messick, Educational Testing Service. Later, sub- committee members included: Richard C. Atkinson, Stanford; William W. Cooley, University of Pittsburgh; Marshall M. Haith, University of Denver; Thomas F. Pettigrew, Harvard; Lauren B. Resnick, University of Pittsburgh; Doxey A. Wilkerson, Yeshiva University.

pilot programs were aired in sixty selected homes in Philadelphia, from 10 to 11 A.M. on July 21 through 25, 1969. In
New York City, four-year-olds also viewed in day-care centers.
Things did not go especially well. Summer temperatures in
Philadelphia rose to above ninety degrees; the children seemed
restless and inattentive. On the first day *Apollo 11* was on the
moon; some children preferred the astronauts to *Sesame Street*.
The television set was stolen from one home, and the set in
another home was reclaimed by a finance company just before
the test series began. Where television sets still were present in
the experimental homes, reception of the little-known UHF
channel owned by the local educational station was poor.

Nevertheless, the attention of the four-year-olds was as high
for the pilot *Sesame Street* programs as for any other children's
programs we had tested. The varied format seemed to work
well and sustained the children's attention over the full hour.
Most important, the children learned much of what was taught
on these shows, with their greatest gains occurring on skills
that were emphasized heavily in the programs. As a dress rehearsal, these test runs did not inspire us with full confidence
about *Sesame Street*'s reception when national broadcasting began in the fall of 1969, but there were enough promising signs
that we were on the right track to keep us from panicking.

Section Three: Broadcasting

Sesame Street *is . . . with lapses, the most intelligent and important program in television. That is not saying much yet.*

Renata Adler,
The New Yorker,
June 3, 1972

Every television series needs a name, but as we approached the beginning of broadcasting in the fall of 1969, we still did not have one. In a preview film we produced to bring the series to the attention of station managers, parents and teachers, David Connell decided to admit our difficulties in finding a name in a Muppet parody of a show-naming conference.

Scene opens with six Muppets assembled around a conference table, engaged in hard thought. The litter of scrap paper around the room indicates that the conference has been going on for several days. Suddenly:

FIRST MUPPET   All right! All right! How about this for a title? *The-Two-and-Two-Are-Five Show?*

CONFERENCE-LEADER MUPPET (*Accompanied by the angry protests of the other Muppets*)   Are you crazy? This is supposed to be an educational show. Two and two don't make five!

FIRST MUPPET (*Dubiously*)   They don't? Then how about *The-Two-and-Two-Aren't-Five Show?*

(*Angry voices from other Muppets*)

SECOND MUPPET   This is a show for kids, right? How about calling it the *Little Kiddy Show?*

ALL MUPPETS   Sounds all right! We like it!

THIRD MUPPET   But we ought to say something about the show telling it like it is. How about the *Nitty-Gritty, Little Kiddy Show?*

ALL   Not bad! Yeah! We like that!

FOURTH MUPPET   Yeah. But "Little Kiddy" can mean any child up to the age of seven or eight. I think that we should aim the show right at the preschooler. So, how about the *Itty-Bitty, Nitty-Gritty, Little Kiddy Show?*

ALL   Ok! Good! Yeah! (*but their enthusiasm is beginning to wane*)

FIFTH MUPPET   But we shouldn't aim the show only at city or country kids, so let's call it the *Farm and City, Dog and Kitty, Itty-Bitty, Nitty-Gritty, Little Kiddy Show!!*

(*Scene fades as conference deteriorates into frustration, with Muppets pummeling each other, the conference table, the furniture, etc.*)

The series' real name would have to be brief, simple, not too cute, and easy for young children to remember. Since we had not found a name that we all liked, we had delayed naming the series until the last moment. Now information about the forthcoming broadcasts was about to be distributed, and we were forced to select the name that we all disliked the least. *Sesame Street* was chosen. We worried that "Sesame Street" had too many *s*'s for young children to pronounce easily and that it might be a bit of a tongue twister for them, but when we tried it out, they seemed to have no serious problems saying it. Originally, the name "123 Sesame Street" was considered, with the numbers identifying the house on the street in which most of the inhabitants lived and also suggesting the number content on the show. To simplify the title, the numbers were dropped.

Sesame Street began broadcasting nationally on November 10, 1969, and the staff of the Children's Television Workshop began an exhilarating ride on a wave of favorable public reaction. The program received great attention in the press and among parents, and was almost universally applauded for its originality and imagination. Reviewers predicted that commercial television would be forced to respond quickly by improving the quality of its own children's programs. Although each commercial network did appoint a high-level executive to children's programing shortly after *Sesame Street* went on the air, the prediction unfortunately never came true.

Sesame Street was carried over public-television stations which led us to worry that some families, especially those in inner cities, might not quickly discover our programs. The Workshop allocated 8 percent of its initial budget of eight million to distributing advance notice about the show, principally in inner-city areas. Abetted by a national preview carried by NBC as a prime-time special, word-of-mouth publicity spread rapidly soon after broadcasting began, so that even at the outset, a large audience of children watched. With about nine million of the twelve million preschoolers in this country within reception areas of the then 190 public-television stations carrying *Sesame Street* (many transmitting weak UHF signals), early estimates indicated that roughly five to six million of these children were watching. Those who did not watch

"SESAME STREET!"

©1970
ORLANDO SENTINEL

"Why isn't that child at home watching 'Sesame Street'?"

were admonished to do so by people who believed it was good for them. Rumors reached us that watching *Sesame Street* was becoming a fad among college students, and that even middle-aged adults and senior citizens without children in their homes were watching in somewhat embarrassed fascination. Some critics, astonished that a program on public-television channels was actually competing for an audience on equal terms with

"FOUR O'CLOCK, DEAR. 'SESAME STREET.'"

Drawing by Weber; © 1972
The New Yorker Magazine, Inc.

the commercial networks, cautioned that novelties subside quickly and that *Sesame Street* might not retain this large audience.

The favorable notices were gratifying. They were also instructive. Reviewers responded to the freshness and humor in the programs and to the appeal of the characters. The early reviews that mattered most to us were those that described children's reactions. Almost every reviewer or parent who commented seemed able to collect a few real examples of how young children enjoyed viewing and were learning from it, instances which included deaf or mentally retarded children. For example, many mothers of mentally retarded children wrote to tell us that although they had been told that their children were incapable of learning, they had actually observed them learning from *Sesame Street* to recite the alphabet, recognize letters and count in sequence. They reported how much pleasure it had given them as parents to be able to praise their children for these real signs of learning and how much pleasure the children took from that praise. Parents of children younger than our intended preschool audience also wrote to describe their children's responses to *Sesame Street*. Apparently we were on the right track.

Some protests we had expected failed to appear. Before broadcasting began, we steeled ourselves against cries of outrage from educators who might feel that we had invaded their territory. They never came. Apparently, fears that *Sesame Street* would render teachers obsolete were not shared by the teachers themselves. From the earliest broadcasts, teachers seemed to believe that *Sesame Street* could help them in their jobs, teaching simple skills that they could build upon through their own personalized instruction. Reactions by school librarians, another anticipated source of resistance, reflected the same sense that *Sesame Street* was aiding them in their work by getting children interested in books and in reading.

There was little time to savor the applause. The producers, fearing that the early programs might not be right, had stockpiled only a few weeks' programs in advance. They launched into their herculean chore of producing five one-hour shows each week for twenty-six weeks. The cast began to discover how to work with each other under great time pressure and, most important of all, how to relate on camera to *Sesame Street*'s spontaneous and unrehearsed children. The Workshop's researchers scrambled to keep up with all the tasks we had assigned to them during the planning period, especially the continuous child-observing that we relied on so heavily. The Workshop's community workers suddenly found themselves in great demand and intensified their efforts to reach inner-city children and parents. Joan Cooney now faced the problem of refining the Workshop's organization so that its initial momentum would be sustained. Amidst this hectic activity, some criticism of *Sesame Street* began to seep into the early acclaim, and the Workshop staff tried to consider these complaints as it went about its business.

Chapter Seven

Criticism

Sesame Street *is a brisk, witty, absorbing series which proves that professional standards of television production aren't necessarily incompatible with intellectual rewards . . . a program of intelligence, sophistication, good humor and noble intent, to be enjoyed by preschoolers, school children and parents alike.*

John Leonard,
Life

Sesame Street *is . . . a poorly conceived, poorly developed, and poorly presented educational program.*

Herbert Sprigle,
Jacksonville *Journal*, July 9, 1971

For the first few months after *Sesame Street*'s broadcasts began, there was virtually no criticism at all. Later, a trickle of complaints filtered through the general acclaim for the series, growing toward the end of the broadcast year and the beginning of the next, and then receding once again to only sporadic comments.

Both *Sesame Street*'s successes and its failures were criticized. Some critics complained about *Sesame Street*'s success in attracting young children, observing that they now would be more seduced than ever to television's passivity and vicariousness. Others found *Sesame Street*'s fast pace and repetition offensive, although they generally exaggerated these characteristics by overlooking the varied style and content of the shows.

Otherwise, each critic seemed to choose to make a different observation about the series.

What was most disappointing in the critical reaction was that it seldom offered constructive suggestions about the problems it raised. It did ask some useful questions, however, about the educational goals we had chosen and our methods for attaining them, about *Sesame Street*'s possible unintended effects, and about the ways *Sesame Street* portrayed minority-group members and women.

Questioning Our Premises

John Holt, a perceptive commentator on teaching practices, and several other educators argued that we are wrong to get children ready to learn what the schools teach. They believe that school is made up of endless arbitrary rituals and any effort to prepare children for these rituals shares their irrelevance. Television should instead teach what the schools never will:

> *Sesame Street* still seems built on the idea that its job is to get children ready for school. Suppose it summoned up its courage, took a deep breath, and said, "We *are* the school." Suppose it asked itself, not how to help children get better at the task of pleasing first-grade teachers, but how to help them get better at the vastly more interesting and important task—which they are already good at—of learning from the world and people around them. [Holt, 1971, p. 78]

We chose to stress school preparation because whatever we think of the schools, they are a crucial part of children's lives, a part that poor children especially must cope with and exploit as best they can. Television's unique potential indeed may be to help children to "learn from the world and people around them," but for inner-city children, the schools might serve as one of the few avenues out of poverty.[1]

---

[1] Christopher Jencks and his research team of social scientists (1972, 1973) question this observation and assert that the schools, as they are, do not reduce the unequal distribution of income between poor and well-to-do. Of course, it remains to be seen what education as it might be could accomplish.

Other educators took the indictment of school preparation a step further, claiming that we not only fail to teach what the schools do not teach but we also miss the chance to instigate a restructuring of American education. For example, Ann Cook and Herbert Mack (1970), two former public-school teachers, argued that *Sesame Street's* success in reaching a large audience of children, parents and teachers places upon it a special responsibility to "broaden our vision of what education can be, to redirect our thinking or pose new questions to the mass viewing audience." (p. 11)

There is a vast distance between our effort to discover how to use television to teach certain skills and the "restructuring of American education," as necessary as this may be. Surely the Children's Television Workshop would be pleased if it had provoked a serious reconsideration of our educational system, but it would have been arrogant and unrealistic to expect anything of this magnitude from a single television series. While it is valuable to be reminded of larger and nobler missions, the Workshop's first obligation is to learn how to achieve its limited objectives well. Perhaps then we can hope to combine with more powerful social and political forces to begin to reconsider American education.

Critics also questioned the value of accelerating the early learning of intellectual skills, a complaint that has two sources. One is the exasperation with regimenting our children's lives at earlier and earlier ages. The other is that children will learn these skills later anyway and will do so more easily when the appropriate time comes. As Helen L. Beck, a school social worker for the Westport, Connecticut, schools, put it: "It is adult anxiety about time running out that gives rise to the attempt to create the 'instant adult.' But reading and number skills can be acquired at many stages of a child's life. They are best acquired when the possibility of practical application arouses the child's interest in acquiring those skills." (Bridgeport *Post*, April 11, 1971)

Our reaction also has two parts. First, the earlier a child learns an elementary set of skills, the earlier he can begin to build upon them. The second is our desire to create a sense of pleasure in acquired competence as early as possible in the child's life. However, neither the objections to accelerating early learning nor its defense can be supported with existing evidence. Each is a statement of faith: young children will grow best if we leave them alone *versus* they will acquire a pleasure in learning if we take the trouble to foster it.

These critics understood our premises accurately. Others distorted our premises and then attacked them. These excerpts from *The Councilor* (Shreveport, Louisiana, July 3–24, 1971) are an extreme instance of biased perception:

> KEY WEST, FLA.—The young mother who sits her child in front of the TV to watch *Sesame Street* might be better off hiring Fidel Castro as a baby sitter! . . . key revolutionists are pouring huge sums into this innocent-sounding TV program.
>
> Here are a few random facts for Moms (and Pops) to ponder:
>
> (1) While parents study the horrors of "communism," *Sesame Street* introduces their tots to real live Reds, and sugarcoats those Reds to make them look like good guys. An excellent example is Pete Seeger, who shows up at nearly every major communist gathering and pro-communist gathering in the world to strum his guitar and warble the praises of Red Revolution. Pete is a *Sesame Street* "lovable."
>
> (2) At a time when small children should be learning the faith of their fathers and love of country, *Sesame Street* indoctrinates them into an anti-Christian, anti-national, faceless, raceless one-worldism.
>
> (3) *Sesame Street* purposely tries to indoctrinate children into complete disregard of racial distinctions and racial pride. Every great civilization in history which dropped racial pride and tribal pride crumbled into oblivion . . .
>
> Can pressure politics influence the propaganda message of *Sesame Street?* Yes! *Sesame Street's* directors admit that they knocked out the housewife-mother image to appease Women's Lib. In early programs a character known as Susan was a housewife, but this seemed to offend the gruff-voiced he-gal types who preach that Mother's place is not in the home. Nowadays, Susan is a wage-earner, instead of just being a housewife.

Where can such pressure lead? Women's Lib is just now getting organized. If Lib becomes strong, isn't it possible that *Sesame Street* will become even more perverted?

Sesame Street is already promoting biracial relationships. Could it not under pressure from the gruff-voice gals gradually "glorify" girl-girl relationships? Is there any real progress in doing away with Robert Louis Stevenson's Treasure Island, and replacing it with the Isle of Lesbos?

Our curriculum also was criticized for being compartmentalized. Since it lists a series of discrete skills, critics contended that children will not know how to combine them to meet real problems. For example, an objective added to the *Sesame Street* curriculum during the first broadcast year is to teach at the children's level certain ideas about ecology, such as limited resources and depletion, and interdependency among living things. These ideas demand the simultaneous application of reasoning skills (such as classifying and anticipating consequences), numerical concepts (such as enumeration and conservation of number), language concepts (such as the use of relational terms), all combined with certain basic facts about the natural and man-made environments. Each is represented separately in *Sesame Street*'s curriculum, but these ingredients must be combined to be of any practical use.

This objection extended the early reservations of our own advisors when they protested the deliberate planning of the curriculum and the dissection of children's minds into component skills. As cogent as this argument may be, we assumed that it was important to say exactly what we were up to. This requires writing things down, which in turn means chopping larger ideas into their component parts.

The curriculum also was attacked for its narrowness, with one educator exaggerating this characteristic to contend that "it is insulting to the simplest inner-city child to think he's only capable of learning the 26 letters and the numbers one to ten." (Frances Hawkins, Pasadena *Star-News*, March 21, 1971). Although *Sesame Street* teaches more than this, we decided that we could not possibly aspire to be comprehensive in providing everything young children need educationally. One such critique by an educational researcher is entitled "*Sesame Street* Can't Handle *All* the Traffic."[2] We agree fully and never intended to try.

Presuming to Choose Goals

The fundamental objection to our goals argued that we have no right or privilege to make any choices whatever, that we are presumptuous to take it upon ourselves to choose goals at all. For example, Jeanette Veatch, a professor of elementary education at Arizona State University, considered the very act of an adult specifying goals for children to be a violation of their freedom, a use of "behaviorist" methods of thought control advocated by people like B. F. Skinner (1958, 1971). Journalist David B. Wilson wrote:

> I am hesitant about applauding such premediated acculturizers (ouch) as *Sesame Street* . . . not because they are so bad, which they are not, but because they represent, in the last analysis, a kind of patronizing altruism, educational welfarism, if you will, and you probably won't.
>
> For I suspect that if the tube arrogates to itself the power to try to inculcate the Golden Rule, the Beatitudes and the Civil Rights Act of 1964, it is perfectly capable of trying to persuade me that Aryans are superior or that the good citizen welcomes the opportunity to pay higher taxes, neither of which propositions ought to be given room in anybody's house. [Boston *Globe*, October 31, 1971]

This is, of course, a philosophic objection that includes *Sesame Street* but goes far beyond it, extending into any area of education (or, indeed, of social, economic or political regulation) where adults assume the responsibility of deciding what

---

[2] Ingersoll, 1971.

may be good for children. The systems of "open education"[3] being tried here and abroad argue that children must learn to be responsible for decisions about their educational activities. The most recent resurrection of open or informal education comes from Great Britain, and criticism of adult "authoritarianism" on *Sesame Street* came vocally from Monica Sims, director of children's programs for the British Broadcasting Corporation. Indoctrination was only one of Miss Sims's denunciations of *Sesame Street*. In a series of statements, including a 1970 statement in *The Guardian* and a 1971 speech before the European Broadcasting Union, she enumerated *Sesame Street*'s:

- lower-class orientation
- middle-class orientation
- emphasis on right answers
- American slang
- failure to "bridge the gap between advantaged and disadvantaged"
- "hard-selling techniques"
- "philosophy of built-in, never-ending repeats"
- encouragement of "passive box-watching"
- aim to "substitute for actual contact between a child and his mother, his companions, or his teacher"
- goal of "preparing children for school but not for life"

Miss Sims's disapproval thus ranged wide, but basically, her criticism amounted to "It is not our job to dictate what young children should learn." (*The Guardian*, December 22, 1970).

But where does it leave us, this rejection of adult responsibility for deciding what young children see on television in the interest of preserving their autonomy and freedom? Surely there should be opportunities for children to decide on their own what to experience and learn. We should nourish the chil-

---

[3] See, for example, Featherstone, 1971; Silberman, 1970; Weber, 1971.

dren's initiative to make their own decisions and their ability to contribute to decisions made jointly with adults. In producing national television programs for children, however, each individual child's interests and preferences unfortunately cannot be accommodated. Although we place the greatest importance upon knowing children's reactions, we cannot ask each child in advance what kind of program he would like to see created, and then—if the child can specify—proceed to create it for him. Nor can we ask children to create their own national programing. Adults must assume the responsibility to approximate as closely as possible the programs that will meet children's needs and interests.

Other Goals Are Better

Critics have suggested goals that we should have selected instead of those we did, most of the suggestions reflecting the view that other aspects of children's lives are far more important than the intellectual skills needed for school preparation. Children's feelings and social reactions were proposed, along with other cognitive skills beyond those in our curriculum. Critics also were perturbed that we did not take on the task of reducing the educational gap between advantaged and disadvantaged children.

Eda LeShan, a psychologist, suggested self-esteem and curiosity; Natalie Shainess, a psychiatrist, proposed curiosity; Robert Shayon, a television critic, advocated self-worth; and Herbert Sprigle, another psychologist, proposed persistence and self-confidence. Other suggestions included the eagerness to explore and confront ambiguity, sex education, concern for human values, a sense of control over one's destiny, and an appreciation of differences among people. Urie Bronfenbrenner,[4] professor of psychology at Cornell University, said: "The makers of *Sesame Street* focus on cognitive skills, they do their job

---

[4] Bronfenbrenner, 1970.

well, and they can't think of everything . . . But character development . . . is being taken over by two other institutions as yet unprepared for the task: the children's peer group and the television screen."

It remained for Eda LeShan, a psychologist who hosts her own television series of advice to parents, to suggest the ultimate: that *Sesame Street* needs to teach . . . "wisdom." She felt that *Sesame Street* failed because of its "goal of smartening kids up with no idea of what wisdom is." (Washington *Post*, November 21, 1971)

The Workshop had decided that television could only be a supplement to other efforts to educate children. In particular, we were uneasy about raising social, moral and emotional issues on a medium that reaches anyone who cares to watch and that cannot guarantee that a competent adult or older child is present to work through aroused feelings with the young child. Until we discovered more about the risks of the medium, we decided to be cautious about raising social and emotional issues, as important as these are in children's lives. Despite these reservations, we hoped that as children learned basic skills, they would develop a feeling of personal competence. We also hoped that children's social and emotional development would be affected when they saw the characters on *Sesame Street* treating one another with kindness, warmth and even simple courtesy, and when they viewed *Sesame Street* as an example of a community appreciative of differences among its inhabitants. The neighborhood initially included children and adults of different colors, language dialects and personalities, and was expanded later to include others, such as children with noticeable physical disabilities.[5] Parents seemed aware of this effort. For example, when "Sedulus," a critic for *The New Republic*, argued that *Sesame Street* distorts the harsh realities of life by its blandness, one parent replied:

Sedulus argues for "genuine" misery, terror, or exultation, as if most kids were not already well acquainted with the first two,

[5] Klebanoff, Klein, and Schleifer, 1971.

and some also with the third. Why do they need to have Gordon and Mr. Hooper engage in a real fight over a pile of trash when Mommy, Daddy and the neighbors can provide them with a steady diet of heated tiffs and brooding acrimony over issues of *even* less importance?

What many—and perhaps most—children need is a few lessons in accepting the faults and foibles of their associates with equanimity. So when Oscar the Grouch blows out all his birthday candles and announces that he wished that all of his fellow celebrants would go away and leave him alone, the breach of etiquette doesn't cause enmity because Oscar is what he is and is fun anyway. Or when Big Bird or Buddy and Jim again display their towering stupidity, they are not scorned or derided but continue in the personal affections of a tolerant community.

Robert D. Jaehnig,
New Republic, June 27, 1970

Although *Sesame Street*'s curriculum already includes many cognitive skills, still others were suggested. Most flowed from the impression that *Sesame Street* teaches facts but not how to use them, with examples usually citing number learning. John Holt said: "In all this talk about numbers, there is nothing about what they are for, or how people use them in the world, or how children use or might learn to use them." (1971, p. 78) Louise B. Ames, a psychologist at the Gesell Institute in New Haven, concluded that "a child who can recite his numbers to 10, or even 20, still is unable to perform even the simplest arithmetic functions." (1971, p. 60)

Sensing a larger social evil at work on *Sesame Street*, Robert L. Levey, a journalist writing in the Boston *Globe*, said: "Collection, collection. What an awful emphasis to place on the use of the human mind. But that has been the story of our age. It has been a time when acquisition of information, like acquisition of money, could gain respect for a man." (July 18, 1970) He illustrated his case by describing a four-year-old viewer of *Sesame Street* who was able to count numbers in sequence but did not know that when he counted objects, the final number counted represented the total number of objects he had. Levey confused two related skills, counting in sequence and enumeration. Children may learn the first skill before acquiring the second. Furthermore, it is questionable that counting is worthless unless it is used in enumerating. Just as children learn to recognize letters before they learn to read, children may need to identify numbers and to use them to count in sequence before they can put them to use enumerating or solving other problems. As much significance as we give to active problem solving in the *Sesame Street* curriculum, the importance of recognizing symbols does not rest solely on children's immediate ability to apply them in problem solving. The understanding of symbols serves in itself as a building block for more advanced skills.

Providing useful information in another area, health and safety, raised a dilemma that we still have not solved. Pediatricians pointed out *Sesame Street*'s potential for showing children how to avoid physical dangers in their environments, noting that if *Sesame Street* could accomplish this, it would surpass any of its other achievements. But to expose danger, television must simultaneously display the dangerous act itself (for example, ingesting a harmful medicine, crossing a street unsafely) as well as its consequences. Since children may not connect the consequences with the activity, or later may not recall the connection,[6] they may imitate the activity instead of learning to avoid it. Again, we strongly felt the need to understand the risks involved.

Others who recommended cognitive skills observed that *Sesame Street*'s curriculum is subdivided into too many small, discrete units, suggesting that larger combinations of skills would be more fruitful. Frank Garfunkel (1970), a psychologist at Boston University, suggested putting chains of reasoning skills together into sustained thought; Ann Cook and Herbert Mack (1970) asked that children be taught how to judge, ask questions, seek information, analyze and evaluate. All of these skills, of course, are critical in a child's development, but no one

---

[6] Leifer and Roberts, 1972.

has yet discovered how to teach them, despite some useful attempts.[7]

John Holt (1971) also suggested that children must learn how to figure things out for themselves and that *Sesame Street* does not teach this. Donald H. Meichenbaum (1971) a psychologist at the University of Waterloo in Canada, has experimented with several ways of teaching children to supply their own internal language to direct their problem-solving behavior. He believes that these self-guidance techniques can be taught effectively by television models and that these techniques fit comfortably into *Sesame Street*'s format.

> There are several activities on *Sesame Street* that provide an excellent opportunity for modeling of thinking and strategy formation as the task is being solved rather than a post hoc explanation. The adults and puppets should model aloud what is to be done, how this is to be accomplished, etc., simultaneously with ongoing performance. [p. 19]

The connections between language and thought have interested psychologists[8] for a long time, including the operation of "private" or silent "inner" speech that is not addressed to a listener, but occurs internally to guide one's thoughts. During our early planning of *Sesame Street*, we had considered the possibility of teaching children to use inner speech, but once again our inexperience with the risks of television made us cautious. For the young child who has not yet learned to use any form of internal self-guidance, teaching may be of considerable benefit. But whatever form our instruction takes in the use of internal cues, it may interfere with forms that some children already use naturally. Even by age three, many children have developed their own forms of inner speech—including, for example, self-verbalization, internal visual images, or some combination of the two. If a child already has developed skill in

---

[7] For example, Anderson, 1965; Crutchfield, 1966; Suchman, 1959, 1961, 1967.

[8] Kohlberg, Yaeger, and Hjertholm, 1968; Luria, 1961; Piaget, 1947.

visualization, instruction in self-verbalization may superimpose a style that is unnatural to him upon the style that he has already developed on his own. If self-verbalization already is used, instruction in visualization may interfere. A national television program cannot be adjusted to all the differing natural styles among children. We have not yet found a way to resolve this dilemma, nor do we know how much of a real dilemma it is.

The Gap between Advantaged and Disadvantaged

Although the Workshop did not undertake to reduce the gap between advantaged and disadvantaged children, some critics felt that this was its proper mission:

> Ms. Cooney's statement of objectives is quite clear in indicating that *Sesame Street* is meant to cause . . . growth in *all* groups of children. However, the reference to stimulating "the growth of all children, *particularly disadvantaged preschoolers*" is ambiguous. It does not make clear whether the objective of *Sesame Street* is to make the economically disadvantaged a special target group for receiving *Sesame Street* as an input; whether a special outcome has to be that those children will learn and grow because of *Sesame Street;* or whether these children are to develop more than their economically advantaged counterparts because of *Sesame Street*. We have chosen the latter interpretation. [Cook et al., 1972, p. 9]

Cook's interpretation ignored several announcements from the Workshop that our effort to reach the largest possible national audience is incompatible with reducing the achievement gap between poor and well-to-do children. For example, in replying to Monica Sims's observations at the BBC, Joan Cooney said: "No single television program is going to bridge the gap in education. What CTW hopes to accomplish with its programs is to move all children across the basic literacy line which is the key to education and later entering the mainstream of American life."

Other critics[9] raised the same issue out of concern that the Workshop's efforts are inadvertently widening the gap. They assumed that although *Sesame Street* can be seen by all children, advantaged families make better use of it than disadvantaged families. Observing the extraordinary response to *Sesame Street* of middle-class children of one and two years of age, they concluded that it is less successful in producing the same response in poor families.

Linda Francke (1971), a writer for *New York* Magazine, took this criticism to the point of accusing the Children's Television Workshop of false pretenses by professing an interest in the poor but ignoring them as soon as funding was secure. She also claimed that the Workshop acts in collusion with outside evaluators of *Sesame Street,* deliberately threatens Head Start's existence, teaches black children to accept the constraints of the ghettos, is rejected or ignored by black families and professionals, has designs to rule the children of the world through international broadcasts of *Sesame Street,* and that all these activities are "The Games People Play on *Sesame Street.*"

Buried beneath this avalanche is the serious question of how effective *Sesame Street* is especially in its efforts to appeal to inner-city children and to collaborate with parents and community organizations in the inner cities. The question, of course, can't be answered with opinion but only with specific evidence. Keeping in mind all of the difficulties of making direct comparisons between advantaged and disadvantaged children, we knew that after the broadcast year ended we would need to examine research findings carefully to see if *Sesame Street* indeed was reaching and teaching the disadvantaged children as well as the advantaged.

[9] For example, Ogilvie, 1970; Sprigle, 1971.

Objections to Our Methods

A general indictment against television's methods, sometimes applied against *Sesame Street* in particular, is that it makes no demands upon children for physical or mental participation. Almost as frequent are complaints about television's impersonality: "With all of our studies and observations, philosophizing and idealizing about teaching and teachers, learning and learners, the only thing that seems to hold up is a personalizing of the process." (Garfunkel, Boston *Globe,* January 1, 1970) Other critics assumed that among the prerequisites for learning are opportunities to see, touch and manipulate objects, opportunities which television can not provide directly. Bernice Nossoff, a kindergarten teacher in California, attacked television for being "not real": "Three through six learns best from experiencing the *real* people and the *real* things in his environment. The more actively his senses are engaged by the *real* people and the *real* things in his environment, the greater the depth of his learning." (1971, p. 57)

According to one cluster of complaints, *Sesame Street's* methods contain "conditioning" and "brainwashing": fast pace; loud noise level; rote teaching of single, right answers; fragmented presentation of disjointed tidbits of information; excessive repetition. Although *Sesame Street* deliberately includes each of these qualities in moderate degrees, critics exaggerated their presence and seemed offended by their resemblance to commercial advertising messages. We had decided to use those elements of commercial messages that—as far as we could tell from our observations of children—evoked substantial attention: change of pace and style, catchy jingles and rhymes, broad comedic devices, and short, simple, straightforward presentations. We had also decided to contrast these features with others. Rapidly paced parts of *Sesame Street* are counterbalanced by others that are calm and peaceful, mixed together to form a varied pace. When a single answer exists, it is taught, but where multiple solutions are possible, these are played out. Many segments are presented as separate episodes; others are

connected within a program, either interrupted or uninter-
rupted by time. Repetition is important but must not be excessive. *Sesame Street's* rapid pace, repetition and episodic
structure are apparent, but a more balanced assessment of
these characteristics comes with extended viewing of *Sesame
Street*. When John Holt (1971) wrote his otherwise well-
informed review and criticized its stress on right answers and
rote learning, one veteran viewer replied: "My father read to
me Mr. Holt's article on *Sesame Street*. I think Mr. Holt has
not seen enough programs of *Sesame Street* to judge it, and I've
watched it for two years or more. Many of the things Mr. Holt
says should be on *Sesame Street* ARE." (Bruce Payne, age 9,
Atlantic Monthly, July 1971)

Other criticisms challenged *Sesame Street's* methods for
teaching prereading skills. Dr. Kenneth Smith (*Arizona Republic*, May 4, 1971) director of the University of Arizona's
Reading Development Center, objected to teaching the sounds
of isolated letters when these sounds are not used in pronouncing whole words. Jeanette Veatch (1970) wrote that she
cringed at the teaching of consonant blends (e.g., two consonants beginning a word) rather than single consonants. "Sedulus" (1971) doubted that children see the connection between
learning letters and reading, claiming that there is little sense
in teaching shapes and sounds of letters if they do not see this
connection. John Holt (1971) observed that *Sesame Street*
never will prepare children to read unless it teaches that behind every written word is a human voice speaking, and that
reading is the way to know what those voices are saying; he
assumed that anything less is simply learning arbitrary, contra-
dictory and obscure rules. Since McLuhan (1970) does not
consider television to be a visual medium at all, he felt that
teaching reading on television is "ridiculous."

Other critics claimed that *Sesame Street's* methods aim above
children's heads and overestimate their abilities. The language
used is too advanced; perhaps three-year-olds can follow it but
"about the only thing a two-year-old could get to understand
would be the colors. They're not able to understand letters and
numbers." (Dr. Francis Kelly, a psychologist at Boston College,

Boston *Herald Traveler,* May 28, 1972). Absurdities and incongruities "may amuse older children and grownups but are a disservice for your three to six," and a program of one-hour's duration is far beyond the attention span of "three to sixes." (Nossoff, 1971) None of these predictions has been confirmed by our child-watching. For example, when a one-hour program is too long, children simply declare their own recesses whenever they desire. We have far more often underestimated children's abilities to learn from television than the reverse.

Many observers noted that *Sesame Street* is dominated by adults, that everything that happens is planned in advance by adults who stick to the lesson no matter what the children on *Sesame Street* do or say. "Grown-ups initiate everything." (Sedulus, 1971) We have held to our decision that children on *Sesame Street* be unrehearsed and spontaneous. Since the adult cast is not made up of professional educators and was not certain of how to respond to the children's spontaneity, they sometimes restricted the children's opportunities to follow their own lines of thought. The cast has gradually learned to respond to the children's spontaneity with spontaneity of their own.

These complaints about *Sesame Street*'s methods form a pattern: "Brainwashing," "conditioning," "mind control" and "producing programmed people," all presumably linked to "behavioristic theories" that force or trick children into learning prescribed content in a predetermined manner. Francis Kelly considers this to be "the Orwellian Big Brother theme" (Boston *Herald Traveler,* May 28, 1972), and Helen L. Beck says, a bit floridly: "Aldous Huxley's *Brave New World* seems indeed to have obtained reality in our living rooms as the young are being drugged into a semi-waking stage by the onslaught of visual and audio stimuli which appeal to the more primitive aspects of the child's personality." (Dallas *Morning News,* April 1, 1971)

The "behavioristic" bag of tricks then is likened to the "hard-sell," "typically American" tricks of Madison Avenue. Having attached the labels "brainwashing," "conditioning" and especially "behavioristic" to *Sesame Street*'s methods, alerts are sounded lest these tactics be transferred to the classroom, and from there proceed to destroy our society:

In the classroom, where human beings are face to face, these cheerleading, commercially oriented types of instruction are wrong. I am quite content as a professional educator . . . to let *Sesame Street,* or anything like it continue its rollicking, charming, cute way. But I am not content to see the adaptation of its techniques of imposed learning used in regular classroom situations . . . There may be a day when this (Skinnerian) school of thought will be destroyed, as it is now destroying one of the most promising nations of the world, but such hopes are discouragingly dim. [Veatch, 1970, p. 58]

Despite exaggerations of "behaviorism's" destruction of society and the degree to which *Sesame Street* relies upon its techniques, Veatch surely is correct in observing that successful methods of televised teaching cannot be transplanted to the classroom or vice versa. Classroom teaching and televised teaching each has its own integrity; there is no reason to assume that successful techniques in one can be applied in the other.

Criticism of *Sesame Street*'s presumed "behaviorism" turned full circle when Roger Ulrich (1970), a research professor at Western Michigan University who espouses this approach to learning, observed that neither *Sesame Street* nor any other television program is in a position to use the approach effectively even if it wanted to. He claimed that television is "foreign" to the behavioral techniques of active interaction between student and teacher, careful evoking of desired responses, and precise reinforcement of these responses. *Sesame Street* thus was accused both of using behavioristic tactics too well and of not being able to use them at all.

A final theme in criticism of *Sesame Street*'s methods was simply that other methods are better. For example, Al Capp proposed the comics:

To pay millions in taxes (or tax-deducted funds) for a TV show that theoretically attracted some of its audience of two million [sic] to reading might be impressive, but not to me. "Li'l Abner" and a half-dozen other comic strips . . . had a far better score than a hundred *Sesame Streets* . . . People with teaching experience testify that, by gosh, now that I'd mentioned it, they recall *they'd* learned to read because they so passionately wanted to read the comics. [New York *News,* 1971]

Unintended Effects

Claims of *Sesame Street's* unintended effects ranged from harm to individual viewers to adverse effects for society. Some blamed *Sesame Street's* success, others its failures. Some accused the Workshop of deliberate maliciousness, others of naïveté. In addition to learning about language, numbers and reasoning, "what else is left scrawled on the child's psyche?" (Bronfenbrenner, *Psychology Today,* 1970). Assumptions included:

- Children will imitate certain physical acts, such as those shown in slapstick episodes.
- Sweet and unhealthy foods are glorified by Cookie Monster, and his sloppy eating habits will be imitated. (One parent unkindly described Cookie Monster as a case of "arrested development.")
- *Sesame Street* keeps children from getting "out in the backyard breathing God's good air, so their bodies can grow healthy and strong." [Francis Kelly, Boston *Herald Traveler,* May 28, 1972]
- The series teaches poor grammar and vocabulary.
- *Sesame Street's* efforts to show that adults are not always smarter than children brought such comments as: "You feature bumbling adults . . . Your two grown men have trouble putting the letter W together. Not only do Larry and Phyllis keep hammering away at the concept of 'cooperation'—which is a fairly abstract concept for three to six—but they have trouble pronouncing it. Are you teaching stuttering?" [Nossoff, 1971, p. 58]
- Children will acquire the false attitude that learning always will be fun and not the serious, tedious business that it really is.

The "monsters" on *Sesame Street* frighten children. (This observation abated soon after broadcasting began as the children discovered that the monsters' outward appearance hid a gruff kindness.)

Robert Shayon, formerly television critic for the *Saturday Review* and now a professor of communications at the University of Pennsylvania, couched his objection in psychoanalytic terms, arguing that displaying adults blundering undermines the assurance of the "loving and supportive relationship" needed during the preschoolers' "Oedipal period." He believes that only when children become older can they "enjoy a laugh at adults" without endangering a needed sense of security. On another psychoanalytically oriented topic, Shayon claimed that *Sesame Street* threatens the child's "orality: animals in cartoons eat up letters and numbers" (*Saturday Review*, February 14, 1970).

Claims of even more sinister emotional damage linked the influence of one form of "artificial external stimulation" (television, and *Sesame Street* in particular) to dependency upon another (drugs). "Drugs are the natural refuge of a child nurtured on television" (Hayakawa, Boston *Globe*, September 21, 1969), and *Sesame Street* is "fostering a new generation of drug-takers because of the restlessness that is fostered, the lack of discipline, the lack of critical judgment and what will literally become a fear of a moment's quiet and silence." (Shainess, Dallas *Morning News*, August 29, 1971) There is, of course, no evidence that television induces dependence on drugs, and the logic leading to such a conclusion is dangerously superficial, but the search for single causes for pervasive social problems often proceeds unfettered by facts.

A more plausible speculation about *Sesame Street*'s unintended emotional effects is the blurring of distinctions between fantasy and reality resulting from the mixing of fantastic characters (puppets, monsters, animated figures) and real ones (live adults and children, live-action film). However, the anticipated confusion never materialized in our observations of children. Apparently, the mixing of fantasy and reality is seen by children as one of television's conventions, one of the magical incongruities peculiar to the medium.

Another set of critics contested *Sesame Street's* view of reality. Life in inner cities is sugar-coated on *Sesame Street*, its dangers ignored or hidden. There are no racial tensions; nobody ever gets mad, no sharp words are spoken.

> The children—whether black, white, or brown—are charming, soft-spoken, cooperative, clean, and well-behaved. When they speak, they say the right things. They never fuss, fear, or fail. In these respects, they take after their adult models . . . who are charming, gentle, smiling and friendly. Unlike the children, they sometimes make mistakes, but these are small ones and easily forgiven (missing on the last jump in hopscotch). Among the adults there are no conflicts, no difficulties, nor, for that matter, any obligations or visible attachments. [Bronfenbrenner, *Psychology Today*, October 1970, p. 14]

Mad Magazine also chided us on *Sesame Street's* view of the ghetto, graphically suggesting what *Sesame Street* would really look like if it were true to life.

A similar protest against *Sesame Street's* vision of life came from abroad. When German educators met to review *Sesame Street* programs in anticipation of developing a German-language version of their own,[10] they too objected to the message (contained, for example, in the song used by *Sesame Street*, "Or Would You Rather Swing on a Star?") that children can aspire to almost unlimited heights, that they can accomplish great feats if they try hard enough. This, they argued, is an unrealistic dream in the real world of boundaries and constraints, giving children false hopes.

John Holt (1971) also accused *Sesame Street* of a "remarkable failure—could it be a refusal?" to show children the reality

---

[10] The Germans did produce their own series, called *Sesamstrasse*, which began broadcasting in 1972.

of their environments by failing to use the visual and learning resources of the city. To which one parent observed:

> Oh, what Mr. Holt has missed! If only he had seen the cine-
> matic poem about a manhole cover, by day and by night, in
> sunshine and in rain . . . or the story of a boy who tests his
> perception of the sights and sounds of the city with "magic
> glasses" . . . or the clip in which shots of a youngster using toy
> trucks and machines alternate with shots of actual earth-moving

equipment at work. Such films not only use the urban setting to convey nonverbal ideas, they evoke the viewers' aesthetic and imaginative powers, subtly encouraging children to view their environment, and themselves, in new ways. [Samuel C. Brown, Jr., *Atlantic Monthly,* July 1971]

Sesame Street's repercussions were presumed to reach several of society's institutions, including racial integration, the family, the schools and their teachers, and other forms of early education. In a highly publicized action, the Mississippi State Commission for Educational Television accused *Sesame Street* of endorsing racial integration (it does) because it uses a highly integrated cast of adults and children. It was banned there for a time but later reinstated. When it also was banned elsewhere in the South, one parent commented:

Sir: The children in South America are certainly lucky, since *Sesame Street* is going there. Our children in north Louisiana aren't so lucky—we had it but lost it. The ostensible reason was that the show was too expensive. Actually it was too black.

Margie Townsend
Shreveport, Louisiana
Time, December 14, 1970

Some thought that *Sesame Street* undermines family life, either because it is used as a baby-sitter and reduces contact within the family (Bronfenbrenner, White House Conference, 1970; Kelly, Boston *Herald Traveler,* May 28, 1972) or because it makes parents "feel guilty if the child is not watching and 'learning'" (Beck, Milwaukee *Journal,* March 24, 1971). Other presumed effects on the family were more positive: It alerts parents to the importance of encouraging learning during the early years (Anderson and Shane, 1971; Kagan, New York *Times,* October 17, 1971); it can provide parents with models of how to do things with their children (Meichenbaum, 1971); it "convinces many proud parents that their kids *can* learn a lot" ("Sedulus," 1970; Rosenthal, 1970).

Speculations about *Sesame Street*'s unintended effects upon schools and teachers were just as varied. Children will be "spoiled" for school and find it dull in comparison with *Sesame Street* (Gunther, 1971; Webster, *Newsweek,* June 1, 1970; Cook, Boston *Globe,* January 10, 1970). School curriculums, especially in kindergarten and the early grades, will need to adjust to better levels of intellectual competence, longer attention spans and improved motivation to learn (Doan, *TV Guide,* July 11, 1970; Groseclose, *Wall Street Journal,* November 13, 1970; Payette, Gloversville, New York, *Leader-Herald,* December 30, 1970). Kindergartens will be rendered obsolete unless they change their educational function (Danbury *News Times,*

Sesame Street it's not.

Copyright © 1970 by Janice and Stanley Berenstein.

March 13, 1971). Teachers are made more sensitive to how they plan and present ideas in the classroom (Rosenthal, 1970).

However, children themselves did not seem to share these predictions that school will suffer by comparison with *Sesame Street.* Despite the cartoon rendition by the Berensteins, children apparently regard the two experiences as separate and make no comparisons.

A serious reservation of educators such as Frank Garfunkel (1970) and Herbert Sprigle (1971, 1972) was that *Sesame Street* would become the yardstick by which other forms of early education (including theirs) will be judged, draining funds from more worthy programs and giving the public the false hope of cheap solutions. Early misgivings were voiced that *Sesame Street* would compete, for example, with Head Start for public support. No evidence to support these misgivings has yet emerged.

The notion that *Sesame Street* would become an inappropriate "yardstick" was applied to other children's television programs as well. Other programs must "counter *Sesame Street* with television of a different, perhaps more reflective pace. There is more than one way to make programs for children." (*Christian Science Monitor* Editorial, October 7, 1971). Agreeing with these remarks, the Children's Television Workshop would have considered its efforts a disservice if they had closed other doors to diversity in preschool education. Although there is no evidence that other experiments in early education, including television, were discouraged by *Sesame Street*, neither unfortunately are there signs that new programs were encouraged.

Poorly Represented Constituencies

Other criticism of *Sesame Street* revolved around social inequities in need of correction: sexism, racism and overpopulation. (Of perhaps greatest social concern when *Sesame Street* began broadcasting was the role of the United States in the war in Vietnam, but no objections to *Sesame Street* flowed from this source.)

Critics observed that females are underrepresented or misrepresented on *Sesame Street*. To monitor the stereotyping of sex roles on *Sesame Street*, Cynthia Eaton and Susan Chase of the National Organization of Women observed *Sesame Street* programs and reported their findings to the Workshop. They concluded that the programs are male-dominated, and when women or girls do appear they are often: timid, passive, fearful, dependent, helpless, vain, unadventurous and unskillful; involved in domestic activities serving other family members, especially while in the kitchen; shown in stereotyped romantic situations; less distinctive in personality than male characters; and shown in a limited number of roles.

These complaints were echoed in the press. Ellen Goodman, a reporter for the Boston *Globe,* concluded: "The females that do live on *Sesame Street* can be divided into three groups: teacher, simp, and mother (which more often than not is a combination of teacher and simp). Oh, yes, a cow." In a report in the New York *Times,* Jane Bergman observed that the female puppets appearing on *Sesame Street* are "a strident, overbearing mother," "a simpering, querulous little girl with pigtails and a squeaky voice," "a trembly, hysterical game show contestant," "a hapless, hopelessly vague mother," "a ponytailed cheerleader." She went on:

> The old sexist stereotypes are alive and well. A recent sequence shows the charming monster Grover falling in love with Maria at his first meeting with her. She arrives, and he is transfixed, after the manner of swains through the centuries; his mouth falls open, he sighs wildly, he becomes entirely hysterical trying to anticipate and fill all her requests. Breathless, feverish Grover is practicing chivalry, a behavior which reduces the adored female to an object; she is, in effect, told, "Your wish is my command—so sit still." Grover is ingenuously explicit about the cause of his passion: "OHHHH, she is so *pret-ty.*" So much for Maria, the ex-person. [New York *Times,* January 2, 1972]

We had decided to stress the importance of strong male-identification figures for inner-city children. Also, in most public education for young children, women teachers predominate, and possibly as a consequence girls seem to meet teachers' expectations with less difficulty than boys. For both reasons, we decided to show men on *Sesame Street* in warm, nurturing relationships with young children. We did not intend, however, to bolster male identification at the expense of misrepresenting or excluding feminine models, and as time went on, we searched for opportunities to present females in positive, distinctive roles. However, since some trade-offs are necessary when competing options are encountered, we knew that we could not be everything to everybody. The education editor of the New York *Times*, Fred Hechinger, wrote with his wife Grace Hechinger a reply to Jane Bergman: "Disconcerting is the equal-time, equal-space technique of criticism employed by each successive power group . . . Recognizing the program's impact, anybody with a cause wants *Sesame Street* to be its advocate." (New York *Times*, January 30, 1972)

Although *Sesame Street*'s racial integration generally was commended, the program was accused of both racism and reverse racism. Most complaints were of reverse racism, that *Sesame Street* is *too* black, *too* integrated, or that black adults and children are shown as better or smarter than others. On the other hand, it was also observed that *Sesame Street* displays racism by not being black enough or by sugar-coating the realities of the ghetto, teaching minority-group children to accept quietly middle-class America's corrupt demands to subjugate themselves.

Another complaint was that we advocated overpopulation. A short musical puppet sequence on *Sesame Street* uses a five-member family (father, mother, sister, and two brothers) to teach enumerating to five. To some critics, this seemed to extol large families or at least did not encourage population control. Also, *Sesame Street* contains no information on sex and reproduction to convey the importance of smaller families. In due course, opponents of population control also had their say in criticizing *Sesame Street* (Randy Engel, a journalist writing in the *Catholic Accent*, March 23, 1971).

The Workshop staff kept track of all these criticisms, partly from vanity and curiosity, partly in the hope that we could discover ways to improve *Sesame Street*. With some exceptions, the criticism was not illuminating. It contained opinions and offered few constructive alternatives. It contained only scattered observations of children when we needed careful and extensive descriptions of their responses. In addition to its own child-watching activities, the Workshop had commissioned some external research and other studies were being done by independent researchers around the country. Perhaps these studies could tell us more about how we were doing with children and how we might do better.

Chapter Eight

Outcomes

We had tried to avoid the trap of making unrealistic advance claims, but by providing a national television series, we made some promises and assumed certain obligations. We needed to attract a sufficiently large audience to justify our expenditures, and we needed to teach young children what we said we would teach them, without producing harmful unintended effects. How well did *Sesame Street* deliver these minimum obligations? What else happened?

Short-term research could begin to provide some answers. But only research over a longer period of time could identify *Sesame Street*'s true effects, either beneficial or harmful or both. If children did learn what we set out to teach, did it make a difference in their school performance? What else did children learn in addition to what we intended to teach? Did parents change their attitudes or their behavior toward their preschoolers? Did *Sesame Street*'s presence strengthen other programs of early education, or was it used as an excuse to discontinue them? It will be a long time before research supplies final answers, but at least some preliminary evidence exists.

Audience Surveys

Who watches? Start with those children and families to whom *Sesame Street* is available. Although television sets exist in virtually every American home, public-broadcasting channels reach only about 72 percent of them (Harris and Associates, 1969–71). Even among those homes within the range of public broadcasting, 31 percent are reached only by UHF signal, impossible to receive without a special television adapter and often weakly received with one. In short, *Sesame Street*'s maximum potential audience when it began broadcasting in 1969 was roughly 60 percent of the nation's households, rising by 1971 to 63 percent. Public-broadcasting channels are more accessible on the Eastern and Western seaboards than in the South and the Midwest, more accessible in large metropolitan areas than in small towns and rural areas.

Public-broadcasting stations have never attracted large audiences. Harris polls have indicated that only about one-third of its potential audience were watching public television "at least once in the last week." In inner cities, viewing of public television is especially limited. All in all, public-broadcasting stations do not provide the best vehicle for reaching a large national audience.

Shortly after *Sesame Street* began broadcasting (November 24 through 30, 1969), however, Nielsen ratings estimated that it was reaching 1,580,000 households. This figure immediately jumped to 2,220,000 and then by midyear to 3,100,000. Since 90 percent of these homes had one or more children of preschool age, and estimating that when one preschooler was watching, there was roughly a 25 percent chance that more than one preschooler was viewing, *Sesame Street*'s early audience was assessed at 3,500,000 to 4,000,000 young children, a substantial part of the estimated maximum audience of 8,000,000. In addition, approximately 50 percent of the children in day-care and other prekindergarten centers in inner cities also were viewing (Taylor and Samuels, 1970). Adding these to the children viewing at home, the size of *Sesame Street*'s early audience seems remarkable, even judged against audiences attracted by popular commercial programs viewed solely for entertainment purposes.

Was this large audience drawn primarily from well-to-do families, or did inner-city children share in the high level of viewing? A series of surveys (Yankelovich, 1970) reported that:

• Ninety-one percent of the at-home children in the low-income Bedford-Stuyvesant area of New York City were viewing, 60 percent of them watching regularly; in East Harlem in New York City, 78 percent of the young children watched, 91 percent of these viewers watching regularly. In both communities, the exceptionally high penetration seemed related to the fact that both a commerical (WPIX, Channel 11) and non-commercial (WNDT, Channel 13) station were carrying the program.

• In Chicago's inner city, *Sesame Street* was carried only by a noncommercial channel (a VHF station, WTTW, Channel 11, that can be received without a special adapter), and no special advance effort had been made to promote the show or to involve the inner-city audience in its use. Here 88 percent of the 307 inner-city families interviewed watched *Sesame Street*, 50 percent of them watching daily.

• Inner-city areas of Philadelphia also received *Sesame Street* through a VHF public-broadcasting channel (WHYY,

Channel 12). Of 252 households interviewed, 72 percent reported watching *Sesame Street*, 86 percent of these saying that their children watched the show four or more times a week (Greene, 1970).

• An additional contrast in inner-city viewing existed in Washington, D.C., where *Sesame Street* was transmitted only by a UHF public-broadcasting channel: 20 percent of the 297 low-income households had no UHF adapter, and only 63 percent of those who did ever watched the UHF channel—usually only for programs such as *Soul* and *Black Journal* before *Sesame Street* went on the air. Here 32 percent of the UHF households watched *Sesame Street*, with 66 percent of these children watching regularly, either daily or at least four times a week.

By the end of *Sesame Street*'s first broadcasting year, having produced, broadcast, and researched 130 one-hour programs, we were tired and feared that *Sesame Street*'s audience might be also. We anticipated that *Sesame Street*'s novelty value had been dissipated and that retaining a large national audience would become difficult, especially after summer reruns in most parts of the country. But by the beginning of the second broadcast year (1970–71), audience estimates remained high and gradually grew still higher. According to Nielsen estimates, the number of households reached now had grown to 3,670,000 by the beginning of 1971, a substantial gain over the comparable period during the preceding year. Not only was this audience large, but it was also loyal. Nielsen's "cumulative audience estimates" (giving the rate of audience turnover from day to day) showed children to be as loyal to *Sesame Street* as the notoriously loyal daytime viewers are to their soap operas. Few higher compliments exist in television.

At the comparable period during the third broadcast year (1971–72), *Sesame Street*'s audience was still continuing to rise, now reaching 4,410,000 households. Since by 1971–72 *Sesame Street*'s conveyor stations could still only be received in about 75 percent of American households, a "coverage factor" was calculated to estimate how many of the households that could receive *Sesame Street* actually were tuning in. This "coverage" had started high (70 percent in 1969–70), rose to 75 percent in 1970–71, and then to 81 percent in 1971–72. By the end of 1972, Nielsen estimates indicated that roughly 8,990,000 children two through five years of age were watching *Sesame Street*.

Over the broadcast years, what happened to *Sesame Street*'s audience in inner cities (Yankelovich, 1971, 1973)? In the Bedford-Stuyvesant section of New York City, the 91 percent of viewers reported in 1969–70 dropped to 77 percent in 1970–71. The program had been carried in 1969–70 by both a commercial and a public-broadcasting station who broadcast it at different times of the day. When in 1970–71 the public-broadcasting station (Channel 13, WNDT) placed *Sesame Street* in the desired 9 A.M. time slot, it was withdrawn from the commercial station (Channel 11, WPIX) and the coverage dropped somewhat. By 1973, the figure rose once again to 92 percent. Comparable figures in other cities were:

	1970	*1971*	*1973*
East Harlem	78%	86%	94%
Chicago	88	95	97
Washington, D.C. (UHF only)	32	59	67

In these sites and several others, attempts by the Children's Television Workshop to attract an inner-city audience apparently succeeded in retaining or extending the high level of initial viewing in these communities.[1]

---

[1] In 1970–1971, *Sesame Street* began broadcasting in many countries outside the United States, often attracting surprisingly large audiences and interest. For example, a survey conducted on the Caribbean Island of Curaçao (Lasker and Casseras, 1971) estimated that 80 percent of the Curaçao children whose homes have working television sets (84 percent of Curaçao families) watch *Sesame Street* occasionally and 59 percent watch it regularly. The lack of other children's programs on Curaçao television may account for these high figures, but comparable data are reported where other alternatives are in greater supply. For example, in experimental runs in certain regions of Great Britain, both parents and children watched *Sesame Street* in large numbers (Alexander, 1971; Blackwell and Jackman, 1971; London Weekend Television, 1972), despite objections to the program by some British educators. Indeed, in Great

Community Use

Many good reasons exist for involving parents and communities in the children's viewing experiences, including the value of parental reinforcement of learning and the possibility of raising parents' expectations for their children. We found the most compelling reason for working directly with parents and organizations to be public television's poor record of attracting large inner-city audiences. Before anything else could be achieved, we had to get children and their families to watch. Only a few public-television programs had succeeded at all—shows for black adult audiences, produced by black professionals, having a strong local appeal (*Soul, Black Journal, Say Brother*). No other public-television programs had succeeded in attracting the inner-city audience, certainly no national educational program for young children had done so. This perhaps was our greatest fear as *Sesame Street* was designed. Even if everything else went well—even if our shows were appealing and our educational plans well-executed—inner-city children might not ever watch. *Sesame Street* thus became an experiment in attracting inner-city children to watch television programs with a serious educational purpose. Viewing commercial television is habitual, once a show's appeal has prompted people to watch one program instead of another. Since viewing public television is a rarity, especially in the inner cities, we needed more than just a good show.

Although we aimed for maximum cooperation with existing inner-city agencies, we knew that they are already overburdened with their own projects and that we could not expect them to do our work for us. Asking personnel at the local public-broadcasting stations themselves to arouse interest for us among inner-city families seemed equally implausible. Realizing this, we knew that our own Children's Television Workshop

Britain the extent of parents watching with children reached a higher level than that achieved in the United States. Other reports of extensive viewing of *Sesame Street* by children and parents have arrived from other countries outside the United States.

staff would be needed to initiate and maintain our activities in the inner cities, and that our staff would need extensive personal and professional experience in those communities.

Getting children and parents to watch, and then designing community projects to sustain interest, would require new techniques as well as direct personal involvement in the communities. Traditional communication through general circulation newspapers, magazines and on-the-air promotion were not going to work. We had to find methods to ignite word-of-mouth communication. These eventually included setting up viewing groups in day-care and neighborhood centers and in homes; soliciting and placing television sets in viewing centers and child-care facilities; enlisting volunteers, especially among the adolescents in a community; placing materials in libraries and other centers; using storefront and distribution centers; encouraging mothers to set up special neighborhood viewing groups; distributing the *Sesame Street Magazine* (which contains games, stories, puzzles and other activities of children) and the *Parent/Teacher Guide* (which contains ideas for parents and teachers for the use of *Sesame Street* and associated materials); creating *Sesame Street* clubs; using organization newsletters and community newspapers; meeting with local merchants; conducting streetcorner and shopping-center rallies; conducting door-to-door, word-of-mouth campaigns; arranging parades and street fairs; distributing flyers; using sound trucks, library story corners, poster contests, giveaways, business and labor involvement; working with the local press and local broadcast media.

Each of these approaches was used at some time in combination with others for maximum effect in a particular community. Research that assessed each component was important only as it later told us how combinations could be formed. But since it is impossible to develop and evaluate all approaches simultaneously, we undertook research into specific promising projects such as the *Sesame Street* Mother Project and the Neighborhood Youth Corps Project.

The *Sesame Street* Mother Project goes beyond the first step of letting parents and children know that *Sesame Street* is available for their benefit. It helps parents to work with their children, and perhaps with others, to reinforce and expand upon the lessons provided by *Sesame Street*. It builds on the most powerful resource available to young children—their parents' interest in them. Evelyn Davis, who heads the Workshop's Division of Community Education Services, observes: "One of the great misconceptions that people have is that because you are poor, because you are black, because you are Spanish, you are not interested in your child. We are asked at CTW 'How do you get parents so involved in your activities?' We answer: 'Because they are for their children.' "

In a project conducted by the Institute for Educational Development under the direction of Robert Filep,[2] over 120 mothers in low-income areas of Los Angeles and Chicago volunteered and were trained to conduct *Sesame Street* viewing sessions in their own homes with small groups of preschoolers, whose combined number was around 400. In Central Los Angeles and in Chicago, all of the mothers were black; in East Los Angeles, all were Mexican-American. During viewing sessions, each mother directed activities so as to reinforce specific lessons on *Sesame Street* and to relate these lessons to the children's experiences.

We tried to learn how much the participating children learned from these experiences by using an ETS test battery designed for its national assessment of *Sesame Street* and, more informally, through the mothers' observations of changes in behaviors and attitudes of the children. The data indicate significantly improved skills across participating groups, with those children who were involved on a more regular basis over a longer period of time gaining more than irregular participants. For example, in the Watts and South Central districts of Los Angeles, children who watched regularly in the *Sesame Street* mother groups over a five-to-seven-month period showed significant improvement in all but three of thirty-four subtests (naming letters, counting, classification, sorting, etc.), while the children who watched less regularly improved in all

2 Filep, Millar, and Gillette, 1971.

but eleven of the thirty-four subtests. *Sesame Street* mothers also reported improvement in the children's social interaction, in their confidence in undertaking new activities, and in their attitudes toward learning. Equally notable, the mothers themselves reported that their training and experiences with the children were personally gratifying and could lead them to further involvement in education for children. Given the detailed planning required for recruitment and training, the *Sesame Street* mother model may not be easily used on a large scale, but the apparent benefits to young children who have no other educational options, and to their mothers as well, are promising.

Adolescents living in inner cities can also be a valuable educational resource for young children, with potential benefits to both. Our perennial assumption has been that adolescence is a period of profound psychological and emotional upset, but at least on the surface, adolescents often seem troubled simply by not having any work that makes them feel good about themselves and not being sure that they have skills or resources that anyone needs or values. There seems little question that many adolescents care enough about smaller children to try to teach them what they know. While teaching, the adolescents may become aware that they are regarded by others as possessing valuable resources to be shared. Perhaps because of the novelty of being taught by older children, the young children seem to respond with interest and enthusiasm. A few educational programs of "cross-age teaching" have tried to harness this power.[3]

The Neighborhood Youth Corps Project run by the Children's Television Workshop enlisted inner-city adolescents in the effort to teach young children. During the summer following *Sesame Street*'s first broadcast year (1970), a pilot program was conducted in New York City, with 240 inner-city adolescents teaching 1,500 young children in viewing centers throughout the city. On the basis of that experiment, during the summer of 1971 the project was extended to over 1,200 teenaged tutors and 15,000 young children in thirteen cities and a

[3] For example, Lippett and Lippett, 1969; Thelen, 1969.

Florida migrant camp. By the summer of 1972 the project involved about 10,000 tutors and 100,000 young children in thirty-three areas throughout the United States, Puerto Rico and the Virgin Islands.

The adolescents were trained to teach some of the skills in the *Sesame Street* curriculum. For eight weeks during July and August, these adolescents worked with groups of children who watched *Sesame Street* in community centers, day-care centers, storefronts, public-housing projects or private homes. In 1971 individual projects ranged in size from Los Angeles, where two separate programs involved 140 Neighborhood Youth Corps tutors and more than 1,400 preschoolers, to Jackson, Mississippi, where 18 adolescents taught 99 preschoolers in four different viewing centers.

The evaluation of the Neighborhood Youth Corps project[4] describes the many practical difficulties in conducting educational programs of this magnitude over a brief period of time. One insurmountable problem in such a short time was gathering reliable tests on the preschoolers to assess the summer program's impact upon them. As a consequence, the formal research includes only the effects upon the participating teenagers. The adolescents were asked to judge their own attitudes, and although some independent judgments were available from the centers' supervisors, the evidence is biased by the usual distortions in self-perception. Nevertheless, the adolescents clearly believed that their attitudes toward themselves, toward school and toward working with other people—especially young children—improved significantly while acting as tutors. Given something useful to do and provided with clear and tangible evidence of their success, teenagers feel good about themselves and the children they teach.

---

[4] Community Relations Department, Children's Television Workshop, 1971, 1972.

Periodic Progress Testing

We were reluctant to wait until the end of the broadcast year before getting some estimate of how much viewers were learning from watching *Sesame Street*. If there were no indications of learning over a shorter period of time—say, after three weeks or fifteen programs—corrections would need to be made in the program immediately. Our earliest assessments were made after three weeks and then checked again after six weeks (thirty programs) and three months (roughly after one-half of the full one-hundred-and-thirty-program broadcast year). We tried to estimate the differences in learning between viewing and non-viewing children, although as time went by it became increasingly difficult to locate children who had never seen *Sesame Street* at all.

Once again, the ETS test battery was used. These eight tests (Letters, Numbers, Body Parts, Forms, Classification, Sorting, Relational Terms, Puzzles) contained a total of 217 separate items and were administered individually to children before their viewing of *Sesame Street* (or for nonviewers, before *Sesame Street* began broadcasting) and then again after viewing the specified number of programs (or, for nonviewers, after that period of time had elapsed). In this early progress testing, in order to collect and analyze the information quickly in case program changes were indicated, the researchers observed and tested children viewing in day-care centers instead of children viewing at home. The children in these day-care centers were randomly assigned to one of two groups—viewers and non-viewers—with approximately 100 viewers in three day-care sites (Maine, New York and Tennessee) watching daily in groups of eight to twelve children while the comparable number of non-viewers in these sites continued their normal classroom activities (Reeves, 1970).

After three weeks (or about fifteen programs) differences between viewers and nonviewers appeared in only a few test areas, with the viewers showing superior ability to label, recognize and match letters and numbers. By six weeks, however, larger

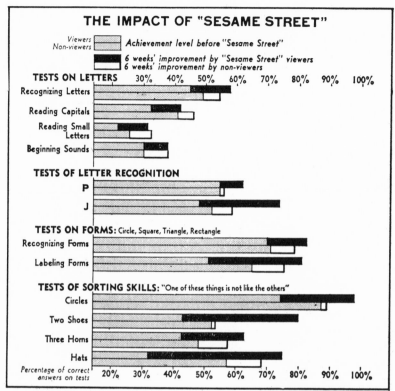

THE IMPACT OF "SESAME STREET"

Viewers
Non-viewers ☐ Achievement level before "Sesame Street"

■ 6 weeks' improvement by "Sesame Street" viewers
☐ 6 weeks' improvement by non-viewers

TESTS ON LETTERS   30%   40%   50%   60%   70%   80%   90%   100%
Recognizing Letters
Reading Capitals
Reading Small Letters
Beginning Sounds

TESTS OF LETTER RECOGNITION
P
J

TESTS ON FORMS: Circle, Square, Triangle, Rectangle
Recognizing Forms
Labeling Forms

TESTS OF SORTING SKILLS: "One of these things is not like the others"
Circles
Two Shoes
Three Horns
Hats

Percentage of correct answers on tests   20%   30%   40%   50%   60%   70%   80%   90%   100%

In most categories charted above, children who were to view "Sesame Street" scored lower on pre-tests than nonviewers. Grouping worked out that way by chance, as result of random selection. In many cases, viewers overtook and passed nonviewers after six weeks of "Sesame Street." In tests of sorting skills, children were shown several identical objects, plus one object that did not match the others, and asked to pick out the latter. In "two shoes" category, children were asked to pick out a single, isolated shoe from among several pairs of shoes. The same principle applied to "three horns."

differences began to appear between viewers and nonviewers, with the average gains from pretest to six weeks being greater for viewers than nonviewers on all eight tests in ETS's battery. As reported in the New York *Times* of January 28, 1970, gains for viewers were substantial on the tests of letters, forms, and sorting.[5]

[5] *Plaza Sésamo,* a Spanish-language version of *Sesame Street,* began broadcasting throughout Latin-America during 1972–73. After seven weeks of daily broadcasts in Mexico, progress testing on approximately 200 Mexican children showed results almost identical to those in the United States. Viewers gained more than non-viewers on all tests, with the differences being especially large for Letters and Words, Numbers, Relational Terms, and General Knowledge.

By the end of three months, the nonviewers in day-care centers had become familiar with *Sesame Street*, apparently watching it in their homes, on weekends, or when they were absent from school. These "nonviewers" began to display learning gains, but the gains of the viewing children continued to equal or exceed the gains of these "nonviewers," especially on the tests of letters, numbers, forms, and puzzles.

By examining the progress of viewers and nonviewers on each of the 217 test items, the researchers could tell the producers what the children were learning and failing to learn. Moreover, this early progress testing suggested that *Sesame Street* was making strides toward teaching what it had set out to teach.

Estimating Overall Effects

Periodic testing during the first broadcast year was intended primarily to guide production; it could give only transient views of what children were learning. The tests were designed only to prevent total disaster. By the end of the year, however, the time for a true accounting had come. What, if anything, had children learned from viewing? To reduce the personal biases that might contaminate this accounting if done by the Children's Television Workshop itself, the evaluation was designed and conducted by the Educational Testing Service of Princeton, New Jersey (Ball and Bogatz, 1970; Bogatz and Ball, 1971a,b; Ball and Bogatz, 1972).

Two basic principles guided these evaluations (Ball and Bogatz, 1972). First, the intended effects of *Sesame Street* were examined, along with some side effects. Next, in addition to examining overall effects on all children, ETS tried to sort out *Sesame Street*'s differential effects on different children: which children it works best with, which children it fails to help, and the conditions that produce these different outcomes.

ETS involved local community members directly in their research teams conducting the studies. Ghetto communities have become increasingly inaccessible to researchers, who often descend upon a community, study the children, and then vanish without leaving any visible benefit either to the children or the community. This exploitation occurs outside inner-city communities too, but the discrepancy between how much help is needed in ghettos and how little is received from researchers is especially vivid, and the ghetto population is justifiably wary. Researchers try two replies, both without success. They admit that others before them have been guilty but argue that they will be different. Or when inner-city parents point out that research has yielded nothing but a long list of invidious comparisons between their children and others, researchers counter that they are testing the educational program, not the children. Neither reply convinces ghetto people that things will be different this time.

ETS followed a different procedure, appointing and training local people as coordinators, testers and observers. Since this approach provides income to some residents, it has been called blackmail: Hire and pay us and we will let you work here. There is, however, real value in involving community members in the research. As part of the research team, they can act on their own behalf to guarantee that the studies will be important to the community. Also, since community members are familiar with local conditions, the research can be made a more natural part of ongoing activities. ETS researchers themselves seemed surprised at the magnitude of these advantages:

> Advantages accrued from our field staff's coming from the community. Many doors were opened to us (both literally and metaphorically) that would not otherwise have been opened. In our house-by-house listing of 3- to 5-year-olds, we had very few refusals (less than 5 per cent). Second, to say the least, no harm was done to the validity of our testing when our testers spoke, dressed, and behaved in ways culturally familiar to the preschool subjects. The third advantage was one on which we had not counted initially. Since the testers were neither sophisticated in test theory nor advanced educationally themselves,

attempts at dishonesty were easily noted when the data arrived at our office. (The literature indicates that with middle-class, well-educated testers and interviewers it is difficult and costly to solve problems of honesty in data collection.) A number of devices were built into our test battery to exercise quality control; as a result, the data from four testers were discarded, and thereby about 130 subjects were lost from the initial 1,300. But since the coordinators were also from the community, they could play unpleasant supervisory roles without much adverse community reaction. The fact that people with low educational levels would be administering the instruments presented problems in constructing the instruments, but this fact too was a blessing in disguise. We had to take a new and patently clear approach to test development, and it is good that we did. [Ball and Bogatz, 1972, p. 7]

The researchers aimed to simplify the testing procedures as much as possible, both for the tester and the child. ETS constructed over two hundred items, which required about two hours of testing, usually distributed over three or four sessions. The only materials were a set of stimulus pictures, and usually the only response required of the child was simple pointing. The child did not need to verbalize his answers, except where verbalization was the goal being assessed. Nor was the child required to interpret the stimulus pictures; he was told what the pictures were. All children were tested individually.

These test items assessed the major curriculum goals of *Sesame Street:*

Body Parts

Pointing to Body Parts
Naming Body Parts
Function of Body Parts (Point)
Function of Body Parts (Verbal)

Letters

Recognizing Letters
Naming Capital Letters
Naming Lower-Case Letters

Matching Letters in Words
Recognizing Letters in Words
Initial Sounds
Reading Words

Forms

Recognizing Forms
Naming Forms

Numbers

Recognizing Numbers
Naming Numbers
Numerosity
Counting
Addition and Subtraction

Relational Terms

Amount Relations
Size Relations
Position Relations

Sorting Skills

Classification Skills

Classification by Size
Classification by Form
Classification by Number
Classification by Function

Puzzles

In addition, a parent questionnaire was administered to learn about the home backgrounds of children in the study. Several aspects of family life, parental aspirations, television viewing habits and socioeconomic status were included in this questionnaire, which parents were paid to fill out both before broadcasting began and at the end of the broadcast season.

Post-broadcast questions assessed also the child's television viewing habits in general and *Sesame Street* viewing habits in particular.

ETS tested over 1,200 children before *Sesame Street* began broadcasting, sampled geographically from middle-class suburbs, urban ghettos in northern and western cities, lower-class sections of a southern town, and from rural areas. These sites included Boston; Philadelphia; Phoenix; Durham, North Carolina; and a rural area in northeastern California. Included were children from well-to-do and poor families, Spanish-speaking children, black children and white children, three- four- and five-year-olds, boys and girls, children at home and those in Head Start and other preschool programs. In addition to testing these children, ETS observed many of them watching *Sesame Street,* analyzed the content of the show, administered questionnaires to teachers whose children were viewing, and developed several techniques to assess the amount of viewing by each child in their study.

The most direct test of *Sesame Street*'s effectiveness came from comparing children who had watched the show regularly with those who had not seen it at all over the course of the broadcast year. The children were divided into four groups according to how much they viewed *Sesame Street.* The highest group watched the program an average of five times a week or more. The lowest group watched rarely or never, although it was difficult to locate a group that had never seen *Sesame Street* at all. Attracting a large viewing audience to an educational series was perhaps *Sesame Street*'s greatest success, but it also meant that there would be few true nonviewers to compare with the viewers. Even in the lowest viewing group many children watched the program occasionally.

Children who watched the most learned the most. For example, the 731 disadvantaged children participating in the ETS study were divided into four groups according to amount of viewing. As shown in ETS's First Year Report Card, 9 percent gains were made by the children who watched seldom if ever, 15 percent gains by those who watched two to three times a week, 19 percent gains by those who watched four to five times

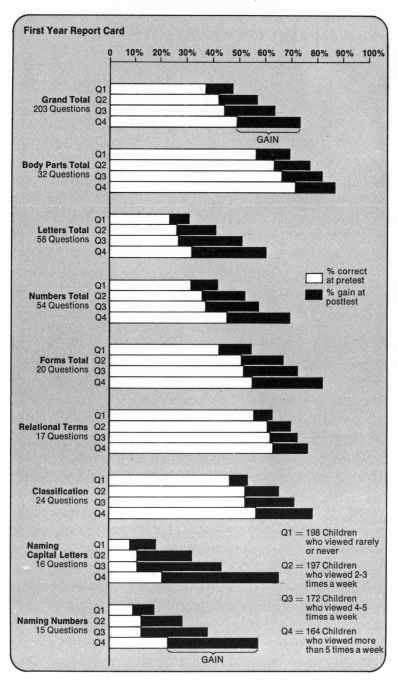

First Year Report Card

a week, and 24 percent gains by those who watched more than five times a week.[6]

The skills that received the most time and attention on *Sesame Street* were, with rare exceptions, those that were learned best. For example, more time (14 percent) was devoted to letter-related skills than to any other single subject, and here children's gains were the most dramatic. In addition to acquiring skills that were directly taught, there was some transfer of learning. Some children, for example, learned to recognize full words or to write their own names, skills not taught directly on the program.

Sesame Street does not demand adult supervision in order for children to learn. Children viewing at home showed gains at least as great as children who watched in school under the supervision of a teacher, a finding that has special significance in light of the fact that more than four fifths of all children three and four years of age, and more than a quarter of all five-year-olds, do not attend any form of school. At the same time, the value of an interested adult watching with the child was apparent. Among the disadvantaged children who watched regularly at home, for example, those who gained most had mothers who often watched the show with them and talked with them about it.

The major finding—that children who watched more learned more—held true for children of different ages, sexes, geographical locations, socioeconomic statuses, and IQ's, as well as for children watching either at home or at school. In all goal areas, gains in learning increased steadily with amount of viewing. Some groups of children, however, showed greater gains than others. The three-year-old children gained the most, five-year-olds the least. That is, although three-year-olds scored lower

---

[6] The finding that viewers learned more than nonviewers also was confirmed for children abroad. For example, in 1973 K. I. Lemercier and G. R. Teasdale of the Flinders University of South Australia reported that children from low-income families in Adelaide who viewed the English-language version of *Sesame Street* showed superior performance to a comparable group of nonviewers on all of the Educational Testing Service's tests with the single exception of Relational Terms.

than four- and five-year-olds before broadcasting began, after broadcasting those three-year-olds who watched regularly scored higher than older children who did not watch regularly. A similar pattern emerged for advantaged and disadvantaged children. Although the disadvantaged children began the broadcast year with considerably lower scores than advantaged children, after broadcasting those disadvantaged children who watched regularly surpassed the advantaged children who watched less. A tentative but provocative finding was that *Sesame Street* seems particularly effective for teaching certain skills to children whose first language is not English. A very small sample of children from Spanish-speaking homes in the Southwest (forty-three children in all) showed more dramatic gains with regular viewing than any other group.

Sesame Street was more successful in teaching certain of its goals than others, with those receiving more attention on the programs being learned better. Relative lack of success sometimes resulted from our initial underestimation of children's prior knowledge. When this happened, we aimed our instruction too low and presented what many children already understood. Learning seemed greatest when skills were presented in a direct fashion (as was letter recognition in animated segments) rather than indirectly (as was recognizing initial sounds in words by providing a long series of examples without pointing out the exact lesson to be learned).

The meaning of some of these findings was obscured by self-selection among the children, where those who viewed the show the most (and therefore learned the most from it) also had higher attainments before broadcasting began. It was not clear whether the gains in learning were a function of greater viewing or of these preexisting faster learning rates for the children who chose to view the most. ETS therefore selected two groups from their full sample who were absolutely alike in age, intelligence and community background, making certain that there were no observable differences between them in previous attainments. Group 1 was composed of about one hundred children who were 53 to 58 months of age *before* broadcasting began. Group 2 was composed of about the same number of children who reached exactly the same age of 53 to 58 months *after* watching the full broadcast season. Group 2 viewers scored about 40 points higher on the 203 test items than Group 1 children, who had reached the same age before *Sesame Street* began broadcasting and who consequently had never watched the show. At all levels of age, intelligence, previous attainments and home background, the frequent viewers made significantly larger gains than nonviewers.

Sesame Street's unexpected popularity created problems for ETS's evaluation of its first year on the air. Before broadcasting began, the evaluators worried that too few children would watch, so they had gone to great lengths to insure a sufficient audience of viewers for their research. For example, they deliberately chose sites with VHF transmission rather than UHF, and encouraged some of the viewers to watch. Some advisors to the Educational Testing Service even argued eloquently that a group of children should be paid to view or there would be too few viewers in the sample. Actually, so many children watched *Sesame Street* that the researchers had difficulty in filling their quota of nonviewers to compare with the viewers.

The scarcity of nonviewers forced ETS to change its strategy when evaluating *Sesame Street*'s second year on the air, during the fall of 1970 to spring of 1971. This second-year evaluation set out to see if a crop of children who had not seen *Sesame Street* during its first year would respond as well as these earlier groups did and also to see if the earlier groups continued to learn.

To find some true nonviewers, ETS went to two communities that had not received *Sesame Street* during its first broadcast year. In Winston-Salem, North Carolina, *Sesame Street* had just become available during 1970 and 1971 with the introduction of cable television. The cost of cable television is high for poor families, so ETS was able to arrange with Tele-Cable in Winston-Salem to install cable free of charge in one hundred randomly chosen homes there. These children became the experimental viewing group, and a comparable group of disadvantaged children living in noncable homes became the nonviewing controls. In Los Angeles, *Sesame Street* was carried only by a UHF station, KCET. Here the Educational Testing Service identified inner-city homes that lacked UHF adapters, and by providing adapters for some of these homes and not others, again insured a control group of true nonviewers.

Since the second-year curriculum for *Sesame Street* had been expanded to include such goals as addition and subtraction, a twenty-word reading vocabulary, and multiple-classification skills, the ETS test battery was also expanded. Comparisons between viewing and nonviewing children in Winston-Salem and Los Angeles clearly confirmed the first year's results. In every goal area measured, the gains of viewers equaled or exceeded the gains of nonviewers. In no case did nonviewers gain significantly more than viewers.

To trace the continuing effects of *Sesame Street* on its first-year graduates, the Educational Testing Service returned in 1970–1971 to Boston, Phoenix, and Durham, North Carolina. All the disadvantaged, at-home children from the first-year study in these sites were included in this follow-up study. Because even the "nonviewers" in the first-year study had seen some *Sesame Street* and others among these control children had watched during the summer reruns in 1970, few true nonviewers were available. By this time almost all the children were viewing, almost all children continued to gain in their test performance, and it was difficult to tease out the effects of first-year viewing. But from all the children who had watched during the first year, two groups could be separated out and compared: those who continued viewing into the second season and those who stopped. ETS compared these two groups in 29 goal areas, with continuing viewers displaying better performance in almost all areas (including most prominently the new goals that had been introduced into *Sesame Street*'s second-year curriculum) while noncontinuing children were better in almost none.

One hundred and sixty children from ETS's first-year study had gone into Head Start, kindergarten or first grade by the beginning of the second season, and this provided an opportunity to study *Sesame Street*'s influence on school performance. To avoid singling out these children from their classmates, teachers of *Sesame Street* follow-up children were asked to rank all children in their classes for their general readiness for school, verbal readiness, quantitative readiness, general intelligence, attitude toward school, relationships with peers, and physical coordination. The teachers were not told how much the children had or had not watched *Sesame Street*. Teacher ratings were obtained for 112 of the 160 children in the *Sesame Street* first-year study who had gone on to school, along with ratings of their classmates. The veteran *Sesame Street* viewers were ranked higher than children who had watched less, especially for general readiness for school, quantitative readiness, positive attitudes toward school, and relationships with peers. Contrary to predictions that *Sesame Street* would produce boredom and restlessness in children when they reached school, teachers judged these veteran viewers to have highly positive attitudes toward school. Their higher ranking for peer relationships also suggested that they were making at least satisfactory adjustment to school life.

The same teachers were asked to rank their children again at the end of the 1970–71 school year, the second year of *Sesame Street* broadcasts. By this time, it became almost impossible to identify "pure" groups of nonviewers. Many children who had not watched *Sesame Street* in its first year began viewing during its second season, while some others who had been viewing now stopped. Despite this, children who remained regular viewers through both seasons or who had viewed regularly during the first season even if they stopped by the second season were ranked higher than their classmates who did not watch in either season. This superiority held across all areas of school readiness, including general readiness, positive attitudes toward school, and relations with peers.

The mothers of school-age children seemed to agree with these judgments of teachers. In a 1973 survey of 1,217 households in inner cities (99 percent of them either black or Spanish-speaking), these mothers were asked if they felt that watching *Sesame Street* had helped their children in school (Yankelovich, 1973). The yes votes were: Bedford-Stuyvesant, 92 percent; East Harlem, 92 percent; Chicago, 89 percent; Washington, D.C., 84 percent.

Nationwide indications of *Sesame Street's* popularity among parents came from a commercial network, in a study financed by the Columbia Broadcasting System. It consisted of in-depth interviews with 1,900 Americans in 1970, and duplicated and updated a similar 1960 study, concluding that "the best-regarded programs are those that are designed to educate and not just to entertain. *Sesame Street* leads the list of favorite programs in 1970 despite the fact that half the samples of parents could not receive an educational television station."[7]

The great impact of *Sesame Street's* first year on the small number of children from Spanish-speaking families in the Southwest led to an effort to trace this effect during *Sesame Street's* second season. A new group of 85 Spanish-speaking children in Los Angeles was located, in order to compare those who watched regularly with those who did not. All but six of these children, however, had actually viewed *Sesame Street* during its second season, and once again the results were obscured by the scarcity of true nonviewers. Although the Spanish-speaking children who viewed did gain more than the few nonviewers, the finding could not be considered definitive.

A distinguishing feature of ETS's evaluation was its attempt to go beyond the program's intended effects to look for unintended effects, certain of which already have been mentioned: reading whole words, writing of names, attitude toward school, relations with peers. When children of comparable ages were compared—one group having watched *Sesame Street* regularly and the other not—*Sesame Street* viewers showed more positive attitudes toward children from other races. Apparently, the respect and appreciation for racial differences displayed by the inhabitants of *Sesame Street* did register with at least some young viewers (Bogatz and Ball, 1971a).

[7] Bureau of Social Science Research, 1973.

The Gap between Advantaged and Disadvantaged

We had decided that the important mission of reducing the achievement gap between advantaged and disadvantaged children could not be accomplished with a nationally televised series,[8] but we did want to be sure that *Sesame Street* was not inadvertently widening it. This could happen if advantaged children were watching more than disadvantaged children or were learning more from similar amounts of viewing. The evidence suggests that neither was the case.[9]

There may have been a period during *Sesame Street*'s first broadcast year when proportionally fewer inner-city children were viewing, but perhaps because of the Workshop's efforts to attract audiences in inner cities, no differences were evident following that time. In addition, Bogatz and Ball (1971a) report that the gains made by disadvantaged children from viewing *Sesame Street* were at least as great as those of advantaged children. *Sesame Street* seems neither to reduce nor widen the gap, a finding reported in other countries as well.[10] Both groups watched in large numbers and seemed to learn effectively from viewing.

Other Studies

The Workshop could afford only to conduct or commission a small part of the research needed for a full evaluation of *Sesame Street*'s effects. When strong public interest developed in response to our early broadcasts, we hoped that independent researchers across the country—in universities and other research centers—would share that interest and produce other studies. Some did, but the studies were far fewer than we had

---

[8] Indeed, Jencks (1972) argues that this reduction may not be achieved through any form of education whatever, but must be faced squarely as a political and social question instead of one that education can solve.

[9] Ball and Bogatz, 1970; Bogatz and Ball, 1971a; Harris, 1970, 1971.

[10] For example, Salomon, 1972.

hoped. Although the Workshop supplied materials and assistance to all researchers who sought its cooperation, only a handful of studies has accumulated.

Even the few studies that were done were unfortunately of limited value, flawed primarily by their false premises about *Sesame Street's* purposes and methods. Cook (1972), a researcher at Northwestern University, decided that we really had set out to reduce the gap between advantaged and disadvantaged children and then, by reanalyzing data collected by ETS and others, concluded that we had failed. He observes that the "most obvious strategy" to narrow the gap is "to slow down the advantaged by taking *Sesame Street* off the public airwaves so that it cannot be viewed by any economically advantaged children at all." This strategy would be an absurd violation of the Workshop's announced aim to stimulate the growth of all children.

Ingersoll (1971), an educational psychologist at Indiana University, felt that he had to question both *Sesame Street* and its ETS evaluation because of the "danger that the educational community will be lulled into tacit acceptance of the series, or its future imitators, as the 'best' form of education for the preschool disadvantaged." We had repeatedly stressed the mindlessness of comparing *Sesame Street* with other forms of preschool education, noting that the most we could hope for children's television is that it might provide a useful complement to other educational experiences.

Herbert Sprigle (1971, 1972) embarked with the largest boatload of false premises about *Sesame Street's* purposes and methods. He accused the Workshop of offering a single, simple solution to problems of preschool education and of attempting to replace more worthy programs (including his "Learning-to-Learn" school in Jacksonville, Florida). He decided that the Workshop did set out to narrow the gap between advantaged and disadvantaged, and then without studying any advantaged children whatever, he decided that we failed. He adopted the deficit model of differences between advantaged and disadvantaged children, arbitrarily elected his own candidate for the disadvantaged child's principal deficit—"the biggest handicap is his detachment from close human relationships"—and then accused *Sesame Street* of failing to remedy this deficit. He assessed *Sesame Street*'s effects, not with measures of its goals, but with his own choice of standardized tests of academic achievement in school.[11] He compared *Sesame Street* viewers with "control" children who were taught in his school in groups of four, each group taught by its own teacher. Pitting *Sesame Street* against his teachers, he reported that children taught in small groups learn more than *Sesame Street* viewers. Although his studies are too flawed technically to demonstrate even this conclusion, who would doubt it? For *Sesame Street* to have educational value, must it be more effective than the personal attention of a teacher? For teachers to be of value, must they demonstrate that they can beat *Sesame Street*? Television and teachers cannot even be evaluated by the same criteria. Each makes a distinctive contribution, and our task is to learn to combine them.

Other independent research on *Sesame Street* has been more illuminating. Sproull (1973), for example, the research coordinator at Western Illinois University, was especially concerned about the unintended messages communicated by the programs. She looked carefully at the responses of thirty four-year-old children viewing individually and in small groups. Although relatively few children were studied, the reactions of each child were videotaped both during viewing as well as during play following the broadcasts so that detailed analyses could be made. Sproull reported that:

• "Eye contact" averaged 47 minutes of the 58 minute program both for individual and group viewing. This high level of viewing, other estimates of "concentration" while viewing, and the maintenance of a high level of attention to the program even when the children talked to each other—all contradicted

11 Although Sprigle probably holds the record for the greatest number of false premises about *Sesame Street* and for the technical inadequacies in his own research, others (e.g., Minton, 1972) share his error in assessing *Sesame Street* with measures of their own choosing that have nothing to do with the programs' announced goals.

the experimenter's "impressionistic" judgment of the children's viewing before the videotapes were analyzed.

· Almost all children (28 of the 30) exhibited both verbal and nonverbal modeling of a variety of behaviors exhibited on the program, including repeating numbers, reciting the letters of the alphabet, singing along with the songs, and imitating various physical movements.

· Each child averaged more than one laugh or smile for every two minutes of the program.

· The children who viewed individually incorporated letters, numbers and other symbols seen on *Sesame Street* into their post-viewing play. Sproull found most of the unintended effects she looked for in a variety of modeling behaviors, including the "girl who kissed the boy next to her after seeing frog and monster kiss on the program" and the "boy who imitated the cow eating an 'O.' "

Salomon (1973b), a psychologist at the Hebrew University of Jerusalem who studied the reactions of Israeli children to *Sesame Street*, looked for other kinds of unintended effects. He reports substantial learning of "media literacy" skills by the Israeli viewers of *Sesame Street*, including the ability to take different points of view, to see how parts go together to make a whole, and to pick out the important elements in a complex problem-solving situation. The learning of "media literacy" was especially great among children from low-income families when their mothers were encouraged to watch the show with their children. Salomon also examined whether viewing *Sesame Street* helped children to learn from other instructional films. It did.

On balance, the research done on *Sesame Street*, when compared to similar evaluations of other educational approaches, looks pretty good. *Sesame Street* apparently amused many young children a great deal and thereby succeeded in holding their attention. It succeeded in teaching some basic intellectual skills. We will not be absolutely sure from the research until more time passes, but those basic skills seemed useful to teachers and parents in getting children ready for their formal school experiences. These achievements alone seemed to justify *Sesame Street*'s existence as a supplement to other educational opportunities. But perhaps its greatest success was its most obvious one: It attracted a large and loyal audience of very young children to a television series with deliberate instructional purposes. This has never before happened in television's history.

Section Four:
Lessons from Sesame Street

To pass through childhood, when one's imagination, one's sense of the possibilities of the world is developing, and have it touched only, or mostly, by a piece of boffo-funny mechanistic claptrap such as McHale's Navy seems a damn shame.

Michael J. Arlen,
McCall's, February 1971

Almost a decade has passed since Joan Cooney and Lloyd Morrisett began the collaboration that led to *Sesame Street*. It was perhaps the most auspicious time for the project to be born. In the early and mid-1960's, the hopelessness, despair and rage of the poor began to enter our national consciousness. Politically, poverty was becoming explosive. Socially, it was disruptive, immoral, and frightening. At the same time, the importance of the child's earliest years in determining his future life was becoming generally recognized. Both principles converged in a concern for helping children from poor, inner-city families by seeking new alternatives in early education. This commitment no longer seems so firm.

Even in 1968, this commitment would not have affected children's television if Joan Cooney had not appeared on the scene with a new idea and with the ability to carry it through. When *Sesame Street* did attract widespread national attention, however, we dared to hope that other, different successes in children's television would follow, that an even more intense commitment to early education would be made, and that the dedication to helping children of the poor would be strengthened. None of these things has happened. How, then, can we claim that *Sesame Street* was a success? What did we learn that seems to matter now or will matter in the future?

The Lessons of Success

Here is *Sesame Street*'s main lesson: It deliberately uses television to teach without hiding its educational intentions and yet it attracts a large and devoted audience of young children from all parts of the country.

To judge success by this standard seems to be playing commercial television's game of get-the-biggest-audience. What is new about *Sesame Street* is that it gained its large audience despite its serious educational purposes and its distribution over noncommercial, public-broadcasting stations. We didn't hide its educational content from children, yet they watched.

Sesame Street also gave us our first real evidence, beyond scattered anecdotes from parents, of the remarkable rate at which young children can learn from television. Dr. Natalie Shainess, a child psychiatrist, criticized us for teaching children specific skills "ahead of the normal time in their intellectual development" (Dallas *Morning News*, August 29, 1971). Our experience with *Sesame Street* makes us question this predetermined "normal" time for development which Dr. Shainess and others claim must not be violated. Existing definitions of normality seem to be simply an artifact of professionals who see certain behaviors appear in children at certain ages and then wrongly decide that these behaviors are the only proper expectations. On *Sesame Street*, when we used existing guidelines of "normal" development, we found that we constantly underestimated how much three-, four- and five-year-olds could learn from *Sesame Street*, and did not even have the foresight to anticipate that our most responsive audience would be children even younger than three years of age. Here then is another of *Sesame Street*'s lessons: We must begin to appreciate how well and how rapidly children can learn at very young ages, especially from visual media.

Sesame Street also has some lessons for researchers and television producers. Except for a few studies of violence[1] and com-

---

[1] For example, Surgeon General's Report, 1972; Feshbach and Singer, 1971.

mercial advertising,[2] researchers have not taken much interest in television's effects upon children; consequently our knowledge is pitifully thin.[3] Television's commercial origins may have made researchers wary about reporting information that could be misused for commercial exploitation. But research on *Sesame Street* may have conferred a new respectability upon studies of the effects of visual media upon children. It also gives young researchers something beyond violence and commercial advertising as materials for study.

Sesame Street may also have lent respectability to producing shows for children, which always has been regarded as a low-prestige job in television, on-the-job training for the more serious (and lucrative) trade of television production for adults. Perhaps the professionalism of *Sesame Street*'s production, and its popularity across the country, will help to change that image. Perhaps some gifted young professionals will now actually seek out that hitherto neglected stepchild of the industry.

Why did *Sesame Street* succeed? Looking back on our experience, we can come up with two different interpretations. We can assign *Sesame Street*'s success to the Workshop's model of careful construction of a professional organization, rational selection of its educational goals, and continuous self-correction based upon the observations of children. Alternatively, we could call the Workshop's "model" a fiction or at least deny that it is the cause of its success. We could credit instead the fortunate combination of Joan Cooney's genius for implementing a novel idea, Lloyd Morrisett's extraordinary skill in locating financial backing, and the propitious social and political climate of the time—along with doses of pure luck. We shall never know which view is right.

If the systematic model was at work, what were the major ingredients that made for its success? We started with the assumption that entertainment could be a useful vehicle for

---

[2] For example, Ward, Levinson and Wackman, 1972; Barcus, 1971.

[3] An annotated bibliography of existing research prepared in 1971 by Atkin, Murray and Nayman for the National Institute of Mental Health does list 496 reported studies. They provide little illumination.

education. Although we did not camouflage *Sesame Street's* educational content, we did try to make it as inviting and amusing as we could. In doing so, we rejected the ideas that learning is not learning unless it hurts, that children never do what is good for them unless they are forced to, and that entertainment (acceptable as a temporary relaxation earned by diligent work but not really good for you) competes with education (which *is* good for you, but is earnest and hard). We relied instead on the children's personal initiative to watch what is interesting (even while being educational) and ignore what is not. It worked. Children watched in numbers that we had not guessed were possible.

Related to the blending of entertainment and education was another key premise, stated in Joan Cooney's original proposal to establish the Workshop. This was the assumption that even very young children today bring a high degree of media literacy to television viewing. By age three, they already have had wide exposure to a range of media techniques, including animation, live-action film, game formats, music, puppets and various camera techniques. We still have only vague insights into the exact nature of this media literacy in young children, but we accepted its existence, and this led to important decisions about *Sesame Street:* the magazine format; the great variety of styles, paces and characters; the incorporation of all of television's techniques in order to hold the children's attention. Joan Cooney viewed the Children's Television Workshop primarily as a creative organization whose justification ultimately rests in the quality of what finally appears on the television screen. From her own background in television production, she knew that the creative staff must be free of all responsibility except that of creating the programs themselves. Giving this condition top priority when organizing the Workshop, she and Lloyd Morrisett built a staff to handle all matters of organization, funding, relations with funding sources, business management and arrangements with the public-broadcasting stations that carried *Sesame Street.*

The educators and researchers at the Workshop played their

own roles, but their ultimate contribution was also to provide sustenance and support to the creative staff. This is not the educators' usual role in educational projects. Usually they are asked to design the instructional content of a program. Often the practitioner who is expected to put the design into operation resents what he perceives to be the role of errand boy or does not fully understand the directives handed down from above. We did not proceed in this way. From the earliest discussions, the educators and creative staff worked together to design the instructional content of *Sesame Street*. This meant that the creative staff had a full opportunity to become acquainted with the ways in which educators and psychologists think about children and to question any decisions that they did not understand or accept. When production began, they could draw upon this knowledge and work with an instructional design that they had helped to create.

The Workshop's researchers also served production, providing the observations of children that the producers needed to improve the series as it was developed. The researchers had to invent ways to make these observations, and the producers had to overcome some obstacles to using the information effectively, including simply recognizing that the series would not be perfect from the start.

The most practical sign of the high priority given to production was the proportion of the Workshop's budget assigned to it. Of the eight million dollars in grants from foundations and government sources to set up the organization and to carry it through a planning period and first broadcast year, seven million was actually spent. Two thirds was spent for production, with the remaining one third rather evenly divided among research, distribution of information, and administrative costs. Although the total Workshop budget has changed somewhat in subsequent years—rising in 1972 to about $13,000,000 as a major new series (*The Electric Company*) was added, and then dropping as public support for education decreased—the proportions spent for each Workshop function remained about the same, reflecting the continuing priority of creative programing.

There were other organizational ingredients in the Workshop's model. Joan Cooney and Lloyd Morrisett had gone after the sum of money that they believed would be needed to do the job well, and they had raised it. They had approached several funding sources, including foundations and government agencies, not only because the total sum was too large to request from any one source, but also because multiple sources of financing seemed advisable. Each of the backers commented on our progress, thus exerting a set of checks and balances upon each other. Joan also insulated the financial backers from the Workshop's creative staff, with all communications from backers fielded by her, Bob Davidson, Tom Kennedy (Vice-President for Finance and Administration) or other members of the administrative staff, who then discussed these messages with the creative staff.

These backers, especially the government agencies that depend upon annual Congressional appropriations, often deal in year-by-year support that makes long-range planning hazardous. However, Joan and Lloyd insisted on a sufficiently long planning period to do the project well, estimating that at least eighteen months would be needed before broadcasting began. The organization would need to shake down, with its personnel getting to know one another before the grind of daily production could begin. The producers and writers would need time to invent the new series, to experiment with formats and techniques, to create show segments and consult with the researchers who were trying them out on children. The researchers would need time to collect information about our target audience, to try out existing television materials on children, and most of all, to learn how to convey these observations to producers in a form they could use. Working contacts with inner-city community groups would need to be established. At the end of the eighteen months, the Workshop was on its way to being a smoothly operating unit, with a sense of mutual trust among its members that would carry them through the rigors of producing 130 one-hour shows within a twenty-six-week season.

If the Workshop's "model" was really what produced *Sesame Street*'s success, these then seem to be its main features: some important assumptions about children and how they learn from television, the priority given to high-quality production, and an organization that fostered mutual confidence among its members. These ingredients are not very different from those that others[4] have identified as important. For example, James Gibbons, a Stanford University professor, surveyed six "successful ventures in the use of technology in education," programs mostly at higher-education levels in Japan, Germany, Poland, United Kingdom, Australia and the United States.[5] He concludes:

1. The educational program must be planned for a specific *target audience*.

2. *Specific educational objectives* that are relevant to the needs and interests of the target audience must be clearly understood and agreed on.

3. A systematic *multi-media approach* must be used in which both knowledge specialists and media specialists are employed.

4. Educators who are capable of learning and understanding the *instructional characteristics* of various media must be found.

5. Clear and careful provision for *personal interaction . . .* must be made.

6. *Evaluation and feedback* arrangements must be made to monitor audience reaction and change the instructional material to suit audience needs.

Although Gibbons' criteria for successful applications of television to education do resemble those that emerged from our *Sesame Street* experience, there is one way in which the experi-

[4] E.g., Bretz, 1972.
[5] Gibbons, 1973.

ences differ greatly. Audiences for the programs reviewed by Gibbons were motivated to watch because of formal matriculation or enrollment in a televised course, often depositing money and receiving academic credit. No such motivations existed for *Sesame Street*'s audience. The appeal of the shows was the sole incentive to viewing.

However, *Sesame Street*'s "model," like all models, may simply be imaginary, a pretense that we understand something we do not. We may wish to believe that a model we understand is at work because it makes us confident that we can achieve similar success by following the model in the future. On the other hand, believing that a program's success has resulted from a combination of personal genius, luck and good timing makes it seem accidental and difficult to duplicate. As uncomfortable as the notion may be, *Sesame Street*'s success probably resulted from just such a combination.

Take the matter of genius. Joan Cooney brought the genius of innovation and organization. Dave Connell combined the imagination needed to design the show with the pragmatism needed to meet an exhausting production schedule. Ed Palmer brought a sensitivity to children's responses. Jon Stone, Jeff Moss, Sam Gibbon, Jim Henson, Joe Raposo and other writers, producers and performers supplied the different forms of creative genius. None duplicated the other.

Take the matter of luck. Creative geniuses are supposed to be solitary and irascible. Those at the Workshop liked each other. No one can plan that such people will get along together, but a strong personal chemistry existed within the group, with each person confident of contributing his share. They had a sense of mission as a group, yet each was willing to assume responsibility for his part in the program's successes or failures.

Or take the matter of timing. Joan and Lloyd launched the project at a time in our country's social and political history when the importance given to reducing poverty and to constructing programs of early education made funding possible. Since there were no existing organizations in the field at the time, the Children's Television Workshop could be built from the ground up, as a special-purpose group designed specifically for our purposes. Although we anticipated that teachers and librarians might regard our efforts as threatening (they didn't), we were otherwise not intruding upon any established organization's territory. Lastly, the timing of *Sesame Street*'s success was unexpected. *Sesame Street* happened, and became popular, with little of the advance fanfare that accompanies new projects and sets unrealistic expectations for them. Never before had there been a really explosive success in children's television programing, and no one was expecting one at that point. Advance hope did not discount the reality when it occurred.

A Lesson of Sesame Street*'s Failure*

Sesame Street failed in some ways too, of course, and these failures carry their own lessons. Our failure to create a movement toward general improvement in the quality of children's programs forces us to recognize that a single instance of success will not be enough to sustain real progress. Chuck Jones, who was appointed by ABC to the newly created post of vice-president for children's programs after *Sesame Street* appeared, said: "*Sesame Street* opened children's television to taste and wit and substance. It made the climate right for improvement." The climate may have been right, but apparently the money wasn't. On commercial television, that improvement never came.

Sesame Street was widely accepted for itself, but expecting more from its success ignores other powerful forces: money (and politics) in the case of commercial broadcasting, politics (and money) in the case of public broadcasting. Economics and politics affect children's television directly and deeply. As these forces now operate, they are likely to impede any momentum that a good children's series can create. Responsibility for upgrading children's programs continues to fall between the cracks, sloughed from commercial broadcaster to advertiser to government agency to public-service organization, with no one taking decisive action and with money always the unspoken issue.

The $ as Test Pattern

Rarely in the world's history has the appearance of a new invention come in such a prophetic form. A young man named Philo T. Farnsworth, working in a darkened San Francisco apartment in 1927, transmitted images for the first time without the use of wires. As a test pattern, Farnsworth used the dollar sign.

That dollar sign has dominated television ever since, and anything that does not attach itself to it stands little chance. The television that has come from the dollar sign has generated public reactions of two sorts, melodramas about its damage to us or romances about its potential. We view with alarm its destructive effects, saying that our intelligence and taste are so offended by its mindlessness that we will have nothing to do with it. Or, we make bright but empty promises for its future, foreseeing a posterity that seems never to arrive.

Television once had (and perhaps still has) the potential to become a principal means toward an informed society. Instead, it has become the butt of a long-running recurrent joke—a symbol of crassness and futility, an irresistible target for disparagement. It is still fashionable for people to proclaim that it is beneath their dignity to watch television or even to harbor a set within their homes. The list of ways in which television menaces us is long and is getting longer: violence, depersonalization, exploitation of children, commercialization, spectatorship, passivity, and most recently, government control over our minds. The mildest indictment is that it wastes our time.

The list of bright, empty promises is just as long. Presumably cable television is coming on a large scale, and when it does, it will provide unprecedented medical, educational and social services. Video cassettes will give people a much wider choice in what they watch. Two-way, interactive television will permit real exchanges to take place between television and its audience. Satellites will allow us to cover the globe with television broadcasts, reaching even the most remote and isolated regions.[6] Maybe all these things will happen, maybe not. Thirty years ago, the promise of television broadcasting seemed equally bright, but the promise was never kept.

Let us look instead at what we can hope to achieve with the system of television broadcasting that we have now. The obstacles are many, with financing anything new or different being only the most prominent problem. Except for its profit motive, television operates today in an almost total vacuum, isolated from social pressures that might force improvement. There are no social institutions that monitor or govern television programing for children.[7] There are no legal or government agencies at work to improve the quality of children's programs.[8] There are no formal means of recruiting and training those professionals who would create new television programs. There is not even an agency responsible for describing and recording what has happened and will happen in the future. With so little leverage toward improvement, and with commercial incentives so overwhelming, it may be hopeless to think about the distinctive benefits that television can provide for children. It also may be too late; perhaps we long ago passed beyond the time when television could be taken seriously as a constructive force in our country. But it is too important not to try.

[6] A useful analysis of the prospects for cable television and satellites is provided by journalist Brenda Maddox (1972).

[7] Action for Children's Television, originally based in Boston, Massachusetts, is expanding its services to the national level. Even this group's heroic efforts, however, have brought increased scrutiny to only one aspect of children's television, the effects of commercial advertising.

[8] The Federal Communications Commission does, of course, provide some regulatory and licensing guidelines. The partially government-funded Corporation for Public Broadcasting does provide some funds for programs like *Sesame Street* and *Zoom*. Neither has had direct impact upon the general quality of television for children.

Children and Television

Television is not an isolated experience in a child's life. Each child uses it in his own way. What a child learns from television is only one element in a complex balancing act of simultaneous influences—peers, siblings, parents and people in his neighborhood as well as television. One example is the simple finding from the Educational Testing Service's evaluation of *Sesame Street:* Among the disadvantaged children who watched at home, those who gained most had mothers who often watched *Sesame Street* with them and talked with them about it. Although Joan Cooney set out to make *Sesame Street* an effective experiment in the use of television, she acknowledged early that it is only one influence among many, saying, "Television has a very important role to play in education. Still, it's just a big cold box, and just can't replace a loving teacher or parent who cares about a child." (*Time*, November 23, 1970)

Children are simply too complex, and the influences upon them too diverse, to expect that a single influence—like television—will have a uniform effect upon their lives. Nevertheless, there are some minimum guarantees that must be assured, the most obvious being that television must avoid damaging any child. Richard H. Granger, a Yale professor of clinical pediatrics,[9] applied to television the basic principle of medical practice: "First do no harm!" That television do no harm is little enough to ask. But can it bring any distinctive benefits to children?

Enjoyment

The simplest benefit we can expect for our children from television is the one that it seems to have been supplying throughout its history and the one that many people attack as exactly

---

[9] Granger, 1973.

what is wrong with television: It gives children an important source of present enjoyment. To describe this as a benefit seems to share in television's traditional defense of itself, that it only provides what the public wants. Haven't we had enough "entertainment" from television? I think it depends upon what we mean by entertainment. Writing about children's movies in the New York *Times*, Benjamin DeMott, an essayist and astute social commentator, gives us his definition:

> The purpose of children's shows is to entertain, and the key to entertainment is involvement: steady, sympathetic, deep-breathing identification with the cares, troubles, and feelings of somebody not myself. . . . Implicit in it is a conviction that involvement isn't a game or holiday—not when experienced by a kid worried about the fate of the hero, and not when assessed by any developmental psychologist with a humane sense of the stages by which a sane, sensitive and effective grownup comes into being.
>
> The act of imaginatively participating in a hero's life, the process of worrying intensely and lovingly about a vulnerable danger-courting small animal—these have moral consequences, they nourish a kid's awareness of other lives and his power of going beyond himself. [September 12, 1971]

Enjoyment in this sense need not be frivolous and empty. The idea even has been applied to the analysis of what happens in schools, long the bastions of earnest nonfrivolity. Failing to find clear evidence that performance in school affects a child's later achievement or income, Christopher Jencks and his colleagues[10] concluded that the only unequivocal basis for evaluating a school should be whether the students and teachers find it a satisfying place to be. Making a child's education useful to his future is important, of course. But making his life more pleasant now is not offered as an excuse for either the schools' or television's inability to do more. It is no small achievement in itself.

---

[10] Jencks et al., 1972.

For Children Who Need It, a Sanctuary

Television does not hover over children with demands and expectations. They can watch without being tested, graded, reprimanded or even observed by others. They are safe from the threat of humiliation or ridicule for not living up to what is expected of them.

There is little doubt that we all need retreats, some sanctuary from forces that correct and direct us. But we have not made up our collective mind about whether they should exist. We fear that they may engulf us in escape and illusion, and that the indulgence may become addictive. Yet periodic escape from surveillance and exacting expectations need not be equivalent to escape from reality. For those children who need it, television used in moderation can provide a temporary refuge.

For Children Who Need It, Another Way to Learn

Television differs from traditional teaching in some major ways. Traditional teaching depends primarily upon oral language; television combines the visual as well as auditory means. Television moves, in contrast to the more static techniques in schools and classrooms. Traditional teaching tries to control the level and pace of the materials presented to children, giving them what we believe they need, organized and sequenced into progressive steps, followed by appropriate reinforcements. Television does not meet these standard criteria, usually being more helter-skelter and richer in surplus meanings. Some children learn very well from traditional techniques; others need an alternative like television.

Using this alternative, what can children learn? From our experience with *Sesame Street,* we know that they can learn certain language skills and number concepts, and that the symbols of words, numbers, shapes and forms are used in thinking. We do not yet know if children can use television to learn how to learn, but there is evidence that it can help children move from "knowing that" to "knowing how," as psychologist Jerome Bruner puts it.[11] First, *Sesame Street* had some success in teaching mental processes that aid learning, such as classifying and ordering objects and events by size, form, function or class; making inferences; generating and testing predictions. Also, other studies seem promising. For example, in a series of reports,[12] Jerome Kagan and his colleagues at Harvard have shown that watching models can "modify an impulsive tempo" —that is, models can teach children to stop to think instead of acting upon the first idea that occurs to them. Gavriel Salomon, a psychologist working at the Hebrew University in Israel,[13] has shown that zoom-in camera techniques can help children learn to pick out the important details in a problem-solving situation, discriminating them from those details to be ignored as irrelevant to the problem being solved. Douglas and Nancy Denney, psychologists now at the University of Kansas,[14] have found that "information-processing strategies" can be taught to young children by televised models. Working with a "Twenty Questions" procedure, the Denneys found that six-year-olds could model constraint-seeking questions—that is, they would learn to ask fewer random, shotgun questions ("Is it the car?" "Is it the dogs?") and ask more questions that narrowed down the choice by eliminating more than one alternative from the array ("Is it a tool?" "Does it fly?" "Is it red?"). Thus, children can not only learn simple intellectual skills from television, but they also may be helped to learn how to think and solve problems systematically.

Through television, we also may be able to portray for children socially valued behavior. Television's ability to teach antisocial behavior is regrettably evident, but our *Sesame Street* experience suggests that we also can teach children to take another person's point of view; to cooperate by combining re-

[11] Bruner, 1972.
[12] For example, Kagan, Pearson, and Welch, 1966. Also: Debus, 1970; Ridberg, Parke, and Hetherington, 1971.
[13] Salomon, 1972, 1973, and 1974.
[14] Denney, Denney, and Ziobrowski, 1973.

sources, taking turns or dividing labor; to understand certain rules that ensure justice and fair play, such as sharing and reciprocity. Other studies have shown that televised models can teach altruism and kindness, self-control, affection, the initiation of social contacts, and the inhibition of deviant behavior.[15] These observations led us to think about additional experimentation that the Children's Television Workshop might conduct with preschoolers or children in the early elementary grades, and we outlined some of our ideas as follows:

> A new experiment by the Children's Television Workshop will be designed to study whether television can be used to increase a child's psychological awareness of his own thoughts and feelings as well as his understanding of the thoughts and feelings of others. In this process, can the child learn that his thoughts and feelings are not unique to him but are shared by others— that he is not alone either in what he enjoys or in what causes him anxiety?
>
> Our expectation is that, if television can help the child to better understand himself, he will:
>
> 1. feel better about himself.
> 2. rely with more confidence on his own resources.
> 3. find constructive outlets for his emotions.
> 4. be more likely to face failure without collapsing.
>
> With a better understanding of others, he will:
>
> 1. be able to take another person's point of view, to understand that person's perspective, thoughts, and feelings.
> 2. anticipate how others will react to his actions, to reflect upon the possible consequences of his actions.
> 3. communicate effectively with others.
> 4. enter groups constructively and work comfortably within them.
> 5. understand the value of sharing, helping, and reciprocity.

---

[15] Some of these studies are noted in Chapter 2.

With a better sense of shared experience, he will:

1. appreciate both the similarities and differences between himself and others.
2. discriminate when to accept and when to reject peer-group influences.
3. discriminate when aggression is appropriate and inappropriate.
4. find alternative forms of resolving conflict with others, without resort to violence.

> Extract from a document prepared by staff of Children's Television Workshop, July 1972.

Any new experiment in teaching socially valued behavior through television would need to involve the whole family. Whereas the teaching of intellectual skills by television benefits from the direct involvement of parents and older siblings, the teaching of socially valued behavior almost demands it. We were proposing, therefore, to design television for family viewing, and there are no precedents for how to achieve this successfully. Clearly, the televised situations used must be familiar to young children yet universal enough to interest all members of the family.

Learning about the World as It Is

Perhaps television's most useful mission for young children is to show them interesting things about the world that they haven't seen before and probably will not see without the benefit of television. It can show children things they have never seen, sounds they have never heard, people and ideas they have not yet imagined. It can show them how things work, how other people use them, what goes on in the world and how to think about it. The events need not be dramatic or exotic. Children are still trying to unravel and understand the ordinary, commonplace world as it is.

Television has always tried for the dramatic, escalating into more and more extreme violence, sex, catastrophe and political encounters. The more extreme, the better. This search for the exotic is shared by films, books, theater, advertising and journalism, which all assume that only new instances of extraordinary human behavior can stimulate our jaded interests. Perhaps adults who are over-familiar with the ordinary do need this escalation of the unusual (although even for them, it quickly seems to reach the point of diminishing returns). And even adults take trips just to see people and places they have never seen before, not because they expect dramas to unfold before their eyes but just to be there, to see what it's like.

For children, television can do more than supply drama. It can show them that there are other people out there in the world, going about their lives, sharing this exact moment in history with them, all having no meaning in terms of drama whatever. It is when the ordinary escapes from the dramatic that television seems to come alive. We saw numerous examples of this on *Sesame Street*.

Some of these we planned. Others just happened. In devising our curriculum, we deliberately included the category of "natural environment." We showed a boy learning to ride a bike. We showed what happens on a fishing ship, in the back room of a bakery, on a farm, on a bus ride around the city. We showed where mail goes, what happens to junk and garbage when it is discarded, what goes on under a manhole cover in the street.

Other unplanned, life-sized events happened on *Sesame Street* to emphasize the power of the ordinary. Kermit the Frog and a little girl are talking about the words "near and far." As they demonstrate being "near" to each other, on impulse they exchange kisses. The girl catches a bit of the puppet Kermit's fuzz on her lips, becomes intrigued by Kermit's fuzziness, and begins to explore it by gently rubbing his head and body. Kermit understands her curiosity and holds patiently, as does the camera. The girl's sense of wonder has been shared by viewing children who encounter other wonderful imponderables in their own lives.

Another example of the ordinary on *Sesame Street* involves an adult cast member, children and puppets discussing the fact that objects have different-sounding names in different languages. One small girl in the group knows both Spanish and English, and as the group relies more and more upon her to supply the names in these languages, her face shines with joy and a modest smile. Her message to the viewer: What pleasure there is in knowing *two* languages, *two* ways to speak!

A final example from *Sesame Street:* John-John, a small, black three-year-old, is counting to twenty with one of the Muppet Monsters. John-John is brimming with confidence, throwing back his head and bellowing each number in turn. Suddenly, reaching fourteen, he falters and realizes he does not know how to proceed. Confusion covers his face, his sublime confidence crumbles. The monster encourages him, telling him that he knows he can do it. And suddenly he does; "Fourteen!!" exclaims John-John. His face clears, his confidence returns, and he bellows the remaining numbers triumphantly. We have seen how one little boy handles an ordinary event, not knowing or remembering something, with strength and poise.

The children's program, *Zoom*, introduced in 1972 over public-broadcasting stations, uses familiar, commonplace activities in children's lives effectively. Episodes include a boy building a raft from the beginning stages to its completion, a group of children laying out a playing field in a vacant lot and then proceeding to play an improvised version of field hockey, and a country girl going about her chores in her home in Virginia. Such episodes of everyday life attracted great attention among viewers.[16]

Even for adults, we probably underestimate the interest of unexceptional televised events. One of the most popular series on the commercial networks during the 1972–73 season was *The Waltons*, a low-keyed collection of stories involving a rural family living during the Depression decades ago. The events were ordinary and unsensational. No one expected the show's great popularity.

If television did begin to balance the ordinary against the dramatic, it would bring a further change with it. Most of what television displays in its search for the dramatic is catastrophic, unhappy, sick or disrupted—at least slightly out of its mind. Perhaps this reflects the actual daily experience of people in this country, but I doubt that most people are usually in the state of sustained hysteria that television presents. Including some ordinary experience in television may bring it closer to our lives, if we are not too glutted from our overdose of the dramatic to accept it.

Another value in television's showing the world as it is would be to display to children how people actually go about trying to solve the typical problems they encounter and the consequences of these attempts. William Kessen, a child psychologist at Yale University,[17] summarized the limited ways in which television currently shows how problems are solved, with almost the only problems ever shown on television stemming from differences in power among people. Solutions are restricted to magic, guile or what Kessen calls "automatic virtue:" somehow it all works out, often because of the stupidity of the authority figure.

[16] Hines, 1973.
[17] Kessen, 1973.

We know almost nothing about how our youngest children, those younger than three, respond to television, although some of them are surrounded by it from the time they are born. Yet we can expect that television's greatest impact of all, for better or worse, is precisely upon these youngest children. Samuel Gibbon, the original studio producer of *Sesame Street* who perennially frets over the mysteries of television's effects upon children, speculates[18] that television is one of the earliest organizers of the young child's experience, a resource for learning how to sort, classify, predict and otherwise process the reality surrounding him, including that portion of the reality, mixed with fantasy, that is provided by television itself. He claims that as soon as the child is able to make some predictions about the reality that surrounds him, it must occur to him that televised reality is easier to predict than most of his other experiences. The recurring formats, the redundancy, the regular schedules, the characters who are never out of character—all present ideal conditions for learning rules about behavior. Joyce Maynard, the Yale undergraduate who at age nineteen reflected upon her childhood,[19] also observed that when she was young, television seemed to her to be one of the most accessible ways to learn about the rules and regularities in life. She says that she found it marvelously comforting to find that at least something in life could be predictable. If these speculations are correct (and it would be a critical experiment to test them), the regularities of television that may be for adults a retreat from the unpredictability in their lives may be for our youngest children a source of help in making life understandable.

However, even this simple function of television—to show young children the world as it is—is not without detractors. Marya Mannes, an incisive journalist, writes under the headline "Has Childhood Been Raped?" that television deprives children of their rightful period of innocence; exposure to mass com-

18 Gibbon, 1973.
19 Maynard, 1972.

munications propels them into an adult world for which they are not ready. Television's presentation of the ever-more-exotic may justify this view. But surely there is no harm in showing children the persons, places and things of this world and what is basic in human life.

Learning about the World as It Might Be

Presenting the world as it is does not mean that television cannot help to lead children to a vision of the world as it might be. Michael J. Arlen, who for a time was television critic for *The New Yorker*,[20] describes the importance of television in creating the myths for children to live by:

> All of us, whether we are aware of it or not, whether we wish it or not, live in relation to myths. In the past, the myths our people lived by were largely religious and literary—myths of Christian love, of family, of conquest, of bravery in combat . . . People, one imagines, have never—or have very, very rarely—done arduous things (such as living) just for the thing itself; and the same is no less true today.

> There is a difference nowadays, though, or so it seems to me. First, the myths we Americans have lived by are not working . . . and we have no new myths to put in their place. The second difference is that the source of mythmaking in our society has changed . . . Increasingly, the sources of our myths are movies, and journalism, and, most pervasive of all, television.

These "myths" need not be modern resurrections of valor in combat, romantic love or religious zeal. Myths for children can be simple presentations of simple goodness. We hear that children are now so worldly wise, so gorged by a wide range of visual experiences, that they avoid sentimentality at all costs. I doubt it. It surely is true that children do not like to be preached at, but television can show simple instances of caring,

[20] Arlen, 1971.

examples of good people in this world who are doing good things for others and for themselves. Perhaps seeing such people at home, on television or wherever is all children need to build their own myths.

Of course, there are other myths that we are providing now. Through them, we provide training in irony and cynicism, rearing what Benjamin DeMott has called "a generation of toddler-ironists." We teach them that the appearance of simple goodness is usually a cover-up for personal selfishness, and they must learn how to see through this. We teach them that caring about another person's life exposes you to disappointment and rejection, and they must learn to remain detached to escape this. We teach them that life is full of tension and deprivation, and they must learn to accept this. Television has helped to create these myths for children. Surely it can create others that help them toward a more humane vision of life.

Money

This history of *Sesame Street* ends where it must: money. Television is not going to go away. There simply is too much money in it.[21] The problem is that a disproportionately small share of it is invested in children.

Commercial networks will continue to spend only the minimum investment necessary to keep the Federal Communications Commission at bay, and since the FCC does not press them too hard, that minimum of dollars and talent will be small indeed. Commercial broadcasters know what works in the ratings, which means they know how to make money, and they are not going to give that up. The recent record of public-broadcasting support is equally disheartening. Foundations regard their proper role as helping to start new, experimental projects, but not to provide funds to sustain them over time.

[21] Detailed descriptions appear in Brown, 1971; Pearce, 1972.

Government funding of public broadcasting is whimsical, totally at the mercy of political forces.

There are no easy solutions, of course, but Joan Cooney suggests the direction for change when she says that the provision of good programs for children must be removed from the free enterprise system and made a public service. For the commercial networks, this would mean that they "half-nationalize themselves,"[22] with television for adults remaining free enterprise but television for children becoming public interest. But this means that commercial broadcasters will have to decide by themselves to do this. Not likely.

For public broadcasting, children's programs would have to be removed from the political pressures that determine funding. Some precedents do exist. We have special school taxes in this country, and the British Broadcasting Corporation levies a special tax on television sets to run its system; both are at least somewhat insulated from politics.

Having ended this record of one episode in children's programs on the topic of money, I am no longer certain that I have been writing about television at all. Perhaps I have really been writing about our society as a whole: its sense of futility, its elation when even small signs of progress appear, its desperate hope that all is not lost even when all seems truly lost, its persisting faith that individual genius still can make everything all right. I do not say this to make this book seem more important than it is. But the state of children's television seems so accurately to reflect our exasperation at what we are doing to ourselves, along with our unwillingness to abandon the dream that somehow our individual genius will magically rescue us from our corporate stupidity.

Television can inform children and create visions of what their lives can be. It also can inter them endlessly in Plato's Cave, watching removed images of life passing them by. Interment is what television has given them so far, with only a rare glimpse of what they need to see and to hear. Maybe we can change that. Edward R. Murrow, one of few who can claim a

[22] Geoghegan, 1972.

lasting contribution to television broadcasting in this country, encouraged us to try:

> This instrument can teach, it can illuminate: Yes, and it can even inspire. But it can do so only to the extent that humans are determined to use it to those ends. Otherwise, it is merely lights and wires in a box.

Epilogue

~~~~~~

During the time it takes to write a book, other things keep happening. This has certainly been true at the Children's Television Workshop. *Sesame Street,* the Workshop's first project, entered its fifth broadcast season in 1973–74, and remained CTW's bread-and-butter activity. But through the years we have added several new projects. Each contains its own story, as yet untold.

In 1971 the Workshop began broadcasting another major television series for children, *The Electric Company,* designed to provide supplementary instruction in basic reading skills for children in the early elementary school grades who are experiencing difficulty in beginning reading. After two years of broadcasting, it appears that many teachers do use the series effectively[1] and that television can help children to learn these reading skills.[2] We are optimistic about *The Electric Company,* and others, sometimes a bit effusively, share our optimism. For example, Martin Mayer, a journalist who writes on the media and on education, observed that "this television show may improve the average level of reading ability in the United States. In fifteen years of examining these matters, I have seen nothing in American education of comparable importance" (*The New York Times Magazine,* January 29, 1973). *The Electric Company* will continue to experiment to improve its reading instruction.

In addition, the Children's Television Workshop is planning

~~~~~~

[1] Herriott and Liebert, 1972; Cazden, 1972, 1973.
[2] Ball and Bogatz, 1973.

a series of broadcasts to provide basic health information and concepts to young adults.

Connected with these television programs, the Community Education Services division of the Workshop continues to develop its programs to reach the target audiences, especially the economically deprived. This division has mounted concerted efforts to assist parents and community groups and institutions in the use of the broadcasts. For example, it supervises summer tutoring programs involving teenagers and college students working with preschoolers in projects based on *Sesame Street;* trains teachers, parents and paraprofessionals in the use of *Sesame Street;* and incorporates *The Electric Company* into adult basic education programs designed to equip participants with skills necessary to enter the labor market.[3]

Reasoning that television programs by themselves will not have continuing long-range effects, and reasoning also that the Workshop will need to support itself financially, a Nonbroadcast Materials Division is creating books, puzzles, games and toys based upon *Sesame Street* and *The Electric Company,* for use both in school and at home.

Internationally, the English-language version of *Sesame Street* is viewed in over fifty countries, from Antigua to Zambia, from Pago Pago to Poland. A Spanish-language version, *Plaza Sésamo,* is produced in Mexico City and shown in Latin America. A Portuguese-language version, *Vila Sésamo,* is produced in São Paulo for use in Brazil. *Sesamstrasse* is produced in Germany. Productions now are planned in other countries. These international activities provide opportunities for new experiments. For example, on the island of Jamaica in the Caribbean, we watched[4] as young children in the remote, nonelectrified Blue Mountains encountered television for the first time, by means of mobile video-cassette equipment. They adapted with amazing speed and soon were learning effectively.

Since the research on children conducted by the Workshop itself cannot extend far beyond its own television programs,

[3] Children's Television Workshop, May 30, 1973.
[4] Lasker, 1973.

several cooperative arrangements have been made with other research centers. For example, a partnership now exists between the Workshop and Harvard University, called the Center for Research in Children's Television, to study certain basic research questions[5] about how young children learn from the visual media.

As this book about *Sesame Street* ended on the topic of money, so does this epilogue. The Workshop's Board of Trustees[6] continues its responsibilities to determine the long-range purposes of the organization and to monitor its business operation and management. It brings to these tasks the same imagination and enthusiasm that the creative staff brings to television production. The future of the Children's Television Workshop rests upon its efforts.

[5] Such as those described on pages 150–152 in Chapter 6.

[6] Lloyd N. Morrisett, Ph.D. (Chairman), President, The John and Mary R. Markle Foundation; Luis Alvarez, National Executive Director, ASPIRA, Inc.; Joan Ganz Cooney, President, The Children's Television Workshop; Eugene H. Cota-Robles, Ph.D., Professor and Head of the Department of Microbiology, Pennsylvania State University; Lawrence A. Cremin, Ph.D., Barnard Professor of Education, Teachers College, Columbia University; James Day, Chairman, Station Independence Project; Gerald S. Lesser, Ph.D., Bigelow Professor of Education and Human Development, Harvard University Graduate School of Education; Robert A. McCabe, Managing Director, Lehman Brothers, Inc., New York City; Mrs. Emmett J. Rice, Director, College Entrance Examination Board, Washington, D.C.; Ralph B. Rogers, Chairman of the Board, Texas Industries, Inc. (Dallas) and Chairman, Public Broadcasting System; Richard C. Steadman, Partner, J. H. Whitney & Company, New York City; Eddie N. Williams, President, Joint Center for Political Studies, Washington, D.C.

References

Alexander, D. "A Report on the Experimental Showing of *Sesame Street*." Great Britain: Harlech Television, June 1971.

Ames, L. "Don't Push Your Preschooler." *Family Circle*, December 1971.

Anderson, R. C. "Can First-Graders Learn an Advanced Problem-Solving Skill?" *Journal of Educational Psychology* 56 (1965): 283–294.

Anderson, R., and Shane, H. G. "A Whistle in the Workshop." *Houghton Mifflin Educational News,* January 1971.

Arlen, M. J. *Living-Room War.* New York: Viking, 1969.

Arlen, M. J. "A Few Sensible Words about Children's TV." *McCall's,* February 1971.

Atkin, C. K., Murray, J. P., and Nayman, O. B. *Television and Social Behavior: An Annotated Bibliography of Research Focusing on Television's Impact upon Children.* Washington, D.C.: U.S. Department of Health, Education, and Welfare, 1971.

Ball, S., and Bogatz, G. A. *The First Year of "Sesame Street": An Evaluation.* Princeton, N.J.: Educational Testing Service, 1970.

Ball, S., and Bogatz, G. A. "Summative Research of *Sesame Street:* Implications for the Study of Preschool Children." In *Minnesota Symposia on Child Psychology,* Vol. 6, edited by Anne D. Pick. Minneapolis: University of Minnesota Press, 1972.

Ball, S., and Bogatz, G. A. *Reading with Television: An Evaluation of "The Electric Company."* Princeton, N.J.: Educational Testing Service, 1973.

Bandura, A. "The Role of Modeling Processes in Personality Development." In *The Young Child: Reviews of Research.* Washington, D.C.: National Association for the Education of Young Children, 1967.

Bandura, A. "Social Learning Theory of Identificatory Processes." In *Handbook of Socialization Theory and Research,* edited by D. A. Goslin and D. C. Glass. Chicago: Rand McNally, 1969.

Bandura, A., Grusec, J., and Menlove, F. "Vicarious Extinction of Avoidance Behavior." *Journal of Personality and Social Psychology* 5 (1967):16–23.

Bandura, A., and McDonald, F. J. "Influence of Social Reinforcement and the Behavior of Models in Shaping Children's Moral Judgments." *Journal of Abnormal and Social Psychology* 67 (1963):274–281.

Bandura, A., and Menlove, F. "Factors Determining Vicarious Extinction of Avoidance Behavior through Symbolic Modeling." *Journal of Personality and Social Psychology* 8 (1968):99–108.

Bandura, A., and Mischel, W. "Modification of Self-Imposed Delay of Reward through Exposure to Live and Symbolic Models." *Journal of Personality and Social Psychology* 2 (1965):698–705.

Bandura, A., Ross, D., and Ross, S. "Imitation of Film-Mediated Models." *Journal of Personality and Social Psychology* 66 (1963): 3–11.

Banfield, E. C. *The Unheavenly City.* Boston: Little, Brown, and Co., 1970.

Barcus, F. E. "Saturday Children's Television: A Report of Television Programming and Advertising on Boston Commercial Television." Action for Children's Television, unpublished monograph, 1971.

Barnouw, E. *The Image Empire: A History of Broadcasting in the United States from 1953.* New York: Oxford University Press, 1970.

Baughman, E. E., and Dahlstrom, W. G. *Negro and White Children: A Psychological Study in the Rural South.* New York: Academic Press, 1968.

Bereiter, C., and Engelmann, S. I. *Teaching Disadvantaged Children in Preschool.* Englewood Cliffs, N.J.: Prentice-Hall, 1966.

Berkowitz, L. *Aggression.* New York: McGraw-Hill, 1962.

Berkowitz, L., and Geen, R. "Film Violence and the Cue Properties of Available Targets." *Journal of Personality and Social Psychology* 3 (1966):525–530.

Berlyne, D. E. *Conflict, Arousal, and Curiosity.* New York: McGraw-Hill, 1960.

Bettelheim, B. *The Informed Heart.* Glencoe, Ill.: Free Press, 1960.

Bissell, J., White, S. H., and Zivin, G. "Sensory Modalities in Children's Learning." In *Psychology and Educational Practice,* edited by G. S. Lesser. Glenview, Ill.: Scott, Foresman, 1971.

Blackwell, F., and Jackman, M. "*Sesame Street:* A Report on a Monitoring Study of the Showings of Ten Programmes from the Series by Harlech Television." Great Britain: National Council for Educational Technology, June 1971.

Bloom, B. S. *Stability and Change in Human Characteristics.* New York: Wiley, 1964.

Bogatz, G. A., and Ball, S. *The Second Year of "Sesame Street": A Continuing Evaluation.* Princeton, N.J.: Educational Testing Service, 1971a.

Bogatz, G. A., and Ball, S. "Some Things You've Wanted to Know about *Sesame Street.*" *American Education,* April 1971b, 11–15.

Bond, G. L., and Dykstra, R. "The Cooperative Research Program in First-Grade Reading Instruction." *Reading Research Quarterly* 6 (1967):5–11.

Bretz, R. "Three Models for Home-Based Instructional Systems Using Television." Santa Monica, Cal.: Rand Corporation, 1972.

Broadbent, D. E. *Perception and Communication.* New York: Pergamon Press, 1958.

Bronfenbrenner, U. "Children and Parents: Together in the World." Report to the White House Conference on Children, 1970.

Bronfenbrenner, U. "Who Lives on *Sesame Street?*" *Psychology Today,* October 1970.

Brown, L. *Television: The Business behind the Box.* New York: Harcourt Brace Jovanovich, 1971.

Bruner, J. S. *The Relevance of Education.* New York: Norton, 1971.

Bruner, J. S. "Nature and Uses of Immaturity." *American Psychologist* 27 (1972):687–707.

Bryan, J. H., and London, P. "Altruistic Behavior by Children." *Psychological Bulletin* 73 (1970):200–211.

Bryan, J. H., and Schwartz, T. "Effects of Film Material upon Children's Behavior." *Psychological Bulletin* 75 (1971):50–59.

Bryan, J. H., and Walbek. N. "Preaching and Practicing Generosity: Children's Actions and Reactions." *Child Development* 41 (1970):329–353.

Bureau of Social Science Research, *Television and the Public.* New York: Harcourt Brace Jovanovich, 1973.

Cartwright, G. P. "The Relationship between Sequences of Instruction and Mental Abilities of Retarded Children." *American Educational Research Journal* 8 (1971):143–150.

Cazden, C. D. "*The Electric Company* Turns on to Reading." *Harvard Graduate School of Education Bulletin* 16 (1972):2–3. Reprinted in *Annual Edition of Readings in Human Development*. Guilford, Conn.: Dushkin Publishing Group, 1973.

Cazden, C. D. "Progress Report on In-Classroom Research on *The Electric Company*." Children's Television Workshop, February 1973.

Chall, J. *Learning to Read*. New York: McGraw-Hill, 1967.

Charlesworth, W. R. "The Role of Surprise in Cognitive Development." In *Studies in Cognitive Development*, edited by D. Elkind and J. H. Flavell. New York: Oxford University Press, 1969.

Cheyney, A. B. *Teaching Culturally Disadvantaged in the Elementary School*. Columbus, Ohio: Merrill, 1967.

Children's Television Workshop. "Proposal for 1973–1974 Production of *Sesame Street* and *The Electric Company*." New York: Children's Television Workshop, May 1973.

Cicarelli, V., Cooper, W., and Granger, R. *The Impact of Head Start: An Evaluation of the Effects of Head Start on Children's Cognitive and Affective Development*. Washington, D.C.: Westinghouse Learning Corp., 1969.

Cloward, R. A., and Jones, J. A. "Social Class: Educational Attitudes and Participation." In *Education in Depressed Areas*, edited by A. H. Passow. New York: Teachers College, Columbia University, 1963.

Coleman, J. S., et al. *Equality of Educational Opportunity*. Washington, D.C.: U.S. Government Printing Office, 1966.

Collins, W. A. "Learning of Media Content: A Developmental Study." *Child Development* 41 (1970):1133–1142.

Collins, W. A. "Effect of Temporal Separation between Motivation, Aggression, and Consequences: A Developmental Study." *Developmental Psychology* 8 (1973):215–221.

Community Relations Department. "The Neighborhood Youth Corps/Children's Television Workshop Pilot Summer Project: Final Evaluation Report." New York: Children's Television Workshop, 1971, 1972.

Connell, D. D., and Palmer, E. L. "*Sesame Street*—A Case Study." In *Broadcaster/Researcher Cooperation in Mass Communication Research*, edited by J. D. Halloran and M. Gurevitch. Leeds, England: Kavanagh and Sons, 1971.

Cook, A., and Mack, H. "Business in Education: The Discovery Center Hustle." *Social Policy* 1 (1970):4–11.

Cook, T. D., Appleton, H., Conner, R., Shaffer, A., Tamkin, G., and

Weber, S. J. "*Sesame Street* Revisited: A Case Study in Evaluation Research." Report to the Russell Sage Foundation, 1972.

Cooney, J. G. *The Potential Uses of Television in Preschool Education.* New York: A report to the Carnegie Corporation of New York, 1966.

Cooney, J. G., with Gottlieb, L. *Television for Preschool Children: A Proposal.* New York: Carnegie Corporation of New York, 1968.

Cowan, P. A., Langer, J., Heavenrich, J., and Nathanson, M. "Social Learning and Piaget's Cognitive Theory of Moral Development." *Journal of Personality and Social Psychology* 11 (1969):261–274.

Crutchfield, R. S. "Teaching for Productive Thinking in Children." Paper presented to the American Psychological Association, 1966.

Culkin, J. "Of Big Media and Little Kids." *Television Quarterly* 9 (1970):43–49.

Day, H. I., and Berlyne, D. "Intrinsic Motivation." In *Psychology and Educational Practice,* edited by G. S. Lesser. Glenview, Ill.: Scott, Foresman, 1971.

Debus, R. "Effects of Brief Observation of Model Behavior on Conceptual Tempo of Impulsive Children." *Developmental Psychology* 2 (1970):22–32.

Denney, D. R., Denney, N. W., and Ziobrowski, M. J. "Alterations in the Information-Processing Strategies of Young Children Following Observation of Adult Models." *Developmental Psychology* 8 (1973):202–208.

Deutsch, M. "The Disadvantaged Child and the Learning Process." In *Education in Depressed Areas,* edited by H. Passow. New York: Teachers College Press, 1963.

Deutsch, M. "Race and Social Class as Separate Factors Related to Social Environment." *American Journal of Sociology* 70 (1965): 474.

Doan, R. K. "Kindergarten May Never Be the Same." *TV Guide,* July 11, 1970.

Dubanoski, R. A., and Parton, D. A. "Imitative Aggression in Children as a Function of Observing a Human Model." *Developmental Psychology* 4 (1971):489.

Durkin, D. *Children Who Read Early.* New York: Teachers College Press, 1966.

Dyer, H. S. "The Discovery and Development of Educational Goals." Princeton, N.J.: Educational Testing Service, 1966.

Educational Testing Service. *Evaluating "Sesame Street": A Pro-*

posal for the Children's Television Workshop. Princeton, New Jersey, 1969.

Erikson, E. *Childhood and Society.* New York: Norton, 1950.

Eysenck, H. J. *Race, Intelligence and Education.* London: Temple Smith, 1971.

Featherstone, J. *Schools Where Children Learn.* New York: Liveright, 1971.

Feshbach, S. "The Stimulating versus Cathartic Effects of a Vicarious Aggressive Activity." *Journal of Abnormal and Social Psychology* 63 (1961):381–385.

Feshbach, S., and Singer, R. D. *Television and Aggression.* San Francisco: Jossey-Bass, 1971.

Filep, R., Millar, G. R., and Gillette, P. T. "The *Sesame Street* Mother Project: Final Report." El Segundo, Cal.: Institute for Educational Development, 1971.

Francke, L. "The Games People Play on *Sesame Street.*" *New York,* April 5, 1971.

Frybear, J. L., and Thelen, M. H. "Effect of Sex of Model and Sex of Observer on the Imitation of Affective Behavior." *Developmental Psychology* 1 (1969):298.

Gage, N. L., ed. *Handbook of Research on Teaching.* Chicago: Rand McNally, 1963.

Gagné, R. M. *The Conditions of Learning.* New York: Holt, Rinehart and Winston, 1965.

Garfunkel, F. "*Sesame Street:* An Educational Dead End?" *Bostonia,* Winter 1970, 19–21.

Geoghegan, T. "Batman in the Heavenly City." *The New Republic,* November 4, 1972.

Gibbon, S. Y. Symposium paper on children and television. Ann Arbor, Mich.: Conference on Creative Activities for Young Children, University of Michigan, April 1973.

Gibbon, S. Y., and Palmer, E. L. *Pre-Reading on "Sesame Street."* New York: Children's Television Workshop, 1970.

Gibbons, J. "Guidelines for the Application of Technology to Educational Objectives Obtained from an Analysis of Successes and Failures." In *The Cable and Continuing Education,* edited by W. S. Baer and R. Adler. Aspen, Colo.: Aspen Program on Communication and Society, 1973.

Gibson, E. J. *Principles of Perceptual Learning and Development.* New York: Appleton-Century-Crofts, 1969.

Goulet, L. R., and Sterns, H. L. "Verbal-Discrimination Learning and Transfer with Verbal and Pictorial Materials." *Journal of Experimental Child Psychology* 10 (1970):257–263.

Granger, R. H. "First Do No Harm." *Yale Alumni Magazine* 36 (1973):25.

Green, R. "Dialect Sampling and Language Values." In *Social Dialects and Language Learning*, edited by R. Shuy. Champaign, Ill.: National Conference on Teacher Education, 1964.

Greene, S. C. "*Sesame Street:* Is the Inner City Watching?" Master's thesis, University of Pennsylvania, 1970.

Guba, E. "Eye Movement and Television Viewing in Children." *Audio-Visual Communication Review* 12 (1964):386–401.

Gunther, M. "What's around the Corner for *Sesame Street?*" *TV Guide*, July 10, 1971.

Gurin, P., and Katz, D. *Motivation and Aspiration in the Negro College.* Washington, D.C.: Office of Education, U.S. Department of Health, Education, and Welfare, 1966.

Hamilton, N. R. "Effects of Logical versus Random Sequencing of Items in an Auto-Instructional Program under Two Conditions of Overt Response." *Journal of Educational Psychology* 55 (1964): 258–266.

Harris and Associates. *The Viewing of Public Television.* November 1969, 1970, 1971.

Henry, J. "Docility or Giving the Teacher What She Wants." *Journal of Social Issues*, 11 (1955):2.

Henry, J. *Culture Against Man.* New York: Random House, 1963.

Herriott, R. E., and Liebert, R. J. "*The Electric Company:* In-School Utilization Study." Center for the Study of Education, Institute for Social Research, Florida State University, in conjunction with Research Triangle Institute, 1972.

Herriott, R. E., and St. John, N. H. *Social Class and the Urban School.* New York: Wiley, 1966.

Hicks, D. "Imitation and Retention of Film-Mediated Aggressive Peer and Adult Models." *Journal of Personality and Social Psychology* 2 (1965):97–100.

Hines, B. W. "Children's Reactions to Types of Television." Charleston, West Virginia: Appalachian Regional Laboratory, 1973.

Holt, J. "Big Bird, Meet Dick and Jane." *Atlantic Monthly*, May 1971.

Hunt, J. McV. "The Implications of Changing Ideas on How Children Develop Intellectually." In *Early Childhood Education Re-*

discovered, edited by J. L. Frost. New York: Holt, Rinehart and Winston, 1968.

Hurst, C. G. *Psychological Correlates in Dialectolalia.* Washington, D.C.: Howard University, Communities Research Center, 1965.

Ingersoll, G. M. "*Sesame Street* Can't Handle *All* the Traffic!" *Phi Delta Kappan* 53 (1971):185–186.

Jencks, C. "Inequality in Retrospect." *Harvard Educational Review* 43 (1973):138–164.

Jencks, C., et. al. *Inequality: A Reassessment of the Effects of Family and Schooling in America.* New York: Basic Books, 1972.

Jensen, A. R., "How Much Can We Boost IQ and Scholastic Achievement?" *Harvard Educational Review* 39 (1969):1–123.

John, E. R., Chessler, P., Bartlett, F., and Victor, I. "Observation Learning in Cats." *Science* 159 (1968):1489–1491.

Kael, P. *Going Steady.* New York: Little, Brown, 1970.

Kagan, J. "The Determinants of Attention in the Infant." *American Scientist* 58 (1970):298–306.

Kagan, J. *Change and Continuity in Infancy.* New York: Wiley, 1971.

Kagan, J., and Kogan, N. "Individuality and Cognitive Performance." In *Manual of Child Psychology,* edited by P. H. Mussen, New York: Wiley, 1970.

Kagan, J., Pearson, L., and Welch, L. "The Modifiability of an Impulsive Tempo." *Journal of Educational Psychology* 57 (1966): 359–365.

Karnes, M. B., Teska, J. A., and Hodgins, A. S. "The Effect of Four Programs of Classroom Intervention on the Intellectual and Language Development of Four-Year-Old Disadvantaged Children." *American Journal of Orthopsychiatry* 40 (1970):58–76.

Kessen, W. "Symposium Paper on Children and Television." *Yale Alumni Magazine* 36 (1973):26–27.

Klebanoff, L. B., Klein, S. D., and Schleifer, M. J. "An Open Letter to *Sesame Street.*" *The Exceptional Parent,* 1971, p. 9.

Kohlberg, L., Yaeger, J., and Hjertholm, E. "Private Speech: Four Studies and a Review of Theories." *Child Development* 39 (1968):691–736.

Krebs, D. "Altruism—An Examination of the Concept and a Review of the Literature." *Psychological Bulletin* 73 (1970):258–302.

Land, H. W. *The Children's Television Workshop: How and Why It Works.* New York: Nassau Board of Cooperative Educational Services, 1972.

Lasker, H. "*Sesame Street* among the Mountains of Jamaica." *Harvard Graduate School of Education Bulletin* 17 (1973):18–22.

Lasker, H., and Casseras, R. "Report on the Impact of *Sesame Street* in Curaçao, Netherlands Antilles." Curaçao: January 1971.

Lazarsfeld, P. F. "Why Is So Little Known about the Effects of Television on Children and What Can Be Done?" *Public Opinion Quarterly* 19 (1955):241–251.

Leifer, A. D., Collins, W. A., Gross, B. M., Taylor, P. H., Andrews, L., and Blackmer, E. R. "Developmental Aspects of Variables Relevant to Observational Learning." *Child Development* 42 (1971):1509–1516.

Leifer, A. D., and Roberts, D. F. "Children's Responses to Television Violence." In Surgeon General's Scientific Advisory Committee on Television and Social Behavior, *Television and Growing Up: The Impact of Televised Violence*, Vol. 2. Washington, D.C.: U.S. Government Printing Office, 1972.

Lemercier, K. I., and Teasdale, G. R. "*Sesame Street:* Some Effects of a Television Programme on the Cognitive Skills of Young Children from Lower SES Backgrounds." *Australian Psychologist* 8 (1973):47–51.

Levin, G. R., and Baker, B. L. "Item Scrambling in a Self-Instructional Program." *Journal of Educational Psychology* 54 (1963): 138–143.

Liebert, R. M., Neale, J. M., and Davidson, E. S. *The Early Window: Effects of Television on Children and Youth*. New York: Pergamon Press, 1973.

Lindsley, O. R. "A Behavioral Measure of Television Watching." *Journal of Advertising Research* 2 (1962):2–12.

Lippett, R., and Lippett, P. "Cross-Age Peer Help." Ann Arbor: Institute for Social Research, University of Michigan, 1969.

Locke, J. *Some Thoughts Concerning Education*. London: For A. and J. Churchill, at Black Swan in Pater Noster Row, 1693.

London Weekend Television. "*Sesame Street:* London ITV Area, Audience Observation Tables." Great Britain: London Weekend Television, January 1972.

Lumsdaine, A. A. "Instruments and Media of Instruction." In *Handbook of Research on Teaching*, edited by N. L. Gage. Chicago: Rand McNally, 1963.

Luria, A. R. *The Role of Speech in the Regulation of Normal and Abnormal Behavior*. New York: Liveright, 1961.

Maccoby, E. E. "Selective Auditory Attention in Children." In *Advance in Child Development and Behavior*, Vol. 3, edited by L. P. Lipsitt and C. C. Spiker. New York: Academic Press, 1967.

Maccoby, E. E. "Early Stimulation and Cognitive Development." In *Minnesota Symposia on Child Psychology*, edited by J. P. Hill. Minneapolis: University of Minnesota Press, 1969.

Maccoby, E. E., and Wilson, W. C. "Identification and Observational Learning from Films." *Journal of Abnormal and Social Psychology* 7 (1957):307–315.

Maddox, B. *Beyond Babel: New Directions in Communications*. New York: Simon and Schuster, 1972.

Mayer, M. *The Schools*. New York: Harper and Row, 1961.

Maynard, J. *Looking Back*. New York: Doubleday, 1972.

McLuhan, M., Reeves, B. F., Peters, H., Shayon, R. L., and Blair, G. E. Children's Programming Seminar. National Association of Educational Broadcasters, Columbia, South Carolina, April 1970.

Meichenbaum, D. H. "Implications of Research on Disadvantaged Children and Cognitive Training Programs for Educational Television: Ways of Improving *Sesame Street*." Paper presented at American Psychological Association Convention, Washington, D.C., 1971.

Meichenbaum, D. H., and Goodman, J. "Training Impulsive Children to Talk to Themselves." *Journal of Abnormal Psychology* 77 (1971):115–126.

Milgram, S., and Shotland, R. L. *Television and Anti-Social Behavior: Field Experiments*. New York: Academic Press, 1973.

Miller, N. E., et al. "Graphic Communication and the Crisis in Education." *Audio-Visual Communication Review* 5, No. 3 (1957).

Minton, J. H. "The Impact of *Sesame Street* on Reading Readiness of Kindergarten Children." Unpublished doctoral dissertation, Fordham University, 1972.

Morris, N. S. *Television's Child*. Boston: Little, Brown, 1971.

Nossoff, B. "Is *Sesame Street* a Dead End?" *Early Years*, Spring 1971.

O'Bryan, K. "Report on Children's Viewing Strategies." Unpublished paper, Ontario Institute for Studies in Education, 1972.

O'Bryan, K., and Boersma, F. "Eye Movements, Perceptual Activity, and Conservation Development." *Journal of Experimental Child Psychology* 12 (1971):157–169.

O'Connor, R. D. "Modification of Social Withdrawal through Symbolic Modeling." *Journal of Applied Behavioral Analysis* 2

(1969):15–22; reprinted in *Classroom Management,* edited by K. D. O'Leary and S. G. O'Leary. New York: Pergamon Press, 1972.

Ogilvie, D. M. "Child Observations of Experimental Segments: A Research Report." New York: Children's Television Workshop, 1969.

Ogilvie, D. M. "*Sesame Street:* Headstart for Advantaged Two-Year-Olds?" Unpublished paper, Harvard University, 1970.

Palmer, E. L. "Formative Research in Educational Television Production: The Experience of the Children's Television Workshop." In *Quality in Instructional Television,* edited by W. Schramm. Honolulu: University Press of Hawaii, 1972.

Payne, D. A., Krathwohl, D. R., and Gordon, J. "The Effect of Sequence on Programmed Instruction." *American Educational Research Journal* 4 (1967):125–132.

Pearce, A. "The Economics of Network Children's Television Programming." Cincinnati, Ohio: Media Services Center, University of Cincinnati, 1972.

Piaget, J. *The Psychology of Intelligence.* London: Routledge and Kegan Paul, 1947.

Piaget, J. *The Origins of Intelligence in Children.* New York: International Universities Press, 1952.

Pick, A. D., Christy, M. D., and Frankel, G. W. "A Developmental Study of Visual Selective Attention." *Journal of Experimental Child Psychology* 14 (1972):165–175.

Pick, H. L., and Pick, A. D. "Sensory and Perceptual Development." In *Manual of Child Psychology,* edited by P. H. Mussen. New York: Wiley, 1970.

Postman, N., and Weingartner, C. *Teaching as a Subversive Activity.* New York: Delacorte, 1969.

Reeves, B. F. "The First Year of *Sesame Street:* The Formative Research." New York: Children's Television Workshop, 1970.

Reeves, B. F. "The Responses of Children in Six Small Viewing Groups to *Sesame Street* Shows Nos. 261–274." New York: Children's Television Workshop, 1971.

Reiss, A. J., and Rhodes, A. L. "Are Educational Norms and Goals of Conforming, Truant, and Delinquent Adolescents Influenced by Group Position in American Society?" *Journal of Negro Education* 28 (1959):252–267.

Ridberg, E., Parke, R., and Hetherington, E. "Modification of Impulsive and Reflective Cognitive Styles through Observation of

Film-Mediated Models." *Developmental Psychology* 5 (1971): 369–377.

Roe, K. V., Case, H. W., and Roe, A. "Scrambled versus Ordered Sequence in Auto-Instructional Programs." *Journal of Educational Psychology* 53 (1962):101–104.

Rosekrans, M. A. "Imitation in Children as a Function of Perceived Similarities to a Social Model of Vicarious Reinforcement." *Journal of Personality and Social Psychology* 7 (1967):307–315.

Rosenhan, D. L. "The Kindnesses of Children." *Young Children* 25 (1969):30–44.

Rosenhan, D. L., and White, G. M. "Observation and Rehearsal as Determinants of Prosocial Behavior." *Journal of Personality and Social Psychology* 5 (1967):424–431.

Rosenthal, A. "The *Sesame Street* Generation Arrives." *Today's Health,* December 1970.

Rosenthal, R. "Teacher Expectations and Their Effects upon Children." In *Psychology and Educational Practice,* edited by G. S. Lesser. Glenview, Ill.: Scott, Foresman, 1971.

Rowe, E. J. "Discrimination Learning of Pictures and Words: A Replication of Picture Superiority." *Journal of Experimental Child Psychology* 14 (1972):323–328.

Rowe, E. J., and Paivio, A. "Discrimination Learning of Pictures and Words." *Psychonomic Science* 22 (1971):87–88.

Salomon, G. "Can We Affect Cognitive Skills Through Visual Media? An Hypothesis and Initial Findings." *Audio-Visual Communication Review,* 20 (1972):401–422.

Salomon, G. "Internalization of Filmic Schematic Operations in Relation to Individual Differences." *Journal of Educational Psychology,* 1974, in press.

Salomon, G. "Cognitive Effects of the Media: The Case of *Sesame Street* in Israel." Paper presented at the International Society for the Study of Behavioral Development, Ann Arbor, Michigan, August 1973.

Salomon, G., Eglstein, S., Finkelstein, R., Finkelstein, I., Mintzberg, E., Malve, D., and Velner, L. *Educational Effects of Sesame Street on Israeli Children.* Jerusalem: Hebrew University, 1972.

Samuels, B. "The First Year of *Sesame Street:* A Summary of Audience Surveys." New York: Children's Television Workshop, 1970.

Schramm, W. "What Do We Know about Learning from Instructional Television." In *Educational Television, The Next Ten*

Years, edited by W. Schramm. Stanford: The Institute for Communication Research, 1962.

"Sedulus." *"Sesame Street." New Republic,* June 6, 1970.

Shayon, R. L. "Cutting Oedipal Ties." *Saturday Review,* February 1970.

Shockley, W. "Negro IQ Deficit: Failure of a Malicious Coincidence Model Warrants New Research Proposals." *Review of Educational Research* 41 (1971):227–248.

Silberman, C. *Crisis in the Classroom.* New York: Random House, 1970.

Skinner, B. F. "Teaching Machines." *Science* 128 (1958):969–977.

Skinner, B. F. *Beyond Freedom and Dignity.* New York: Knopf, 1971.

Slaby, R. G., and Parke, R. D. "Effect on Resistance to Deviation by Observing a Model's Affective Reaction to Response Consequences." *Developmental Psychology* 5 (1971):40–47.

Snow, R. E., and Salomon, G. "Aptitudes and Instructional Media." *Audio-Visual Communication Review* 16 (1968):341–357.

Sprigle, H. A. "Can Poverty Children Live on *Sesame Street?*" *Young Children* 26 (1971):202–217.

Sprigle, H. A. "Who Wants to Live on *Sesame Street?*" *Childhood Education* 49 (1972):159–165.

Sproull, N. "Visual Attention, Modeling Behaviors, and Other Verbal and Nonverbal Meta-Communication of Prekindergarten Children Viewing *Sesame Street." American Educational Research Journal* 10 (1973):101–114.

Stein, A. H., and Friedrich, L. K. "Television Content and Young Children's Behavior." In *Television and Social Behavior,* Vol. 2, edited by J. P. Murray, E. A. Rubinstein, and G. A. Comstock. Washington, D.C.: U.S. Government Printing Office, 1972.

Stein, G. M., and Bryan, J. H. "The Effect of a Television Model upon Rule Adoption Behavior of Children." *Child Development* 43 (1972):268–273.

Steiner, G. A. *The People Look at Television.* New York: Knopf, 1963.

Stevenson, H. W. "Television and the Behavior of Preschool Children." In *Television and Social Behavior,* Vol. 2, edited by J. P. Murray, E. A. Rubinstein, and G. A. Comstock. Washington, D.C.: U.S. Government Printing Office, 1972.

Stodolsky, S. S., and Lesser, G. S. "Learning Patterns in the Disadvantaged." *Harvard Educational Review* 37 (1967):546–593.

Suchman, J. R. *Training Children in Scientific Inquiry.* Urbana, Ill.: University of Illinois, 1959.

Suchman, J. R. "Inquiry Training: Building Skills for Autonomous Discovery." *Merrill-Palmer Quarterly* 7 (1961):147–170.

Suchman, J. R. "The Pursuit of Meaning: Models for the Study of Inquiry." In *Behavioral Science Frontiers in Education,* edited by E. M. Bower and W. G. Hollister. New York: Wiley, 1967.

Surgeon General's Scientific Advisory Committee on Television and Social Behavior. *Television and Growing Up: The Impact of Televised Violence.* Washington, D.C.: U.S. Government Printing Office, 1972.

Taylor, M., and Samuels, B. "Audience Development Research." New York: Children's Television Workshop, 1970.

Thelen, H. "Tutoring by Students." *School Review* 77 (1969):229–244.

Thelen, M. H. "Modeling of Verbal Reactions to Failure." *Developmental Psychology* 1 (1969):297.

Torrey, J. W. "Learning to Read Without a Teacher: A Case Study." *Elementary English* 46 (1969):550–556.

Travers, R. M. W. *Man's Information System.* Scranton, Pa.: Chandlers, 1970.

Travers, R. M. W. "Transmission of Information to Human Receivers." *Audio-Visual Communication Review* 12 (1964):373–385.

Ulrich, R. E. "A Behavioral View of *Sesame Street.*" *Educational Broadcasting Review* 5 (1970):57–60.

Veatch, J. "Program Review: *Sesame Street.*" *Educational Broadcasting Review* 4 (1970):57–60.

Walbek, N. "Charitable Cognitions and Actions: A Study of the Concurrent Elicitation of Children's Altruistic Thoughts and Deeds." Unpublished master's thesis, Northwestern University, 1969.

Walters, R. H., Leat, M., and Mezei, L. "Response Inhibition and Disinhibition through Emphatic Learning." *Canadian Journal of Psychology* 17 (1963):235–243.

Walters, R. H., and Parke, R. D. "Influence of Response Consequences to a Social Model on Resistance to Deviation." *Journal of Experimental Child Psychology* 1 (1964):269–280.

Walters, R. H., Parke, R. D., and Cane, V. A. "Timing of Punishment and the Observation of Consequences to Others as Determinants of Response Inhibition." *Journal of Experimental Child Psychology* 2 (1965):10–30.

Ward, S., Levinson, D., and Wackman, D. "Children's Attention to Television Advertising." In Surgeon General's Scientific Advisory Committee on Television and Social Behavior, *Television and Social Behavior: Television in Day-to-Day Life, Patterns of Use.* Washington, D.C.: U.S. Government Printing Office, 1972.

Weber, L. *The English Infant School and Informational Education.* New York: Prentice-Hall, 1971.

Weikart, D. P. *Preschool Intervention: A Preliminary Report of the Perry Preschool Project.* Ann Arbor, Michigan: Campus Publishers, 1967.

Westley, B. M., and Barrow, L. C., Jr. "Exploring the News: A Comparative Study of the Teaching Effectiveness of Radio and Television." *Audio-Visual Communication Review* 7 (1959):14–23.

White, B. L., Watts, J. C., et al. *Major Influences on the Development of the Young Child.* Englewood Cliffs, N.J.: Prentice-Hall, 1972.

White, S. H. "Evidence for a Hierarchical Arrangement of Learning Processes." In *Advances in Child Development and Behavior,* edited by L. P. Lipsitt and C. C. Spiker. New York: Academic Press, 1965.

Wodtke, K. H., Brown, B. R., Sands, H. R., and Fredericks, P. "Scrambled versus Ordered Sequencing in Computer-Assisted Instruction." University Park, Pa.: Pennsylvania State University, 1967.

Wolf, T. M. "A Developmental Investigation of Televised Modeled Verbalizations of Resistance to Deviation." *Developmental Psychology* 6 (1972):537.

Yamamoto, K. "Stimulus Mode and Sense Modality: What's in It for Education?" *Teachers College Record* 70 (1969): 513–521.

Yankelovich, D. "A Report of Two Studies on the Role and Penetration of *Sesame Street* in Ghetto Communities." New York: April 1970.

Yankelovich, D. "A Report of Three Studies on the Role and Penetration of *Sesame Street* in Ghetto Communities (Bedford-Stuyvesant, East Harlem, Chicago, and Washington, D.C.)." New York, June 1971.

Yankelovich, D. "A Report on the Role and Penetration of *Sesame*

Street in Ghetto Communities (Bedford-Stuyvesant, East Harlem, Chicago, and Washington, D.C.)." New York: April 1973.

Zigler, E. "The Nature-Nurture Issue Reconsidered: A Discussion of Uzgiris' Paper." Paper presented at Conference on Sociocultural Aspects of Mental Retardation, Peabody College, Nashville, Tennessee, June 1968.

Index

Walden (Thoreau), 42
Wall Street Journal (newspaper), 197
Walter, Marion, x
Waltons, The (TV programs), 252
Washington *Post* (newspaper), 182
weather reports, learning to read from, 20
weather and seasons, curriculum on, 70
Webster, 197
Weeks, Edward, 132
Weil, Joyce, ix
Weingartner, C., 75
well-to-do families, 141, 145, 204
Western Illinois University, 228
Western Michigan University, 191
what to think *vs.* how to think, 48–49
White, Burton, x
White, Dr. Sheldon, x, 45, 60
White House Conference, 196

WHYY (television station), 204–5
Wilson, David B., 179
wisdom, teaching, 182
WNDT (television station), 40, 204, 206
women's liberation, 143, 177–78; *see also* sex roles and sexism
WPIX (television station), 204, 206
Wright, Norton, ix
writing skills, 6–7, 12–13, 47–48
WTTW (television station), 204

Yale University, 252, 253
Yankelovich surveys, 204, 206, 224–25
Yogi Bear (TV program), 139

"zombie viewer," 82
Zoom (TV program), 251–52
zoom-in camera techniques, 83, 84, 247
Zornow, Edith, ix

About the Author

GERALD LESSER, Chairman of the Board of Advisors of Children's Television Workshop, is Bigelow Professor of Education and Developmental Psychology and Director of the Laboratory of Human Development at Harvard University. He received his B.A. and M.A. from Columbia and his Ph.D. from Yale, and taught at Adelphi College and Hunter College before coming to Harvard. He is the author of many articles and several books on educational psychology.